P9-BHX-390

The 1984
Olympic Scientific
Congress
Proceedings
Volume 6

Sport
Pedagogy

Series Editors:

Jan Broekhoff, PhD
Michael J. Ellis, PhD
Dan G. Tripps, PhD

University of Oregon
Eugene, Oregon

The 1984
Olympic Scientific
Congress
Proceedings
Volume 6

Sport Pedagogy

Maurice Piéron and George Graham
Editors

Human Kinetics Publishers, Inc.
Champaign, Illinois

Library of Congress Cataloging-in-Publication Data

Olympic Scientific Congress (1984 : Eugene, Or.)
    Sport pedagogy.

    (1984 Olympic Scientific Congress proceedings ;
v. 6)
    Bibliography: p.
    1. Physical education and training—Study and
teaching—Congresses.   2. Physical education and
training—Curricula—Congresses.   I. Piéron, Maurice.
II. Graham, George, 1943-   III. Title.
IV. Series: Olympic Scientific Congress (1984 :
Eugene, Or.).   1984 Olympic Scientific Congress
proceedings ; v. 6.
GV565.O46   1984 vol. 6   796 s   85-18113
[GV363]   [613.7′07]
ISBN 0-87322-013-7

Managing Editor: Susan Wilmoth, PhD
Developmental Editor: Susan Wilmoth, PhD
Production Director: Sara Chilton
Copyeditor: Kristen LaDuke-Gallup
Typesetter: Theresa Bear
Text Layout: Gail Irwin
Cover Design and Layout: Jack Davis
Printed by: Braun-Brumfield, Inc.

ISBN: 0-87322-006-4   (10 Volume Set)
ISBN: 0-87322-013-7

Printed in the United States of America

10 9 8 7 6 5 4 3 2 1

Human Kinetics Publishers, Inc.
Box 5076, Champaign, IL 61820

Contents

Series Acknowledgments

The Congress organizers realize that an event as large and complex as the 1984 Olympic Scientific Congress could not have come to fruition without the help of literally hundreds of organizations and individuals. Under the patronage of UNESCO, the Congress united in sponsorship and cooperation no fewer than 64 national and international associations and organizations. Some 50 representatives of associations helped with the organization of the scientific and associative programs by coordinating individual sessions. The cities of Eugene and Springfield yielded more than 400 volunteers who donated their time to make certain that the multitude of Congress functions would progress without major mishaps. To all these organizations and individuals, the organizers express their gratitude.

A special word of thanks must also be directed to the major sponsors of the Congress: the International Council of Sport Science and Physical Education (ICSSPE), the United States Olympic Committee (USOC), the International Council on Health, Physical Education and Recreation (ICHPER), and the American Alliance for Health, Physical Education, Recreation and Dance (AAHPERD). Last but not least, the organizers wish to acknowledge the invaluable assistance of the International Olympic Committee (IOC) and its president, Honorable Juan Antonio Samaranch. President Samaranch made Congress history by his official opening address in Eugene on July 19, 1984. The IOC further helped the Congress with a generous donation toward the publication of the Congress papers. Without this donation it would have been impossible to make the proceedings available in this form.

Finally, the series editors wish to express their thanks to the volume editors who selected and edited the papers from each program of the Congress. Special thanks go to Maurice Piéron of the University of Leige and George Graham of the University of South Carolina for their work on this volume.

Jan Broekhoff,
Michael J. Ellis, and
Dan G. Tripps

Series Editors

Series Preface

Sport Pedagogy contains selected proceedings from this interdisciplinary program of the 1984 Olympic Scientific Congress, which was held at the University of Oregon in Eugene, Oregon, preceding the Olympic Games in Los Angeles. The Congress was organized by the College of Human Development and Performance of the University of Oregon in collaboration with the cities of Eugene and Springfield. This was the first time in the history of the Congress that the event was organized by a group of private individuals, unaided by a federal government. The fact that the Congress was attended by more than 2,200 participants from more than 100 different nations is but one indication of its success.

The Congress program focused on the theme of Sport, Health, and Well-Being subdisciplines of sport science such as sport medicine, biomechanics, sport psychology, sport sociology, and sport philosophy. For the first time in the Congress' history, these disciplinary sessions were sponsored by the national and international organizations representing the various subdisciplines. In the afternoons, the emphasis shifted toward interdisciplinary themes in which scholars and researchers from the subdisciplines attempted to contribute to crossdisciplinary understanding. In addition, three evenings were devoted to keynote addresses and presentations, broadly related to the theme of Sport, Health, and Well-Being.

In addition to the scientific programs, the Congress also featured a number of associative programs with topics determined by their sponsoring organizations. Well over 1,200 papers were presented in the various sessions of the Congress at large. It stands to reason, therefore, that publishing the proceedings of the event presented a major problem to the organizers. It was decided to limit proceedings initially to interdisciplinary sessions which drew substantial interest from Congress participants and attracted a critical number of high-quality presentations. Human Kinetics Publishers, Inc. of Champaign, Illinois, was selected to produce these proceedings. After considerable deliberation, the following interdisciplinary themes were selected for publication: Competitive Sport for Children and Youths; Human Genetics and Sport; Sport and Aging; Sport and Disabled Individuals; Sport and Elite Performers; Sport, Health, and Nutrition; and Sport and Politics. The 10-volume set published by Human Kinetics Publishers is rounded out by the disciplinary proceedings of Kinanthropometry, Sport Pedagogy, and the associative program on the Scientific Aspects of Dance.

Jan Broekhoff,
Michael J. Ellis, and
Dan G. Tripps

Series Editors

Preface

An Olympic Scientific Congress provides the unique opportunity for researchers in the sport sciences to gather and appraise the knowledge and development that has occurred throughout the world over the past 4 years in both general and specific areas of scientific interest. Moreover, a Congress provides the opportunity to identify new problems, issues, and research trends in addition to stimulating certain areas of research that may have evolved since the last Olympic Congress.

For these reasons, the 1984 Olympic Scientific Congress, which was held in Eugene, Oregon, prior to the Los Angeles Olympics, was important in the area of sport pedagogy. Sport pedagogy is currently in its adolescence. Analysis of teaching physical education through systematic observation has increased substantially during the past few years, as reflected in the papers contained in these proceedings. As a research area, sport pedagogy has not yet matured, but the progress and development in this area has been significant.

In Eugene, seven invited speakers and 72 referred papers were presented under the heading of sport pedagogy. Eight years earlier at the Olympic Scientific Congress in Quebec City, Canada, four invited keynote speeches and 12 papers were delivered. This difference is striking and reflects the tremendous increase of interest in sport pedagogy as a research area.

In addition to the obvious increase in the number of papers presented, sport pedagogists enjoyed three other significant events at the Congress. The first event was the presentation of the Association Internationale des Ecoles Superieures d'Education Physique (AIESEP) Award donated by Juan Antonio Samaranch, the President of the International Olympic Committee, to a sport pedagogist, Dr. Daryl Siedentop, of The Ohio State University. Professor Siedentop received the $5,000 award for his book *Developing Teaching Skills in Physical Education* (2nd ed.). It is an important milestone in sport pedagogy for one of its researchers to receive an award of such magnitude.

A second major event at the Olympic Scientific Congress in Eugene was the creation of the International Committee of Sport Pedagogy. The purposes of this organization will be to promote research and research dissemination in sport pedagogy throughout the world.

The third major event was naming of AIESEP to be responsible for creating the sport pedagogy program at the Congress. For this, as well as for the excellent conference itself, our sincerest appreciation is extended to Jan Broekhoff, Mike Ellis, Dan Tripps, and the countless other volunteers who made the Congress an important and worthwhile meeting.

In many ways the papers themselves are at least as significant as these three events. Unfortunately the space allowed for each of the areas did not allow for all of the sport pedagogy papers to be published. A number of good papers had to be rejected for this reason, forcing the editors to make a number of very difficult selections. Priority was given to papers that related to different aspects of sport pedagogy and that were thought to have a potential to influence research, teaching, and/or teacher education practices. A number of the papers correspond to recent trends toward systematically observing physical education teachers and coaches and teacher-student interaction. Teacher effectiveness (process-product) was also the topic of several papers.

In addition to data-based papers, several theoretical papers were also selected for inclusion in the proceedings. This was in recognition of the fact that progress in any academic field of study depends upon the quality of the theoretical reflection as well as the need for empirical validation of these theories. Theories unsupported by data and data unsupported by theories have the potential to be equally debilitating to an emerging area of study such as sport pedagogy.

The papers are divided into three sections. The first section, Teacher Preparation, begins with an invited address by Daryl Siedentop. In his paper he advocates a behavior modification paradigm arguing that teacher preparation needs to be systematic and organized to elicit specific outcomes as opposed to haphazard and random.

The section includes papers from four other authors. Borys uses the motor engagement time of students as the dependent variable for assessing the effectiveness of an in-service teacher education program. The topic of Armstrong's papers is learning to observe and analyze movement. One interesting section of the paper asks and answers the question, Are skillful performers necessarily good observers? The topic of the paper by Agnew-Sweeney and Cheffers is the socialization of preservice teachers. Using qualitative methods, they determine that experience at a residence camp is more valuable for socializing teachers into the profession than experience at a university campus. In the last paper in this section Mitchell and Lawson select teacher educators as the topic for investigation. The paper reveals some important characteristics about both the career paths and the knowledge base of educators of physical education teachers.

Analysis of Teaching and Coaching is the title of the second section of the proceedings. Authors of the majority of papers in this section use systematic observation as a vehicle for analyzing teaching and coaching. The introduction to this section is an invited paper by Beverly Yerg in which she discusses several models for conducting research on teaching.

The physical activity levels of Finnish students in physical education is the focus of the second paper by Telama, Varstala, Heikinaro-Johansson and Paukku. One of their interesting findings is that students who spend less of their leisure time in physical activity are less positive about physical education classes than their more active counterparts. Metzler, in the third paper, finds that a mastery system of personalized tennis instruction is superior to a more traditional method of instruction on the process variables measured by Academic Learning Time-Physical Education (ALT-PE). Paese required two groups of preservice teachers to teach an Experimental Teaching Unit. One of his somewhat puzzling findings is that students who have yet to student-teach exhibited more desirable teaching patterns than the undergraduates who are actually in the process of student teaching.

The next study reports the results of systematically observing experienced teachers in Quebec, Canada. Lirette, Paré, and Caron compared their observations of 12 teachers with the data reported in the early 1970s by Anderson and Barrette and find few major differences. The topic of Schempp's study is the impact that students in different grade levels, K-6, have on one teacher. He finds that the teacher's behavior, as measured by CAFIAS, changes according to the grade level taught. In the study by Peckman, Tainton, and Hacker, classroom teachers are the subjects in the examination of Australian Daily Physical Education. Although few observable differences were noticed in the children taught by a control group and those who experienced a program of daily fitness, some important recommendations for future study are included in their discussion. The final paper in this section on analysis of teaching physical education is by Crum. He summarizes the results of his investigation in the Netherlands on the use of learner reports as a vehicle for gaining insight into students' perception of physical education classes.

The final five papers include studies systematically analyzing coaches and athletes. Sherman and Hassan introduce this section by reporting the results of several descriptive studies which use the Coaching Behavior Analysis System. Gymnasts in Scotland are the subjects in Cox's study. He finds that a reciprocal style of coaching is superior to more direct styles of coaching. The practice patterns of three male United States Olympic volleyball players are described by McKenzie in a study that uses an adaptation of ALT-PE. ALT-PE is also used to analyze the practice time of college women volleyball players in the next study by Wuest, Mancini, van der Mars, and Terrillion. Coaches' use of metaphors is described and analyzed by Griffey, Housner, and Williams in the final paper in the section.

The final section of the proceedings, Curriculum: Theory and Practice, commences with two invited papers. The first, by Patt Dodds, is a research-based discussion of the inequities consciously and unconsciously perpetrated by teachers in their gyms. Herber Haag argues against the dualism that seems to exist between curriculum and instructional theory and argues for a dialectical blending of the two within the context of sport pedagogy.

Four fundamentals of the games curriculum comprise the theoretical discussion in the next paper by Thorpe, Bunker, and Almond. The next two studies, by Underwood and Kneer, respectively, are similar in design and findings. Both authors examine the relationship between curriculum theory and practice in secondary schools. Underwood surveyed 800 secondary schools in England and Wales; Kneer surveyed 20 schools in the state of Illinois. Each author reports an obvious dearth of the use of both objectives and evaluation in secondary schools. Jewett reviews three studies that focus on understanding and maintaining health-related fitness beyond the extent of a formal university course.

The proceedings conclude with a final report by Maurice Pieron in which he examines the research that has been completed to date on teaching physical education. Rather than reporting the results of these studies, however, he reviews the studies from a research design viewpoint. In essence his paper asks, What have we done so far in research on teaching physical education? Who has done it? How well have we done it? and What do we need to do to improve the quality of our research?

We are very grateful to those authors whose papers are included in these proceedings, to those authors who presented papers at the Congress in Eugene, and to all of those individuals who made the Congress such a success for sport pedagogy. It is our sincere hope that during the next 4 years, prior to the 1988 Olympics in Seoul, the area of research on teaching physical education will continue to grow and improve in three ways. First, we hope that the number of scholars who choose to do research on teaching physical education will continue to increase. Second we hope that collaboration among sport pedagogy researchers from different universities will emerge as a trend. Finally, and most importantly, we hope that we will continue to improve the quality of our research work. This last point is especially important if sport pedagogy expects to emerge from adolescence into one of the respected adults of the sport science community in the the next few years.

Maurice Piéron
George Graham
Editors

The 1984
Olympic Scientific
Congress
Proceedings
Volume 6

Sport
Pedagogy

PART I

Teacher Preparation

1

The Modification
of Teacher Behavior

Daryl Siedentop
THE OHIO STATE UNIVERSITY
COLUMBUS, OHIO, USA

Behavior modification is no longer the new kid on the block. During the past 20 years a sufficient amount of human behavior modification research has been completed to put to rest questions about the degree to which earlier work dominated by laboratory research on infrahuman species is generalizable to human behavior. Some of the experimental work has taken place in schools, and here too it appears that student academic/social behavior is modifiable through systematic application of environmental contingencies.

The influence of behavior analysis on psychology and education is clear but primarily superficial. While it is true that the term *reinforcement* is used widely in education and is part of the verbal repertoire that most teachers learn in their preparation programs, it is also true that the term is used in areas as diverse as architecture and military science—and with about the same level of imprecision. Analysis of general psychology tests reveals a stereotyped stimulus response view of behavior analysis that is 80 years old, if indeed it ever did exist. In education texts (Cook, 1984), the treatment of behavior analysis ranges from slipshod to overtly incorrect. A few education tests written by behavior analysts (Alberto & Troutman, 1982; Siedentop, 1983; Sulzer-Azaroff & Mayer, 1977) present accurate theoretical descriptions as well as evidence for and examples of the many behavior analysis strategies that have been applied successfully in schools.

Thus, while some of the language and tactics of behavior analysis have been mainstreamed, mixed evidence exists concerning their correct utilization. Teacher praise is no doubt the most widely known behavior analysis strategy in education. One suspects that most teachers prepared in the past decade have learned that their verbal and nonverbal behavior can be used to improve student academic/social performance. But Brophy (1981) has shown that teacher praise

3

is not always a functional event in the classroom. Substantive and practical differences exist between teacher praise and contingent teacher reinforcement. Educational researchers typically count the frequency of praise statements with no reference to their correct application or functional effects. To classify as reinforcement, a praise statement must be contingent upon appropriate student behavior and be related functionally to an increase in the frequency of that behavior. Behavioral researchers (Strain, Lambert, Kerr, Stagg, & Kenkner 1983) have found that praise is often delivered noncontingently, sometimes mistargeted completely, and typically so thinly scheduled that it could have only weak effects. Thus, it is no surprise when process-product researchers do not always find strong positive relationships between frequency of teacher praise and indices of student achievement. The finding only shows that labels should not be mistaken for operations, given that there are literally hundreds of ecologically valid experimental studies in which some form of student academic/social behavior has been accelerated by and functionally related to contingent teacher praise.

Does this mean that teachers do not often behave in ways that approximate the behavior analysis paradigm? No. Process-product research has provided at least two kinds of indirect evidence which support the use and efficacy of quasi-behavioral teaching strategies (I use the term *quasi-behavioral* to refer to strategies that ''look like''strategies advocated by behavior analysts but were not applied as rules taught from that perspective). Research in teacher effectiveness has produced an inductively derived constellation of strategies associated with academic and affective gains in regular classrooms. These strategies closely approximate those used in behavior analysis classrooms. This constellation of teacher strategies, referred to most often as direct instruction, features strong teacher stimulus control, high rates of student academic responding, a supportive classroom environment, frequent student success, gradual approximation of learning goals, and the consistent application of consequences.

Even more obviously similar to behavioral strategies are the patterns of teacher behavior in the first few days of school that predict achievement throughout the academic year. Many are familiar with the intriguing research (Emmer & Evertson, 1980) which analyzed the teacher tactics in the first days of school that seem to predict achievement across the school year. The prescriptions that derive from those analyses (Evertson et al., 1981) include the establishment of behavioral routines and rules, frequent early prompting, high densities of praise, practice in the relevant routines with specific feedback, and gradual fading of prompts concurrent with a shift to intermittent feedback and reinforcement. Even though this picture was developed inductively through naturalistic research—and, from a nonbehavioral perspective—it is virtually identical to what behavior analysts have suggested for many years.

I do not mean to imply that the effective teachers in these studies utilized quasi-behavioral strategies because they were taught to do so in their preservice training. Quite to the contrary, one suspects that most of the teachers developed these approaches contingently during their early teaching experiences and had them differentially reinforced by the outcomes—managerial, social, and academic—that followed their use.

The point of this beginning overview is to emphasize that behavioral and quasi-behavioral strategies are now widely known in professional education, albeit their specificity and technical applications are not widely practiced or appreciated. These strategies are identifiable, they appear to work, and they appear to be amenable to training.

Why is it then, when one turns from teaching to teacher education, that one sees so few programs in which systematic behavioral change is sought? As effective teaching strategies become more clearly linked to indices of student achievement, why is it that the acquisition of these strategies has not become the central goal of teacher education programs?

Can the teaching behavior of trainees be changed? Are any training interventions both effective and economical? Will behaviors changed in the training program generalize to the early stages of teaching? What kinds of intervention strategies are available to the teacher educator? These are the central questions to be addressed in this paper, and, given the current direction of the education reform movement in teacher education, they need to be attended to seriously. But first the available research must be delimited to ensure that the evidence cited is relevant to the questions asked.

Delimitations

The topic of teacher behavior modification is not as broad as that of teacher behavior change and not as narrow as that of teacher behavior change brought about through specific application of behavior modification strategies. Undoubtedly, teacher behavior does change across time, sometimes gradually and sometimes abruptly. But in many cases the changes are not measured consistently, and even less often an attempt is made to analyze the variables to which the changes can be attributed. Thus, teacher change is too broad an area for purposes of this report.

On the other hand, it is far too narrow to rely only on research in which teacher change is brought about through the specific application of behavior analysis strategies. Gleissman (1981), for example, includes in his important review a section on behavioral teacher training, which is defined by the application of reinforcement strategies. This focus is too narrow simply because it relies solely on classification on the label which is used to identify the intervention strategy.

A more useful approach to delimiting this area is to invoke the characteristics of a natural science of behavior and to consider as relevant all data which approximate these characteristics. The criteria for inclusion then would rest on three primary features. First, the studies would have to focus on teacher behavior as a natural phenomenon studied for its own value rather than as an epiphenomenon studied only to infer something about other less accessible variables. This would rule out all psychometrically oriented research as well as the growingly popular cognitive-developmental work. The measurement of behavior should be direct and continuous, but for purposes of this paper some pre/post kinds of efforts will be included. Second, the training intervention would have to be defined with sufficient specificity to allow for replication. And finally, the research design would have to allow for some internally valid means for attributing changes to the presence and absence of the training strategy.

These delimitations rule out some very interesting research. For example, teacher socialization research is outside the limits for this analysis. In socialization research, the changes are sometimes specified in behavioral terms. But often no way exists to understand clearly when they occur and analyze the specific variables responsible for the changes. It is of little value to suggest that forces in the school change teacher behavior during the induction period. Which forces? When? In what ways? This is not to suggest that an experimental analysis of teacher socialization cannot be accomplished. It just has not been done yet.

The delimitations do allow teacher education research to be included in the analysis even though it is not developed from or identified with the traditions of behavior analysis. Behavior modification occurs when environmental variables are manipulated to produce specific changes in behavior. Whether one calls it behavior modification or not is irrelevant. Whether one labels the independent variables with language that derives from the experimental analysis of behavior or not is also irrelevant. A terribly common misunderstanding is assuming that behavior modification occurs only when a behavior modifier is at work. In a research sense, it occurs whenever the criteria for a natural experimental analysis are satisfied. That is the spirit within which this report has been developed.

A Related Question

It is also important to address a related question at the outset of this report. Relationships among teacher practices and indices of student growth and performance are eventually crucial to the topic of teacher behavior modification. That point seems unarguable. But it is not fair to suggest that teacher education programs do not or should not attempt to change the behavior of preservice trainees in specific directions just because we do not yet know enough about which teaching strategies are appropriate. In the first place, teacher educators have never been without their visions of how teachers should best operate in educational settings. The fact that those visions in many instances were, and continue to be, based on theories, hopes, and beliefs rather than on empirically validated relationships to indices of student growth is interesting but not crucial for answering the questions addressed in this report. One cannot honestly argue that teacher behavior modification has not or should not be attempted because we have not identified fully, either through consensual agreement or empirical validation, the repertoire of skills needed by the beginning teacher. Many good training programs happen to train invalid or irrelevant skills, a fact which in no way diminishes their efficacy as training programs.

Until teacher educators achieve some consensus on what repertoire of skills the beginning teacher needs to provide safe, minimally competent teaching in schools, they will be doomed to shadow status in the eyes of the public. They cannot hope to achieve consensus without first agreeing to some criteria by which teacher effectiveness should be judged or, even better, to alternative sets of criteria which represent different answers that educators might have to the fundamental question, What are schools for? Once such criteria are designated and the repertoire relevant to them is identified, one could then begin to ascertain what levels of skill that meet minimal standards for effective teaching (however defined) are necessary to produce changes among students.

Although some certainly would not agree (Popkewitz, Tabachnick, & Zeichner, 1979), it is my judgment that a great deal of empirically validated knowledge about teaching skills is present. In a major review of teaching research, Good (1980) reached a similar conclusion. He suggested that (a) teachers do make a difference individually, (b) schools do make a difference collectively, (c) the manner by which teachers make a difference has been and continues to be analyzed, and (d) the identified teaching skills and strategies are such that they can become the focus of preservice education. As an example of the then current level of knowledge, Good pointed to evidence that supports the usefulness and trainability of direct instruction strategies.

> That direct instruction is associated with increased learning gains in a common, almost universal conclusion of recent naturalistic research. However to accompany the naturalistic studies are three recently completed field experiments. These studies illustrate that teachers can be taught direct instructional principles in relatively simple training programs that lead to changes in teachers' classroom behavior and student achievement. (pp. 8-9)

The fact that such conclusions from competent and thoughtful researchers continue to be ignored by teacher educators is interesting and perhaps even directly relevant to answering some questions about the topic of teacher behavior modification. But some things are known about teaching effectively, certainly enough to warrant a systematic effort to help preservice trainees to acquire such skills.

The Hope

In the *Second Handbook of Research on Teaching*, Robert Peck and James Tucker (1973) reviewed the state of the art in research on teacher education up to 1971. They began the review by citing the paucity of published teacher education research prior to the mid-1960s. But then a quantum leap occurred in both the quantity and the quality of teacher education research. Their review in the *Second Handbook* reflects the early optimism engendered by that research movement. Much of the research they reviewed qualifies as relevant to the topic of teacher behavior modification. Some of their conclusions are therefore important to note, not only historically but also substantively.

After reviewing research on systematic approaches to teacher education, they concluded that "In short, there is a substantial amount of evidence that specifying objectives and teaching to them is effective" (p. 945). After reviewing research on performance feedback for teachers, they concluded that "All in all, the research evidence looks quite consistent in confirming the utility of giving teachers objective feedback about specific aspects of their teaching behavior" (p. 947). The microteaching review received a generally favorable conclusion, as did training in interaction analysis, which was the dominant observation system of the day. In contrast, a brief review of the effects of traditional approaches to teacher education produced results that were disheartening to say the least.

The final paragraph of the Peck and Tucker review was unabashedly critical of traditional models and excitedly optimistic about what might lie just ahead.

> Teacher education can no longer remain in a happily ignorant, ineffectual state consisting of romanticized lectures, on the one hand, and fuzzy or unplanned "practical" experience on the other. We are genuinely in sight of the theoretical principles, the operational measures, and even the developmental technology for moving onto a performance-based method of appraising teaching. A great deal of research remains to be done to discover additional theoretical principles which would lead to more effective training. Even more extensive and more expensive evaluative research will be absolutely necessary in order to test and refine instructional systems so that we can be sure they will have beneficial effects under carefully specified, differentiated conditions of application. The day is still quite a long way off, but it is no longer merely wishful thinking to foresee a performance-based system for the certification of teachers. More importantly, we can foresee an objective, extremely helpful system of continuing, lifelong development for all members of the profession who want to keep improving their skills. (p. 971)

Needless to say, the programmatic hope expressed in this landmark review has not been achieved. Not only have their optimistic visions remained largely unrealized, but most current educational reform documents suggest directions for teacher education that are philosophically and practically opposite to those suggested by Peck and Tucker. What happened along the way? What does more recent research say about teacher behavior modification? Are the current reform suggestions or the lack of systematic program effort derived from a more recent research base with less promising results?

The More Recent Research Evidence

Larry Locke (1984) recently reviewed (a) individual studies that are relevant to the questions and (b) several major reviews of research in teacher education (all of which contain evidence that is responsive to the questions). The review is among the most important our young area has yet produced.

What I will try to do is document what I judge to be the general findings of this research area. I will also add some research developed within behavior analysis which seldom gets included in education reviews. And occasionally I will refer to an analogous body of research in counselor education, simply because they have done a great deal of research on training clinical and counseling skills, the skills are used in a helping profession practice, and the history of training research in that field is very similar to teacher education. I would take any similarities in outcomes between the counselor/clinical area and teacher education to provide strong convergent validity for the training methods.

Aside from the now largely defunct competency-based teacher education movement, relatively few efforts over the past quarter century have been made to develop systematic training programs to alter the teaching repertoires of preservice candidates. While there is certainly a heightened awareness of behavior analysis and teacher effectiveness strategies, skill development programs based on them have yet to appear. No doubt they receive at least passing mention in the lecture/discussion, outside reading, and field-based experiences formats that dominate most teacher preparation programs. But lecture/discussion, reading assignments, and field experience do not a systematic training make. In short, while the "technician" metaphor has increasingly dominated much of the literature and rhetoric of teacher education, it seems to not have been reflected in actual program change. Even the rhetoric is currently in eclipse as reformers move very dramatically away from any training model and embrace a liberal arts apprenticeship model.

Can one infer from this persistent unwillingness to adopt systematic training models that the more recent research brings such tactics into question? No.

Gleissman (1981), in a major (National Institute Education) review, suggested that there is ample evidence that "shows that teaching skills can be learned and teaching performance modified through methods that provide for control and guidance of experience" (pp. 2-13). Gleissman (1981) further suggested that teacher educators have more ways to accomplish these goals than is commonly assumed.

> For some time, it has been my impression that teacher educators may be both unnecessarily restricted in their conceptions of how to improve teaching performance, and unnecessarily lacking in confidence that teaching performance can be improved.
>
> In completing a recent review of the teacher training literature, I became aware that we have far greater resources to bring to bear on the improvement of teaching than is often assumed. (p. vii)

Gleissman's model for reviewing the research, adapted by Locke (1984) for his review in physical education, includes learning to teach through observation, concept formation exercises, practice (such as in microteaching, peer teaching, and other methods), from direct feedback on teaching performance, through reinforcement of appropriate teaching skill performance, and through information in the form of directives and/or recommendations.

Joyce and Showers (1981) review 200 studies, evaluating them in the first instance for methodological soundness. This initial effort led to some matrix conceptualizations that they then used to even more extensively review the preservice and inservice education literature.

Some of their summary statements are relevant for our purposes.

> What was most striking about that first cut was that the better designed studies demonstrated the effectiveness of a variety of training components in assisting teachers toward skill acquisition. Intensive structured feedback, modeling, intensive practice, careful discrimination training, all in their various ways helped teachers acquire the targeted behaviors. (p. 1)

In the second search 281 papers were identified but 204 were discarded because of insufficient specification of skills, insufficient measurement, and other problems. Because this research team was interested in the problem of transfer of acquired skills, they also identified 174 papers dealing with that issue. But most of those did not report data, and some of those that were data based had serious methodological flaws.

Sixty-seven studies were included in the final review. While it is clear that in education there is no *Zeitgeist* in support of data-based articles, 67 studies of reasonable methodological soundness is a fair number. Joyce and Showers concluded that training generally accomplished the objectives toward which it was directed. Indeed, 60 of the 67 reviewed studies "successfully changed or created behavior at the level targeted" (p. 13).

The general finding that training "works" is accepted and is evidenced by the current concern with transfer from training program to workspace. For example, in a more recent review of the generalization of behavioral teacher training, Robinson and Swanton (1980) began their review article by simply stating that there is "substantial evidence" (p. 486) that teachers can be trained to utilize various types of behaviorally oriented teaching strategies. Robinson and Swanton provide a few citations dealing with classroom management, teacher praise, token economies, self-recording, and other techniques. Then they move immediately to the issue of generalization of changes in nontraining settings and across time.

A very similar picture appears to be true for the research literature in the training of counselors and clinicians. While this research literature evidently was nonexistent in the mid-1960s and was reasonably sparse even into the early 1970s, Ford (1979) found over 100 empirical studies for his 1979 review. What is remarkable about this literature is the similarity with the teacher training literature both in the kinds of dependent variables trained and in the training strategies employed. In his conclusion, Ford suggested the following:

> The research on training counselors and clinicians has demonstrated that several behavioral training components, particularly when combined in systematic and comprehensive training packages or programs delivered via multiple sources and presented with parametric precautions, effectively aid counseling and clinical trainees to acquire relatively discrete therapist skills. (p. 119)

More recent research in this area (Brock, Fawcett, & Lichtenberg, 1982; Isaacs, Embry, & Baer, 1982; Iwata, Wong, Riordan, Dorsey, & Lau, 1982; Whang, Fletcher, & Fawcett, 1982) serves both to validate Ford's general conclusion and to extend it. Recent efforts not only support the notion that training works, but that when clinicians and therapists utilize their newly acquired skills, the clients improve. This establishes the crucial linkage between the acquisition of process skills by trainees and their effects when used in practice.

This point is not to suggest that research on teacher behavior modification is without flaws, methodologically or conceptually. Nor is it to suggest that several crucially related questions have been answered with any satisfaction— namely, what skills should be trained and how they should be trained so as to persist from the training program to the work setting and across time within the work setting. However, these problems should not detract from acknowledging what seems to be the unequivocal results of 30 years of teacher training research. Training programs which have sufficient specificity and contingency are capable both of "fine tuning" interactive skills that are no doubt already within the behavioral repertoire of most trainees and also of helping them to acquire brand new skills. These training gains can be effected through a wide variety of training interventions.

This general proposition is clarified when one considers the research on "traditional" teacher training. Just as the positive benefits of systematic training appear to be consistent in the literature, so do the nonbenefits of unsystematic teacher education. Peck and Tucker's (1973) negative conclusions about traditional models have been further substantiated, including (within the traditional paradigm) the recent trend toward increased field experiences. Gleissman (1981) reported that the supposed benefits of practicum, internship, and student teaching experiences are vastly exaggerated and that no evidence suggests that experience alone improves teaching, and some evidence suggests that teaching deteriorates through these experiences. This conclusion is similar to that stated in physical education by Locke (1979) in his important review of student teaching. Thus, the general conclusion supporting the positive benefits of systematic training appears to be even more important when compared with the noneffects or potentially deleterious effects of unsystematic, conventional approaches.

The Question of Generalization

As stated earlier, a major issue in reviews of teacher education research is whether or not changes effected in a training program generalize across settings to the initial workplace and persist across time. Locke (1982) reflects on the consensus view of this issue when he suggests that lack of generalization—teachers not using the newly acquired skills—is the pessimistic message that balances the more optimistic conclusions that teacher education, when done systematically, does work. The available evidence does not warrant such a conclusion.

The argument for the conclusion that trained skills do not generalize rests on the inappropriate association of some known facts. Research supports the notion that teachers can be trained (in the specific sense that their teaching repertoires can be systematically changed in directions thought to be associated with effective teaching). But this research is reasonably limited in scope and does not suggest that even 5% of the newly certified teachers in any given year are so trained. A basic mistake is assuming that because a reasonably few teachers have been systematically trained in research operations, the same training operations have been applied to most trainees.

When descriptive/analytic research in education and physical education reveals the sad picture of teachers in-service behaving in ways that do not reflect the goals of effective training programs, the conclusion is sometimes reached that a problem of generalization has occurred. It could be a problem of generalization only if the subjects studied in the worksetting (whether in student teaching or as teachers in-service) had been trained to some criterion or mastery level in a training program prior to the time when the descriptive research was done. To assume that because teachers come from certain programs which supposedly emphasize effective practices is insufficient—unless "emphasis" is operationalized as criterion skill performance. In this instance, I disagree with Locke's (1982) conclusions. As suggested, little evidence is available to answer the questions about generalization. But what little there is certainly does not warrant a negative finding. Borg's (1972) often-cited study showed that teachers exhibited about half of the skills they had acquired 3 years previously. Robinson and Swanton (1980) concluded that about 50% of the few studies which attempted to assess generalization of teacher training found positive results. Leith (1982), in a study assessing the delayed effects of microteaching, concluded that "the long term followup made clear that the advantage in classroom teaching performance given by microteaching with personal feedback persists over a prolonged period without further microteaching" (p. 108). In physical education, Mancini, Frye, and Quinn (1982) studied the generalization of training in interaction analysis (IA) and reported the following:

> The effects of instruction and/or supervision in IA on the overall teaching environment, including teacher behavior, effectiveness, and attitudes, were maintained 1 to 4 years after the cessation of training in interaction analysis. (p. 185)

Joyce and Showers (1981) reported substantial evidence of what they called *horizontal transfer* (meaning transfer of trained skills to nontraining settings) but not *vertical transfer* (meaning incorporation of trained skills into new, more complex repertoires).

Thus, much of the speculation about why training effects "wash out" is based on both the erroneous assumption that in most instances specific training effects are achieved in preparation programs, and a misreading of the small research evidence that assesses whether or not generalization occurs among trained subjects. But the relative absence of data warrants immediate attention to the problem of generalization both as a research endeavor and as an area where one might apply what has been learned from basic research about generalization. After all, *generalization* (or transfer of training in more mainstream psychology) is not exactly a new topic.

One technical comment and one theoretical argument should be added to the debate. First, the strategy of "train and hope" represents a primitive approach to the problem of generalization. One of the most commonly cited slogans in behavior analysis is that generalization should be programmed rather than expected or lamented. And, starting from the work of Stokes and Baer (1977), there has been substantial attention paid to a technology of generalization. Strategies such as training sufficient examplars, programming common stimuli, introducing behaviors to natural maintaining contingencies, using indiscriminable contingencies, and mediating generalization through self-control procedures have all been applied successfully to problems of generalization within education (Baer, & Fowler, 1984). Joyce and Showers (1981) provide similar nonbehavioral training model to enhance generalization. The fact is that teacher education has not paid much attention to generalization of training changes either as a research subject or as an objective of the training program. Until both have been done, it seems premature to conclude that training should not be done, because it will not generalize even if it is accomplished.

I have always been intrigued by those who bemoan the fact that teacher education does not produce lasting changes in the teaching repertoires of trainees. Some demonstrations of "permanent" behavioral change exist in the experimental literature, but the contingencies that produce them are extraordinarily powerful and typically aversive. The major assumption of a behavioral approach is that the human organism is tremendously adaptive and particularly responsive to local environmental contingencies. In teacher education, criticisms of training research and assumptions about generalization are based on what used to be trait-theories and now are popular as development theories; that is what needs to be changed some inner essence which, once changed, is permanent and for which overt behavior is simply an epiphenomenal manifestation. From a behavioral perspective one would expect teacher behavior to be responsive to student behavior. Behaviorally, the problem of generalization is to bring teacher behavior under the control of certain student behaviors rather than others, to have teacher behavior controlled by signs of academic progress among students, and to provide trainees with the skills that allow academic outcomes to become conspicuous among the many others which inhabit the classroom. As Doyle (1979) has pointed out, far too many teachers capitulate to the dynamics of classroom life by coming under the control of managerial and social behavior of students' rather than their academic progress. The point is, when it comes to generalization, the assumptions one has about human behavior are absolutely crucial to what strategies one believes might promote generalization from training program to workplace.

Clearly, skills developed in the training program would generalize more completely if some component of the early work experience could serve to reinforce and further refine them. This, in essence, is the common assumption that brings together the many suggestions as global as internships, extended teacher education models, and temporary certification with those as specific as coaching (Joyce, & Showers, 1982). From a behavioral point of view, the issue hinges on the degree to which the training program (or a cohort agency) can continue to operate during the induction period.

Specificity Needed in Training

One training question, which has a very clear answer, deals with the kinds of interventions which might be effective. The answer seems to be that, given sufficient specificity and contingency (i.e., given appropriate contingencies) many different training strategies are effective. When one thinks of training, the kinds of strategies that come to mind are microteaching, minicourses, and practice with feedback. But many others have been shown to be functionally related to changes in teacher behavior. Among these are modeling, discrimination training, learning through observation, role playing, and behavioral rehearsal.

Some of these methods are clearly more cost effective than others, and one suspects that comparative studies with relative time and personnel costs as criterion variables need to be undertaken. Gleissman's (Gleissman & Pugh, 1981) interesting research on behavior change through concept formation is particularly noteworthy because of its relative cost effectiveness.

The research on training counselors and clinicians also is helpful in this area because of the detailed specification of their training procedures (Ford, 1979), which lend particular support to role playing and behavior rehearsal as successful strategies. Here, too, there appear to be training methods that are successful and reasonably cost effective. For example, Wang, Fletcher, and Fawcett (1982) used written instructions, audiotapes of criterion performance, and a problem-solving card file (everyday problems, alternative solutions, and likely consequences to the alternatives) as preliminary training for three major skill groups in a counseling program. Trainees then role played skills. The generalization test was two consecutive therapy sessions in which the skill was demonstrated with 100% accuracy. Trained skills were later assessed for inclusion into more complex repertoires. Student study time for the program took 16 hrs. Training time with a trainer took 26 hrs. Eventually, these kinds of data will be crucial for comparative training studies.

Although these training strategies are diverse, it is clear that they each have both specificity and contingency. If you get the impression that "you get what you train for," you are exactly right. It reminds me so much of the time-honored dictum from sports coaching—you play as you practice. In teacher education, the data suggest that sloppy training leads to sloppy teaching.

One observation might serve to illuminate this area a bit. Good training programs have criterion goals. Students are held accountable for performance at whatever stage constitutes that mastery or criterion level. This training literature is similar to Doyle's work on task structures. Doyle (1981) has suggested that if there is no accountability in the classroom then there is no task. Under those conditions, what results is due to the student's own interests or other unplanned contingencies. The same analysis has held true for physical education teaching (Tousignant & Siedentop, 1983), and it appears to fit student teaching in physical education also (Tinning, 1983). Clearly, teacher educators are teachers too. How many teacher education programs are there where performance demands are traded for trainee cooperation in the managerial aspects of the program and some trainee social approval? One suspects that some teacher educators like for "things to go smoothly" and to "be close to the students" and willingly barter specificity and contingency for these outcomes.

Performance Enhancement

Virtually all of the research literature relevant to this report focuses on skill acquisition and skill refinement. That is no doubt appropriate because that is the first agenda of teacher education. Some critics have pointed out that most skills trained are discrete and that blending them appropriately in a discriminative skill repertoire is not guaranteed—and they are right. But this literature is reasonably young and it has started correctly by doing what is doable. And some of the recent experimental work (Good, 1980) indicates that the current level of skill training is sufficient to produce performance increments among students.

One can expect that future research will focus on more complex teaching skills and the blending of skills into a discriminative repertoire. But I hope that some efforts will be directed toward the performance enhancement of newly acquired skills; that is, motivational training to encourage trainees to consistently maintain and appropriately utilize previously acquired skills. This kind of effort would likely have an impact on the generalization of acquired skills and certainly would require a systematic effort to influence what are typically referred to as "values".

But performance enhancement cannot be achieved without three prerequisite conditions. First, the attention of the teacher educator must be reinforcing to the trainee. This variable is crucial to the approach tendencies of the trainee toward program experiences, to the impact of trainer feedback, and to the impact of trainer modeling.

Second, social reinforcement is extraordinarily powerful but is best exerted in situations which have a sufficient intimacy. In these situations notions about the social value of our work and of professional commitment can be addressed with some expectation for outcomes.

Third, achieving performance enhancement within a teacher education program would require systematic treatment across different program components. For example, there are important skill variations in delivering contingent teacher praise to elementary, middle, and senior high school students. While contingent teacher praise may be a skill acquired initially in one part of the program, it should be refined as students move through the various components which focus on different school levels. But the trainers would have to be systematic and consistent in their own commitments to contingent teacher praise as an important skill, to the subtle variations needed to bring that skill to a level of minimal competence, and to enhancing trainees performance of that skill.

If these conditions exist, the chances are that trainees will use the skill, and use it more appropriately. It will be more resistent to extinction and to contingencies which might shape up and support incompatible skills. If these conditions do not exist, it should not be expected that the teacher will use trained skills diligently, nor should we lament the fact that they do not.

Summary

Can teacher behavior be changed? Yes! Do the kinds of changes that might be achieved have sufficient valence to influence student performance? Yes, at least early reports so indicate. Will the trained behaviors generalize to the work setting? Yes, if trained with sufficient specificity and contingency. Are the kinds of intervention strategies utilized within the reach of most teacher educators? Yes, it appears that a willingness to use them and a commitment of time and effort are all that stand in the way. Is any or all of this consistent with what is known about the analysis of human behavior? Yes, it is about what you would expect from a behavior analysis perspective—that is, a lot of "yes, but" answers.

Given this basically optimistic data base, why then is teacher behavior modification not the central issue in most teacher education programs? Why are there so few systematic efforts? No clear answers to these questions exist, and virtually no research on teacher educators has been done. Because there is no research on teacher educators, these questions cannot be answered, even tentatively, in the same way as the questions were answered above. One can only speculate.

While behavior analysis has superficially influenced psychology and education in the past quarter century, it has yet to achieve any major impact except in clinical psychology and special education, two areas where outcomes are important. In the current *Zeitgeist* behaviorist positions are in eclipse and cognitive psychology sits atop the intellectual mountain. Proof of this can be found in the titles of papers and symposia in the American Educational Research Association Program for 1984.

Current reform manifestos, which argue for more preparation in the liberal arts and content areas followed by an internship in an apprentice model, clearly do not derive from any behaviorist position. It appears that the old argument between education and training is currently being decided in favor of education. But when examined closely, that traditional distinction seems to come down to this—when we know what we are doing we call it training, and when we do not know what we are doing we call it education (Skinner, 1969). Many argue the cognitivist position that education provides a deeper, broader, more lasting ability or predisposition. But little evidence supports such a view and it remains mostly an article of faith rather than a legitimate premise on which to build a preservice program.

Just as this nation and its educational establishment have managed to ignore completely the clear data-based message of early compensatory education research (Lindsley et al., 1984) teacher educators will probably mostly ignore the literature referred to in this paper and other reviews. This is a point that should be remembered discretely the next time any of us begins to bemoan the fact that most teachers do not pay attention to research.

However, pessimism about the current scene is tempered when one steps back and views the events in proper historical perspective. Charles Darwin wrote *The Origin of Species* in 1859, establishing a natural science of phylogeny and moving biological evolution clearly within the realms of a deterministic science. Fifty years later, just after the turn of the century, Darwinian notions were extremely unpopular in the university and at odds with the basic preconceptions of society. In 1984, the Darwinian model is the accepted model in the university, and the State of Texas has recently decided that it is safe enough to be included in textbooks used in Texas schools.

In 1938, B. F. Skinner published *The Behavior of Organisms,* establishing a natural science of ontogeny and moving individual development and cultural evolution clearly within the realms of a deterministic science. Nearly 50 years later, behaviorism seems to be in eclipse in the university and is still vigorously opposed in many parts of society. But as Isiah Berlin (Gay, 1979) always insisted, any attempt to reconcile determinism with a free-will position borders on the sleight of hand. The issue will not go away, and in my judgment those who embrace cognitivist positions will increasingly be called upon to reconcile their views to the emerging data. Until that evolution progresses a bit more, it is too much to expect that teacher education programs will be conceptualized and implemented as behavior change systems. The current contingencies simply do not support such efforts. But contingencies change. Cultures do evolve. And increasingly we have the knowledge and the technology to control the direction of that evolution.

> In what we may call the prescientific view (and the word is not necessarily perjorative) a person's behavior is at least to some extent his or her own achievement. He or she is free to deliberate, decide, and act, possibly in original ways, and he is to be given credit for success and blamed for failures. In the scientific view (and the word is not necessarily honorific) a person's behavior is determined by a genetic endowment traceable to the evolutionary history of the species and by the environmental circumstances to which as an individual he has been exposed. Neither view can be proved, but it is in the nature of scientific inquiry that the evidence should shift in favor of the second. As we learn more about the effects of the environment, we have less reason to attribute any part of human behavior to an autonomous controlling agent. And the second view

shows a marked advantage when we begin to do something about behavior. Autonomous man is not easily changed: In fact, to the extent that he is autonomous, he is by definition not changeable at all. But the environment can be changed, and we are learning how to change it. (Skinner, 1971, p. 101)

References

Alberto, P., & Troutman, A. (1982). *Applied behavior analysis for teachers.* Columbus, OH: Charles E. Merrill Publishing.

Baer, D., & Fowler, S. (1984). How should we measure the potential of self control procedures for generalized education outcomes? In W. Heward, T. Heron, D. Hill, & J. Trap-Porter (Eds.), *Focus on behavior analysis in education* (pp. 145-161). Columbus, OH: Charles E. Merrill Publishing.

Borg, W. (1982). The minicourse as a vehicle for changing teacher behavior: A three year followup. *Journal of Educational Psychology, 63,* 572-579.

Brock, L., Fawcett, S., & Lichtenberg, J. (1982). Training, counseling and problem-solving skills with university students. *American Journal of Community Psychology,* **10,** 225-237.

Brophy J. (1981). Teacher praise: A functional analysis. *Review of Educational Research,* **51** (1), 33-84.

Cook, N. (1984). The behavior model in preservice textbooks. In W. Heward, T. Heron, D. Hill, & J. Trap-Porter (Eds.), *Focus on behavior analysis in education.* Columbus, OH: Charles E. Merrill Publishing.

Doyle, W. (1979). Classroom tasks and students' abilities. In P. Peterson & H. Walberg (Eds.), *Research on teaching: Concepts, findings, and implications.* Berkeley: McCutchan Publishing Co.

Doyle, W. (1981, April). *Accomplishing writing tasks in the classroom.* Paper presented at the annual meeting of the American Education Research Association, Los Angeles, CA.

Emmer, E., & Evertson, C. (1980). *Effective management at the beginning of the year in junior high school classrooms.* Research and Development Center for Teacher Education, Austin, TX (Order No. 6107).

Evertson, C., Emmer, E., Clements, B., Sanford, J., Worsham, M., & Williams, E. (1981). *Organizing and managing the elementary school classroom.* Research and Development Center for Teacher Education, Austin, TX.

Ford, J. (1979). Research on training counselors and clinicians. *Review of Education Research,* **49** (1), 87-130.

Gleissman, D. (1981). *Learning how to teach: Process, effects and criteria.* Washington, DC: National Institute of Education. (ERIC Document Reproduction Service No. ED 200 516).

Gleissman, D., & Pugh, R. (1981). Developing teaching skills through understanding. *Action in Teacher Education,* **3** (1), 1-18.

Good, T. (1980). Research on teaching. In G. Hall, S. Hord, & G. Brown (Eds.), *Exploring issues in teacher education: Question for future research.* Austin, TX: Research and Development Center for Teacher Education, The University of Texas at Austin.

Isaacs, C., Embry, L., & Baer, D. (1982). Training family therapists: An experimental analysis. *Journal of Applied Behavior Analysis,* **15,** 505-520.

Iwata, B., Wong, S., Riordan, M., Dorsey, M., & Lau, M. (1982). Assessment and training of clinical interviewing skills: Analogues, analysis, and field replication. *Journal of Applied Behavior Analysis,* **15,** 191-203.

Joyce, B. & Shower, B. (1981, April). *Teacher training research: Working hypotheses for program design and directions for further study.* Paper presented at the annual meeting of the American Education Research Association, Los Angeles, CA.

Joyce, B. & Showers, B. (1982). The coaching of teaching. *Education Leadership,* **39** (1), 4-10.

Leith, G. (1982). The influence of personality on learning to teach: Effects and delayed effects of microteaching. *Education Review,* **34** (3), 100-109.

Lindsley, O., Ramp, E., Becker, W., & Greer, R.D. (1984, May 31). The political coverup of behavior analysis in education: Follow through. Symposium presented at 10th Convention of the Association for Behavior Analysis, Nashville, TN.

Locke, L. (1979). Supervision, schools and student teaching: Why things stay the same. *The Academy Papers,* 65-74.

Locke, L.F. (1984), Research on Teaching Teachers: Where are we now? Monograph #2, Journal of Teaching in Physical Education, Summer, 1984.

Mancini, V., Frye, P., & Quinn, P. (1982). Long-term effects of instruction and supervision in interaction analysis on teacher behavior, effectiveness, and attitudes of inservice physical educators. In M. Pieron & J. Cheffer (Eds.), *Studying the teaching in physical education.* Liege, Belgium: AIESEP.

Peck, R., & Tucker, J. (1973). Research on teacher education. In R. Travers (Ed.), *Second handbook of research on teaching.* Chicago: Rand McNally.

Popkewitz, T., Tabachnick, B., & Zeichner, K. (1979). Dulling the senses: Research in teacher education. *Journal of Teacher Education,* **30**, 52-60.

Robinson, V., & Swanton C. (1980) The generalization of behavior teacher training. *Review of Education Research,* **50**(3), 486-498.

Siedentop, D. (1983). *Developing teaching skills in physical education* (2nd. ed.). Palo Alto, CA: Mayfield Publishing.

Skinner, B.F. (1969). *Contingencies of reinforcement: A theoretical analysis.* New York: Appleton-Century-Crofts.

Skinner, B.F. (1971). *Beyond freedom and dignity.* New York: Alfred A Knopf.

Stoke, T., & Baer, D. (1977). An implicit technology of generalization. *Journal of Applied Behavior Analysis,* **10**, 349-367.

Strain, P., Lambert, M., Kerr, M., Stagg, V., & Kenkner, D. (1983), Naturalistic assessment of children's compliance to teachers' requests and consequences for complicance. *Journal of Applied Behavior Analysis,* **16**(2), 243-249.

Sulzer-Azaroff, B., & Mayer, G. (1977). *Applying behavior analysis procedures with children and youth.* New York: Holt, Rinehart, and Winston.

Tinning, R. (1983). *A task theory of student teaching: Development and provisional testing.* Unpublished doctoral dissertation, The Ohio State University, Columbus.

Tousignant, M., & Siedentop, D. (1983). A qualitative analysis of task structures in required secondary physical education classes. *Journal of Teaching in Physical Education,* **3**(1), 45-57

Whang, P., Fletcher, K., & Fawcett, S. (1982). Training counseling skills: An experimental analysis and social validation. *Journal of Applied Behavior Analysis,* **15**, 325-334.

2

Development of a Training Procedure to Increase Pupil Motor Engagement Time (MET)

Andrea H. Borys
THE UNIVERSITY OF ALBERTA
EDMONTON, ALBERTA, CANADA

The purpose of this paper is to discuss the development of a training procedure for helping secondary school physical education student teachers increase pupil motor engagement time (MET) in the gymnasium. Pupil MET is the time pupils spend exercising, practicing, and game playing.

Results of descriptive-analytic studies reveal that pupil engagement in motor activity during physical education classes is low. Pupils spend less than one third of their class time engaged in motor activity (Costello, 1977; Godbout, Brunelle, & Tousignant, 1983; McLeish, Howe, & Jackson, 1981; Metzler, 1980; Pieron & Haan, 1980). Moreover, MET varies depending on the pupil. Reasons given for low pupil motor activity include waiting, teacher talk, inefficient class management techniques, and the physical activity itself.

Researchers, comparing most and least effective physical education teachers, have indicated that the time pupils spend engaged in motor activity is the most important criterion in determining an effective teacher (McLeish et al., 1981; Phillips & Carlisle, 1983). Most effective teachers spend less time in management tasks, provide more practice time, and have more practice opportunities at an easier difficulty level than teachers categorized as average or poor (McLeish et al., 1981).

During the past decade intervention strategies have been used successfully in physical education settings during student teaching. Research findings suggest that pupil MET can be increased (Birdwell, 1980).

Development of a Training Procedure

This intervention procedure was developed using the descriptive-analytic and supervision research findings in physical education. The first task was to identify the training package components, which included teaching an activity unit to establish baseline data on pupil activity time in the gymnasium, attending a weekend and two follow-up workshops, and reteaching. In addition, a workbook, describing the techniques for increasing pupil MET, was written and used in conjunction with the workshops (Borys, 1982).

Pilot Testing

After the workbook was written, eight pilot tests were conducted. Based on the feedback received from professional educators and student teachers, the techniques and clinical tasks were refined. This procedure ensured that the class organizational and management techniques selected were the most effective ones for increasing pupil MET.

Pilot Test 1 involved trying the training procedure with one student teacher in a junior high school. As a result, the videotaping procedure was established, an evening and all day workshop was added to the training package, more examples of techniques were added to the workbook, and the training procedure was used during the final (high school) student teaching round.

During Pilot Test 2, teacher educators gave their opinions about the techniques included in the workbook. Subsequently, the number of techniques was reduced.

The revised training package was used during Pilot Test 3 with four student teachers in a high school setting. Consequently, the changes made to the training procedure included extending the workshop hours to include Friday evening, all day Saturday, and Saturday evening. The changes to the workbook added further examples of techniques and a section on planning, teaching a basketball unit, and developing a checklist for monitoring the techniques implemented. Also, the investigator became a faculty consultant to the control teachers.

In Pilot Test 4 the investigator taught a volleyball unit to a high school class to determine the effectiveness of the organization and managerial techniques checklist for gathering information about the techniques implemented during teaching. After teaching each lesson the checklist was completed. Subsequently, the number of instrument items was reduced.

For Pilot Test 5, secondary school physical education teachers examined the techniques outlined in the workbook. As a result of their input, jargon was eliminated and the number of techniques was reduced.

Pilot Test 6 involved obtaining feedback from teacher educators who reviewed the revised workbook. Subsequently, the negative impression of time spent in nonmovement activities was eliminated and a section in the workbook was written. It recognized the time pupils need to recover from vigorous exercise, to engage in cognitive and social activities, and/or to reflect upon their performances. The checklist was revised again to allow teachers to indicate the match between techniques planned and those actually implemented.

During Pilot Test 7 three high school teachers used the revised checklist. As a result of the feedback, techniques were divided into four categories, and trainees were asked to reflect on their teach lessons by describing the techniques used, suggesting alternatives, and selecting the most appropriate techniques for the particular teaching situation. Also, a journal was kept by the trainees to describe what happened when they tried to increase pupil MET.

The final pilot test, occurring after the preliminary field test, involved obtaining feedback on the workbook format and content from school physical education supervisory staff and doctoral students in curriculum and teaching. Subsequently, the workbook included color pages denoting each category of techniques, a reduction in the number of graphics, and a list of common problems for each of the three categories of techniques. Also, trainees were cautioned not to sacrifice safety, quality of practice, need for instruction, and/or rest periods for attaining a higher pupil MET.

Preliminary Field Test

Following the pilot testing phase, a preliminary field test was conducted to assess the feasibility of using the training procedure under field test conditions and to determine its impact on pupil MET. Although pupil MET was increased, changes were made to strengthen the intervention package. For example, the techniques outlined in the workbook were reorganized around three categories: (a) techniques for establishing the learning environment and organizing the class to move pupils quickly into activity, (b) designing and conducting activities to encourage high pupil activity levels, and (c) using monitoring techniques to correct inefficiencies in organization and practice.

Trainees were encouraged to use techniques which increased the opportunity for practice. Therefore, structuring ideal practice conditions and increasing the number of practice trials were emphasized during the field test.

The weekend workshop was extended to Sunday morning to include additional time for planning. Also, the Hawthorne effect was reduced by having the control teachers view their teach and reteach videotaped lessons and discuss these lessons with the investigator.

Field Test

The final phase of the study included a field test to evaluate the effectiveness of the training procedure for helping student teachers to increase pupil MET.

Evaluation Design

A pretest-posttest evaluation control group design was used. Four treatment and four control teachers, randomly selected from a pool of 19 volunteers, participated in the field test. The experimental variable included attending a weekend and two follow-up workshops, completing the workbook clinical tasks, and teaching while the control group received a conventional student teaching experience.

Procedure

The field test began with both treatment and control teachers teaching a 5-day teach/reteach basketball unit. For each teacher, two teach and two reteach lessons were videotaped. After the fourth teach lesson, the control teachers viewed their second and fourth videotaped lessons. In contrast, the treatment teachers attended a weekend workshop that included viewing videotaped lessons, coding pupil behaviors, determining teach pupil time in activity, analyzing and evaluating the techniques used, and planning the reteach lessons incorporating the techniques outlined in the workbook. Following this workshop, all teachers retaught the unit to a different class. After teaching the second and fourth reteach lessons, the treatment teachers viewed their videotapes, coded pupil time in activity, analyzed and evaluated the techniques used, compared the reteach and teach lessons, and suggested alternatives for the next lesson. The control teachers, on the other hand, viewed their videotaped lessons only.

Collection of Data

To determine the effects of the training procedure, an array of information was gathered. In addition to collecting pupil MET data for the teach/reteach lessons, questionnaires, teacher journals, completed clinical tasks, checklists, lesson plans, interviews, an investigator's diary, and observations of videotaped reteach lessons provided information necessary for determining the extent to which the intervention procedure was implemented.

Bestped, a systematic observation tool developed by Laubach (1975) to code pupil behavior in the physical education classes, was used by four trained independent coders. When observer reliability reached the .90 level, training ceased and the 32 videotapes were coded. Reliability checks were conducted throughout the coding period.

Three 5-min lesson portions and five target pupils were randomly selected and coded every 5-sec. Each coder coded a teach and reteach lesson for each student teacher. Codes were key-punched onto IBM computer cards, and an appropriate program analyzing the resulting pupil behavior data was used.

Because of the nature of the quantitative data collected, descriptive statistics were used to analyze the pupil behaviors during the teach and reteach lessons. Also, because the sample size was small, no tests of statistical significance were conducted to compare the treatment group with the control group.

Findings

Because the purpose of the intervention package was to increase the percentage of pupil MET occurrences during reteach lessons, pupil MET is examined first.

Pupil MET

During reteach lessons, treatment teachers as a group showed greater gains in pupil MET occurrences (+12.4%) than the control teachers (+2.3%; see Table 1).

The mean percentage of pupil MET occurrences during teach/reteach lessons for the treatment group was 43.4% and 55.8%, and 40.2% and 42.5% for the control group (see Table 1). When each lesson is examined, pupil MET for the treatment teacher group increased dramatically from reteach Lesson 1 (49.6%) to reteach Lesson 2 (61.9%).

Table 1. Mean percent occurrences of pupil MET during the teach/reteach lessons

Group	Teach lessons 1 %	Teach lessons 2 %	Teach lessons 1 & 2 %	Reteach lessons 1 %	Reteach lessons 2 %	Reteach lessons 1 & 2 %	From teach to reteach lessons %
Treatment teachers (n = 4)							
M	41.4	45.4	43.4	49.6	61.9	55.8	+ 12.4
SD	14.9	19.4	15.2	4.2	19.7	11.2	
Control teachers (n = 4)							
M	32.4	48.1	40.2	42.7	42.3	42.5	+ 2.3
SD	10.5	9.1	7.9	13.4	17.7	8.0	

Pupil MET Components

When pupil MET was broken down into its three components—exercise, practice, and game playing—the mean percentage of practice occurrences for the treatment group increased sharply during the reteach lessons (from 17.8% to 31.7%; see Table 2). Game playing increased slightly (16.8% to 17.8%), and exercise decreased (8.7% to 6.1%). In contrast, the percentage of practice occurrences for the control group decreased during the reteach lessons (from 23.6% to 17.9%).

Table 2. Mean percent occurrences of pupil time in activity during the teach/reteach lessons

Activity	Control teachers Teach lessons %	Control teachers Reteach lessons %	Control teachers Teach/Reteach shift %	Treatment teachers Teach lessons %	Treatment teachers Reteach lessons %	Treatment teachers Teach/Reteach shift %
Practice	23.6	17.9	− 5.7	17.8	31.7	+ 13.9
Game playing	11.0	20.7	+ 9.7	16.8	17.8	+ 1.0
Exercise	5.5	3.8	− 1.7	8.7	6.1	− 2.6
Explore	0.0	0.0	0.0	0.0	0.0	0.0
Express/ communicate	0.0	0.0	0.0	0.0	0.0	0.0
Relocate	4.6	5.3	+ 0.7	3.0	4.7	+ 1.7
Equip	7.6	8.9	+ 1.3	9.8	11.0	+ 1.2
Assist	1.2	4.2	+ 3.0	1.5	0.0	− 1.5
Diverge	0.9	0.7	− 0.2	1.2	1.0	− 1.0
Receive info	29.7	23.6	− 6.1	27.5	16.6	− 10.9
Give info	1.1	1.1	0.0	1.2	0.9	− 0.3
Await	12.6	11.6	− 1.0	12.0	8.6	− 3.4
Off − monitor	1.9	1.9	0.0	0.4	1.4	+ 1.0

In an effort to increase the percentage of practice occurrences during reteach lessons, the treatment teachers decreased the percentage of occurrences of receiving information (-10.9%) and await (-3.4%; see Table 2).

Techniques Used by Treatment Teachers for Increasing Pupil MET

When techniques used by treatment teachers were examined, the treatment teachers implementing the highest number of techniques were also the ones showing the highest gains in the percentage of pupil MET occurrences during reteach lessons. Techniques used most frequently included obtaining and arranging equipment prior to beginning the class, distributing equipment from strategic locations, starting activity when the first pupil arrived, involving all pupils in activities, using small sized groups, and giving teaching points as pupils practiced.

Discussion

The application of the research and development model was unique to this study. After the initial workbook was written, a series of cycles of product tryout, evaluation, and revision were repeated until the field test data indicated that the training procedure met the intended objectives. This lengthy process ensured that when the training program was developed it would help student teachers to increase pupil MET.

Although the intervention package helped treatment teachers as a group to increase the percentage of pupil MET occurrences during reteach lessons, the individual teachers varied considerably. Depending on the teacher and the setting, the training procedure had different effects. These results confirm the complexity of implementing an intervention package that attempts to change teacher and pupil behavior within a short time frame. Because teaching in the gymnasium is a complex activity and teachers experience a multiplicity of settings, it is impossible for a training procedure to be too prescriptive. In addition, pupil MET is influenced by variables other than those in the intervention package. These variables include the cooperating teacher, teaching style, pupil familiarity with subject matter, task difficulty, initial level of pupil MET, student teacher background, response to treatment, length and intensity of practice episodes, physical fitness levels, length of class, size of class, and pupil motivation.

References

Birdwell, D. (1980). The effects of modification of teacher behavior on academic learning time of selected students in physical education. (Doctoral dissertation, the Ohio State University, 1980). *Dissertation Abstracts International,* **41**, 1472A-1473A. (University Microfilms No. 8022239)

Borys, A.H. (1982). *Development and evaluation of a training procedure to increase pupil motor engagement time.* Unpublished doctoral dissertation, Teachers College, Columbia University, New York, N.Y..

Costello, J.A. (1977). *A descriptive analysis of student behavior in elementary school physical education classes.* Unpublished doctoral dissertation, Teachers College, Columbia University. New York, N.Y..

Godbout, P., Brunelle, J., & Tousignant, M. (1983). Academic learning time in elementary and secondary physical education classes. *Research Quarterly for Exercise and Sport,* **54** (1), 11-19.

Laubach, S.A. (1975). *The development of a system for coding student behavior in physical education classes.* Unpublished doctoral dissertation, Teachers College, Columbia University. New York, N.Y..

McLeish, J., Howe, B., & Jackson, J. (1981). *Effective teaching in physical education.* Unpublished paper, University of Victoria, British Columbia. New York, N.Y..

Metzler, M.W. (1980). The measurement of academic learning time in physical education. (Doctoral dissertation, The Ohio State University, 1979). *Dissertation Abstracts International, 40,* 5365A. (University Microfilms No. 8009314)

Phillips, A.D., & Carlisle, C. (1983). A comparison of physical education teachers categorized as most and least effective. *Journal of Teaching in Physical Education,* **2** (3), 55-67.

Pieron, M., & Haan, J. (1980). Pupils activities, time on task and behaviours in high school physical education teaching. *FIEP Bulletin* **50** (3-4), 62-68.

3

Research on Movement Analysis: Implications for the Development of Pedagogical Competence

Charles W. Armstrong
UNIVERSITY OF TOLEDO
TOLEDO, OHIO, USA

The instructional task of administering feedback has long been recognized for its importance in promoting learning. While some researchers debate about the specific role of feedback, it is generally accepted as essential if learning is to occur. The fact that physical activity instructors do administer substantial amounts of feedback suggests that this is clearly recognized (Pieron & Dalmelle, 1982). However, the variability and lack of specificity that characterizes teacher feedback suggests that many instructors lack the knowledge and skills necessary for effective feedback administration. Assuming that most teachers possess the innate intellectual and perceptual capacity to administer good feedback, their failure to do so would appear to be most likely a function of inadequate training.

Competence in delivering feedback goes far beyond simply one's facility for communicating a feedback message. Within the instructional process, motor performance must be observed and analyzed before feedback can be administered. It seems quite logical that feedback from teachers who are skilled in this prefeedback process is likely to supply the information necessary for response modification. Thus, competence in movement analysis appears to be an important precursor to competence in feedback administration. Given the clearly established role of feedback in learning, the importance of developing competence in movement analysis becomes apparent.

Research on Movement Analysis

The significance of movement analysis has been recognized by teacher educators for many years. Yet little has been done to provide prospective teachers with instruction in this critical task. Perhaps the greatest obstacle has been the lack of objective data upon which to base instruction in movement analysis. Unlike more narrowly defined topics, movement analysis has failed to generate the enthusiasm of the related research disciplines. Over the past 20 years, however, there has been a small but significant group of studies done on various components of the movement analysis process. Collectively these studies provide a tentative research base upon which appropriate strategies for the development of competence in movement analysis can be initiated. The purpose of this paper is to review this research base with a specific focus on the implications of this information for developing pedagogical competence.

Performance Experience

It has long been thought that important information regarding the analytic process could be gleaned from investigations of the analytic proficiency of various populations. These have generally taken the form of studies comparing the analytic proficiency of those with various types or levels of experience/expertise.

Of the many definitions for experience, the one that has generated considerable interest pertains to experience in performing the skill(s) to be analyzed. In practical terms this relates to the age-old question of the necessity of motor skill instructors to be experienced athletes themselves. It has been hypothesized that to effectively analyze motor skills, physical activity instructors must themselves have extensive experience in the performance of those skills. Only one study showed evidence in support of this (Girardin & Hanson, 1967). The error detection proficiency of a group of subjects was found to be positively correlated to their abilities to actually perform the skills they were evaluating.

More recently, a study by Gordon and Osborne (1972) examined the relationship between proficiency in tennis and accuracy in rating tennis performance, and a study by Armstrong (1977) investigated the influence on analytic proficiency of systematically varied experience with a novel movement pattern. Neither of these studies was able to demonstrate a relationship between performance experience and analytic proficiency. On the basis of these, as well as a number of related studies, it seems appropriate to conclude that requiring physical activity instructors to acquire experience in sport performance does not insure their proficiency in movement analysis.

Instructional Experience

Beyond the issue of performance experience, another aspect of experience that has been examined relates to the influence of varied levels of teaching/judging/rating experience on analytic proficiency. It has long been hypothesized that the analytic proficiency of physical activity instructors is enhanced through experience with tasks involving movement analysis.

Virtually all studies of this issue have demonstrated a positive relationship between level of experience and analytic proficiency. Of particular interest is the finding in two of the studies that proficiency in analyzing one type of skill does not appear to readily transfer to other types of skills. Biscan and Hoffman (1976) found that the analytic proficiency of physical education teachers was superior to that of classroom teachers when a tumbling task was used, but not when the task involved a novel movement pattern. Similarly, Hoffman and Sembiante (1975) found that the performance of little league baseball coaches was superior to that of physical education and classroom teachers on an analytic task involving batting, but again not when a novel task was employed. These results suggest that various components of the analytic process may be specific to individual skills or possibly categories of skills. Additionally, the findings of Hoffman and Sembiante also provide an indication as to the role of various types of experience in influencing analytic proficiency.

Although the coaches in their study all had ample experience in coaching baseball, none had formalized training in biomechanics, teaching methodology, movement analysis, or anything else that would appear to enhance their analytic proficiency. On the other hand, the physical education teachers all had received some of this training. Yet in analyzing the batting task, the performance of the coaches was superior. This may indicate that experience with the specific analytic tasks associated with a category of skills may be a more powerful factor in influencing the development of analytic proficiency than the generalized training often given physical education teachers.

Finally, several studies have demonstrated a positive correlation between instructional expertise and analytic proficiency (Armstrong & Hoffman, 1979; Bard, Fleury, Carriere, & Halle, 1980; Imwold & Hoffman, 1983). If instructional expertise reflects the ability to produce positive changes in a learner's motor behavior, it would appear that it may be appropriate to conclude that physical activity instructors should be provided with extensive experience in the administration of systematic movement analysis strategies, in both clinical and field-based settings.

Observation

In spite of the abundance of information linking experience to analytic proficiency, relatively few studies indicate the mechanism through which this relationship operates. One possibility involves the process of observation. Sport performance is characterized by diverse movement patterns often performed at high rates of speed. Under these circumstances the observer must prioritize the movement components and determine a visual search strategy that will ensure that those of greatest importance are seen. On this basis it has been hypothesized that knowing where to look and how to look enhances one's analytic proficiency.

Utilizing a technique for recording eye movement, Bard et. al. (1980) found that the visual search patterns of experienced observers (coaches and judges) were less random than those of inexperienced observers and involved eye fixation periods of greater duration. It is well known that increases in eye fixation time produce an increase in the amount of information that can be extracted from a visual display. This study, as well as others from industrial settings, illustrates that experienced observers develop strategies that permit them to efficiently search for the most relevant movement components and extract from them a maximum amount of information. It would appear logical to conclude, then, that physical activity instructors should be provided with techniques to develop effective visual search strategies and should receive extensive practice in the application of these strategies.

Memory

While observation appears to play an important role in movement analysis, the role of memory would seem to be of equal importance. Detecting movement errors and determining their causes are dependent on the ability to recall movement elements that have been acquired through observation. It has been hypothesized that analytic proficiency is enhanced through techniques that expand one's capacity for memory and/or limit what must be remembered. Several studies have examined characteristics of memory that relate to movement analysis. As an example, Imwold and Hoffman (1982) varied the information load in a recognition task. Their findings indicated that as the number of movement components increased, the recognition accuracy decreased. This study, as well as other studies on similar aspects of perception, indicates that performance on analytic tasks is influenced by the amount of information that must be remembered. It follows then that strategies designed to decrease information load are likely to enhance memory and, in doing so, improve analytic proficiency.

Techniques for Enhancing Memory

One memory strategy that has been of particular interest in movement analysis involves the use of mental imagery. It has often been suggested that individuals rely on the formation of mental images (pictures) to assist in the process of analyzing previously observed movements. Studies by Moody (1967), Hoffman and Sembiante (1975), and Hoffman and Armstrong (1975) have addressed this issue. While the results are somewhat inconclusive, evidence suggests that under certain conditions imagery may play a role in movement analysis. This appears to be particularly true with respect to the ability, through memory, to control and manipulate mental images.

A second means of enhancing memory, discussed by Imwold and Hoffman (1983), involves the concept of information chunking. They indicated that through experience with a category of tasks, individuals may gain the ability to form the observed characteristics of a movement into a meaningful whole. This, they suggested, may enhance the ability to retain information and provide a basis for the comparative process involved in the identification of movement errors. In terms of enhancing pedagogical competence, these studies indicate that physical activity instructors should be provided with strategies for reducing the amount of information to which they must attend in movement analysis. Additionally, they should be given experience in the use of techniques that will aid in the recall of previously observed motor performance.

Auxillary Information Sources

Beyond the information acquired through observation, there may be additional information that influences analytic proficiency. Various authors have suggested that knowledgeable instructors are able to use information regarding the outcome of a movement to help determine the errors that may have occurred within a movement. This was examined in two studies: one involving golf (Skrinar & Hoffman, 1979) and the other, tennis (Armstrong & Hoffman, 1979). Although neither study was able to demonstrate this phenomenon in a laboratory setting, both showed indications that the experienced subjects (professional instructors) relied on this information in actual practice. This may reflect that the ability to use such information is important, but also that the methodologies employed to study it have been faulty.

A second consideration regarding supplemental information pertains to the potential that it possesses for biasing the outcome of an analysis. It has been clearly shown that expectancies, established on the basis of prior information about a performer, may negatively influence the accuracy of a rating or analysis (Ansorge, Scheer, Laub, & Howard, 1978; Hatfield & Landers, 1978). It has also been suggested, however, that information acquired prior to analysis about a performer may be used to predict the type and location of errors that may occur (Armstrong & Hoffman, 1979). Thus, it may be appropriate to conclude that instructors must recognize the potential biasing effect of supplemental information, as well as the potential use of such information in movement analysis.

Specialized Training

Of particular relevance to the general issue of developing pedagogical competence are those studies that have attempted to enhance analytic proficiency through specialized training. Of the three studies in which this has been attempted, all but one showed that training improved analytic proficiency (Armstrong & Nash, 1983; Hoffman & Armstrong, 1975; Stephenson & Jackson, 1977). The specific characteristics of the training program were clearly shown to influence the extent of improvement; programs involving extensive visual experiences and examples of errors produced the best results. Of particular significance was the finding in one of the studies that the effects of movement analysis training appeared to be relatively persistent. On the basis of this research, it may be concluded that prospective physical activity instructors should be provided with structured training experiences focusing specifically on the development of competence in movement analysis.

Summary

Past concern for the development of competence in movement analysis has been very limited. It has been assumed that the associated skills are acquired through courses such as biomechanics, motor learning, and teaching methodology and are rehearsed through various types of clinical teaching experiences. The ineffectiveness of this process is clearly evident in the limited ability of many teachers to administer appropriate feedback. Research has shown that many factors influence analytic proficiency and that through the manipulation of these factors, effective training in movement analysis can take place. This cannot occur haphazardly, however. It must be the result of systematically employed training with a specific focus on the development of proficiency in movement analysis. Whether this can best be provided through a specific course, or perhaps through a series of experiences embedded within a variety of courses, remains to be seen. Regardless, certain areas of knowledge and specific skills must be developed if analytic proficiency is to be maximized.

References

Ansorge, C. J., Scheer, J. K., Laub, J., & Howard, J. (1978). Bias in judging women's gymnastics induced by expectation of within team order. *Research Quarterly, 49*, 399-405.

Armstrong, C. W. (1977). Skill analysis and kinesthetic experience. In R. S. Stadulis (Ed.), *Research and practice in physical education* (pp. 13-18). Champaign,IL: Human Kinetics.

Armstrong, C. W., & Hoffman, S. J. (1979). Effects of teaching experience, knowledge of performer competence, and knowledge of performance outcome on performance error identification. *Research Quarterly, 50*, 318-327.

Armstrong, C. W., & Nash, M. (1983). Performance error identification as a function of visual and verbal training. *Abstracts,* AAHPERD National Convention.

Bard, C., Fleury, M., Carriere, L., & Halle, M. (1980). Analysis of gymnastic judges visual search. *Research Quarterly, 51*, 267-273.

Biscan, D., & Hoffman, S. J. (1976). Movement analysis as a generic ability of physical education teachers and students. *Research Quarterly, 47*, 161-165.

Girardin, Y., & Hanson, D. (1967). Relationship between the ability to perform tumbling skills and ability to diagnose performance errors. *Research Quarterly, 38*, 556-561.

Gordon, M. E., & Osborne, M. M. (1972). An investigation of the accuracy of rating a gross motor skill. *Research Quarterly, 43*, 55-61.

Hatfield, B. D., & Landers, D. (1978). Observer expectancy effects upon appraisal of gross motor performance. *Research Quarterly, 49*, 53-61.

Hoffman, S. J., & Armstrong, C. W. (1975). Effects of pretraining on performance error identification. *Mouvement,* Proceedings of Actes du en Symposium Apprentissage Psychomoteur et Psychologie du Sport (pp. 209-214). Quebec, Canada.

Imwold, C. H., & Hoffman, S. J. (1983). Visual recognition of a gymnastic skill by experienced and inexperienced instructors. *Research Quarterly for Exercise and Sport, 54*, 149-155.

Moody, D. L. (1967). Imagery differences among women of varying levels of experience, interest, and ability in motor skills. *Research Quarterly, 38*, 441-447.

Pieron, M., & Delmelle, R. (1982). Augmented feedback in teaching physical education. In M. Pieron & J. Cheffer (Eds.), *Studying the teaching of physical education* (pp. 141-150). Leige, Belgium: AIESEP.

Skrinar, G., & Hoffman, S. J. (1979). Effects of outcome information on analytic ability of golf teachers. *Perceptual and Motor Skills, 48*, 703-708.

Stephenson, D. A., & Jackson, A. S. (1977). The effects of training and position on judges rating of a gymnastic event. *Research Quarterly, 48*, 177-181.

4

Measuring Change in Preservice Teacher Preparation Experiences

Michele Agnew-Sweeney
BOSTON UNIVERSITY,
BOSTON, MASSACHUSETTS, USA

John T. F. Cheffers
AUSTRALIAN INSTITUTE OF SPORT
BELCONNEN, AUSTRALIA

A recurring criticism of teacher preparation programs throughout most of this century concerns the sequencing and timing of the student's ecological experience, that is, that period of time when the preparing teacher comes in contact with real students. So much of our teacher preparation is embedded in the discussion of theoretical perspectives and the examination of research data that contact with the real world is put off until the final moments of the overall preparation. This practice has resulted in frustration from many dimensions. University lecturers despair in their failure to bridge the gaps between theory and application. Student teachers accumulate debilitating stress to the point where their efforts diminish and sometimes collapse.

Continued frustration with this sequencing has led to the concept of the prepracticum, where theory work and practical experience are encouraged to coexist from the first day the student enters college. Research is quite strong in its condemnation of the former system, but little work has been done in determining the efficacy and effectiveness of the ongoing system. It was decided that the purpose of this research would be to investigate teacher socialization in a selected section of this ongoing system, specifically the spring semester of the third year of the teacher preparation program at Boston University.

Qualitative methods (interviewing, participant observation, and logs) were chosen as the techniques needed to investigate such a system. Until the 1960s educators were comparatively silent on the topic of using qualitative data techniques. Socialization studies were rare. Templin and Griffin (in press) favored the use of data collection techniques which concentrated on naturalistic and real-world behaviors. McCall and Simmons (1969) believed that the researcher was the key instrument in recording observable behaviors through personal perspectives. Bodgan and Biklen (1982) believed that process events, rather than simple outcomes and products, best described a phenomenon because of their use in the natural setting. The meridian of researchers who have developed observation systems to describe ongoing behaviors were similarly persuaded (Cheffers, 1972; Cheffers, Mancini, & Martinek, 1980).

The major concern of those researchers turning in interest to the use of qualitative techniques was summarized by Schempp (1982) when he asserted that we know little of how the prospective teacher gives meaning to personal experiences. The meaning underscores the purpose, legitimizes the techniques, accounts for the theoretical persuasion, and distills the societies that gather around a naturally recurring, real-life phenomenon.

The professionalized socialization of a recruit into a highly sophisticated functioning institution is a process that has been neglected in teacher education research. The medical world has provided the most prolific data to date, particularly through the use of participant observation and intense interview (Olesen & Whittaker, 1968; Becker, Greer, Hughes, & Strauss, 1961). Therefore, it is evident that the purpose of this study, to investigate the professional socialization process of third year university students studying to be teachers, was of more than usual import.

Methods

Thirteen students majoring in Human Movement, 7 males and 6 females, constituted the sample. Students were required to enroll in a 10-credit-hour course conducted throughout the semester on Tuesdays and Thursdays and attend a residential field experience for 4 weeks at the end of the semester. The curriculum consisted of 44 hours of theoretical classroom discussion time, 55 hours of on-campus teaching experience, and 4 weeks of supervising and teaching at an off-campus camping site entitled the residential field experience.

Data-gathering procedures included interviews, participant observation, nonparticipant observation, and log writing. Undergraduate interviews were conducted by the investigator at four intervals throughout the semester. Graduate students acting as supervisors also observed the teaching of the undergraduates. Therefore, additional information concerning the undergraduates was obtained by conducting three intermittent interviews with the graduate supervisors as well. The investigator practiced participant observation during the residential field experience and nonparticipant observation of the undergraduates during the on-campus teaching experience. Daily journals recording personal thoughts and feelings of the undergraduates contributed invaluable data and also provided a comparative check of the theoretical study and the planned curriculum on a flowchart basis.

Interviews were recorded on tape. Participant and nonparticipant observations were recorded on paper, and journals were obtained from each undergraduate for analysis.

Information pertaining to each individual student was reviewed separately. An adjectival and verbal analysis was completed utilizing interviews as the main sources of data, and 18 conceptual variables/topics of concern were extracted from the collected data.

Observations and logs were read in their entirety, and notes were made in the margins to highlight substantial information related to the conceptual variables. Utilizing interview dates, a flowchart was established for each individual subject including the 18 conceptual variables and related individualized data. Through the development of flowcharts, the abundance of data collected was reduced so the researcher could formulate an accurate perception of the data.

Results

It was concluded that the socialization process of the 13 undergraduate Human Movement majors exhibited nine major characteristics:

1. Change in adversion and uncertainty towards teaching
2. Self-perceptual change in self-concept
3. Change in assuming teacher role identity
4. Evidence of preconceived notions
5. Concerns of self, teaching situations, and student needs
6. Reversion to past experiences
7. Development of analytical process
8. A specificity to the experience
9. Attitude changes (see Table 1)

The most significant finding in the study was the dramatic turn around in attitude and feelings of confidence expressed after the 4 weeks of residential field experiences. Some changes occurred during the 3 months of on-campus clinical experience, but dramatic change was both observed and expressed as a result of participation in the off-campus camping experiences where the undergraduates were required to expand teaching duties to 24-hr supervision, informal social interaction, and a very different set of interaction skills in their work with the school children.

Why did the residential field experience succeed? The following reasons are advanced to explain the dramatic success of the residential field experience as a change agent:

1. The students enjoyed the greater responsibility placed on them.
2. Feedback through change in their pupils' attitudes was immediate.
3. All parties were exposed to a new invigorating environment.
4. The curriculum was much more challenging by using advanced methodologies and demanding creativity and adaptation skills.

Table 1. Factors that evolved from the socialization process

Factor	Number of students in which factor occurred (out of total of 13)	Number of students in which positive change occurred (out of total of 13)	Sample Evidence B: Before change A: After change
1. Adversion and uncertainty towards teaching	10	10	B: "This class won't help with my profession." A: "It gave me a new outlook on teaching."
2. Perceptual change in self-concept	13	12	B: "I'm not capable." A: "I feel good about myself."
3. Identity to role of teacher	7	7	B: "I don't think of myself as teacher." A: "I feel like a teacher."
4. Preconceived notions	13	11	B: "Little kids are brats." A: "I enjoyed the younger kids."

Table 1. cont.

5. Concerns of self, teaching situations, and student needs	13	0	Developmental cycle moved from "Will they like me?" to "What are their needs?"
6. Reversion to past play	6	0	B: "I'm teaching a game I used to play."
7. Analytical processes	0	13	A: Not mentioned B: No analytical thinking present A: "Current systems are unchallenging."
8. Specificity of the experience	7	0	Although confident over prepracticum experience, insecure over student teaching
9. Attitude changes	11	11	B: "I don't want to teach." A: "I'm looking forward to teaching again."

5. The use of risk activities helped place many students and teachers in a position of growth, stimulation, success, and even pride.
6. The 24-hr teaching responsibility helped draw students and teachers into greater cohesion.

Discussion of Results

Virtually all change occurred as a result of the residential field experience. The finding that the on-campus prepracticum experience did not appreciably influence the undergraduates in the nine disclosed characteristics adds further weight to the discomfort teacher educators are feeling over current teaching practice effect. It appears that too little real change takes place and that feelings of insecurity, even persecution, interfere in the teacher development process.

The 24-hr prepracticum experience, however, was spectacularly successful. Perhaps the outdoor setting, a honeymoon effect, the reduction of normal community restrictions, and the absence of parental overseers were the salient reasons. It is also evident that opportunities for different, more idealized curricula teaching methodologies and supervision techniques invoke significantly different attitudes on the part of the participant (Childs, 1980; Weidner, 1971).

The multidimensional nature of investigation into teacher socialization has the additional advantage of offering these techniques as appropriate in program review. The Boston University program was not as effective in the clinical on-campus phase as it was in the clinical off-campus residential field experience phase. It is interesting to speculate about how effective teacher preparation programs really are in current form and what dramatic change might be affected if 24-hr or somewhat broader teacher responsibility programs were introduced.

One final observation is pertinent: The use of problem solving and guided discovery teaching techniques, along with command and task style with genuine reason, forms the basis of the residential field experience teaching approach. Such diversity in teaching methodology was not observed in the on-campus teaching practicum. These approaches during the residential field experience provided the undergraduate teachers with genuine responsibilities and ownership in the enterprise. Their successes and failures were instantly appreciated and analyzed. Adjustments were made to bring genuine effect, and the results were successful and exhilarating. In the words of one of the students

"I felt an intimacy and a closeness with the kids. I was surprised, but I've definitely grown. The experience has been substantial."

References

Becker, H., Greer, B., Hughes, E., & Strauss, A. (1961). *Boys in white, student culture in medical school.* Chicago: University of Chicago Press.

Bodgan, R., & Biklen S. (1982). *Qualitative research for education: An introduction to theory and methods.* Boston: Allyn & Bacon.

Cheffers, J. T. F. (1972). *The validation of an instrument designed to expand the Flanders system of interaction analysis to describe nonverbal interaction, different varieties of teacher behavior, and pupil responses.* Unpublished doctoral dissertation, Temple University, Philadephia.

Cheffers, J., Mancini, V., & Martinek, T. (1980). *Interaction analysis: An application to nonverbal activity* (2nd ed.). Association for Productive Teaching.

Childs, S. (1980). *Adventure deprivation - a social disease. Self-concept through school camp.* Transerve City, MI: Paper presented at the National Outdoor Education Conference (ERIC Document Reproduction Service No. ED 197 911).

McCall, G., & Simmons, J. (1969). *Issues in participant observation: A text and reader.* Reading, MA: Addison-Wesley Publishing.

Olesen, V., & Whittaker, E. (1968). *The silent dialogue: A study in the social psychology of professional socialization.* San Francisco: Jossey-Bass.

Schempp, P. (1982). *Learning the role: The transformation from student to teacher.* West Lafayette, IN: Paper presented at the Big Ten Symposium on Teacher Education, Purdue University.

Sweeney, M. A. (1984). *Teacher socialization: The pre-practicum experience with third-year human movement majors.* Unpublished doctoral dissertation, Boston University.

Templin, T., & Griffin, P. (in press). Ethnography: A qualitative approach to examining life in physical education. In J. Nixon & L. Vendient (Eds.), *Physical education teacher education: An introduction to teaching.* New York: John Wiley & Sons.

Weidner, E. (1971). Environmental education: Value reorientation. In R. Cook & G. O'Hearn (Eds.), *Processes for a quality environment.* Green Bay: The University of Wisconsin.

5

Career Paths and Role Orientations of Professors of Teacher Education in Physical Education

Murray F. Mitchell
THE OHIO STATE UNIVERSITY
COLUMBUS, OHIO, USA

Hal A. Lawson
MIAMI UNIVERSITY
OXFORD, OHIO, USA

> Those who can, do.
> Those who can't, teach.
> Those who can't teach,
> teach teachers.
>   (Anonymous)

Teacher education professors are a much maligned group in the status-conscious environment of higher education. They are, however, select individuals who play important roles in the preparation of future teachers. These professors have a large measure of control over entry and exit requirements, course content, and teacher placement and evaluation. In other words, the professor may be particularly significant for the degree and kind of training received by prospective teachers.

Even in such a potentially powerful position, the understanding of who university professors are, what they do, and why they do it has not proceeded much beyond Wilson's (1942) pioneer work of over 40 years ago. And work in the area remains scarce (Hall & Hord, 1981). Further, the quality and use of related literature are as much a problem as the quantity of literature. As Locke (1982) observes, "as a body of knowledge and a domain for inquiry in physical education, teacher education remains uneven, unpopular and largely unread" (p. i). Locke should know. In an earlier paper, Locke and Dodds (1981) reviewed research published between 1960 and 1980 that related to teacher education in physical education. Locke (1982) later continued this work by reviewing 40 additional reports that spanned 1980 to 1982. In total, four dissertations that were listed related to leadership characteristics. Beyond that research, the authors raised questions similar to those raised throughout this study (Locke & Dodds, 1981, p. 15).

Clearly, all physical education professors involved with teacher education have some impact upon prospective teachers. Consequently, information about them must better illuminate the teacher education process. Locke and Dodds (1981) observed that, unfortunately, teacher educators "have been remarkably nonintrospective as a professional group" (p.15). This lament also serves as an indication of need. The investigation reported here was designed to address this need. More specifically, the purpose of this explorative study was to begin to build a foundational understanding of career paths accompanying socialization experiences, and role orientations of former-teachers-turned-professors of teacher education in physical education.

Procedure

The subjects selected for study were former teachers who held doctoral degrees and were involved with university courses in curriculum, instruction, and other courses related to pedagogy and school programs in physical education. The criterion of teaching experience was employed because of the hypothesized prevalence of such experience in teacher education faculties. It was also employed to facilitate a more specific identification of the sample. The subjects were identified by their associations with specified courses listed in the most recently available university calendars at four local institutions. These four institutions were selected on the basis of their proximity and their reputations as different types of schools: One American school and three Canadian institutions including one of international repute, one known as a teacher training center, and one established as an experimental university.

Eighteen subjects who met the above criteria were located and contacted. Of these potential subjects, two refused to participate and one was preparing to leave the country and hence was unable to be involved. This left 15 subjects, 4 females and 11 males, who consented to be interviewed. Data was collected by interview using a structured questionnaire. After reviewing relevant but diverse literature, concepts were needed to give structure to the literature and possible findings in such a study. Consequently, specific attractors, facilitators, and other important factors surrounding the decision to become a teacher educator in physical education were accomodated in questions. These questions were then field-tested and revised prior to actual data collection.

Findings

The findings are presented under three headings: Public School Teaching, Career Change, and Current Role Orientations.

Public School Teaching

Subjects generally cited more than one reason for choosing to teach in the public schools. They listed an array of experiences from involvement at the YMCA or YWCA to a love of sports, to the desire to emulate the role model of a former teacher. While public school teachers most wanted to develop skill in students, others wanted to facilitate participation, to enhance respect for the profession, and to create the desire to learn in students. Two subjects admitted that they simply wanted to continue working in a job they liked.

Subjects were asked when they thought they had acquired their skills as physical education teachers. Generally, more than one time and place was credited with this skill acquisition. Interestingly, few subjects cited their teacher training and student teaching experience, and one subject stated the following about teaching skill: '' You're born with it. You teach with your personality.''

Subjects generally found what they expected to in the public school while teaching, and all were happy at that time in their lives. Moreover, most considered themselves to be successful teachers. So why did they leave teaching?

Career Change

The decision to change careers can be identified by two related decisions: (a) the decision to leave teaching, and (b) the decision to pursue a position as a university professor. The ensuing presentation of these two decisions by subjects is organizational and not necessarily chronological.

The most common response to why the decision was made to leave teaching at the public school level was the result of the offer of a job—an offer which was typically unsolicited. This dominant pattern of job placement contrasts sharply with the sponsored mobility system identified by Massengale and Sage (1982). Perhaps today's job placement patterns would be different for teachers-turned-professors with the advent of new doctoral programs and the premium placed on research in teacher education. This is an interesting question for future research.

For subjects in this investigation, the reasons cited for leaving public school teaching are contrary to the reasons cited in earlier studies on teachers. As mentioned, these subjects were happy and generally satisfied rather than dissatisfied (Kahnweiler, 1980; Sarason, 1977). Further, they were generally successful and found what they had expected in the school system rather than becoming frustrated and bored (Beam, 1981).

Subjects' reasons for leaving teaching were very closely related to their motives for choosing to become professors. The most prominent explanation was the mere offer of a job. Less frequently mentioned was the advice of a professor, the perceived impact on students from having something to offer them, blocked aspirations elsewhere, and the need for money as well as job security and stability associated with a professorship.

Current Role Orientations

All of the subjects suggested general satisfaction both in having left the public school system and in their positions at the university level. Beyond this overall satisfaction, a number of qualifications were added. For example, dissatisfaction with the comparatively low pay, the personal shortcomings in the performance of the job, and a lack of congruence between personal perceptions and the opinions of decision-makers with respect to a job description were named.

Subjects had clear perceptions of the professorial role prior to completing their doctoral programs. The programs apparently had little, if any, impact upon their perceptions of the role of professor. Most of the subjects did not change their perceptions either of what the role was or should be.

Subjects could not agree on either characteristics or traits of an outstanding physical education teacher. Neither could they agree on the elements constituting the ideal physical education program. Subjects' differential language, however, may have posed a hermeneutic problem here. It is suspected that the concept of skill development was in the minds of most subjects, but as a method for some and a goal for others. Perhaps these differences stem from the fact that 11 of the 15 subjects had no formal training in the areas they control—curriculum, instruction, and supervision.

Faced with the following role descriptions—teaching, coaching, research, and service—all ranked teaching as the most important. This finding was not surprising, for it is consistent with Rog's (1979) findings. Twelve of the 15 subjects' rankings were at odds with their parent university's reward systems, and all were aware of this conflict. The 3 remaining subjects whose priorities were congruent with their institutions' were all from different universities. Thus role stress for teacher educators emerged in all four universities.

When asked to identify the qualities of an outstanding physical education teacher educator, a number of factors were named, but a lack of consensus is evident. Differences exist in both degree and kind of factors identified. For example, formal knowledge, teaching ability, research skills, publishing ability, the phrase "practice what you preach," and empathy were mentioned. Interestingly enough, the first factors identified—subject knowledge, teaching ability, research skills, and publishing ability—are the only specialized talents named. In each case these qualities are so general that they still allow a great deal of diversity.

Equally revealing is the finding that subjects could not agree on the components of a successful teacher education program. Methods coursework was the most frequently identified component. This diversity of views was not unexpected. For example, Alley (1982) cited results of a study of 230 departments of physical education from which the only course required in all departments was practice teaching (p. 985).

In identifying personal measures of success, however, results were somewhat different. Only 1 of the 15 subjects tested felt unsuccessful. This perception was based on the performance of former students as teachers 5 years into their careers—suggesting that these former students did no better than their predecessors and generally did not employ skills or knowledge learned at the university. The remaining 14 subjects perceived themselves as successful. This finding was supported by the work of Ladd and Lipsett (1975), although differences existed as to how this success was measured. The criteria identified by subjects reflected their priorities for teaching, research, and service. It is interesting to note that just one subject identified the resultant teaching effectiveness of students as a criterion for success as a teacher educator. Furthermore, the majority of subjects, even if given the opportunity, would not change anything about their roles.

Conclusions

Five conclusions seem warranted on the basis of the findings reported here. The first stems from the fact that 11 of the 15 subjects had no formal training in curriculum, instruction, pedagogy, and school programs. Surely this is a reason why the development of a "shared technical culture" for teachers (Lortie, 1975) has been impaired, and this influences the substance and impact of teacher education.

Second, because subjects' role orientations are at odds with institutionally defined role expectations, some bitterness exists over university policies related to promotion and tenure. Consequently, questions must arise as to the likelihood of subjects having continued feelings of satisfaction in such a setting and, because subjects view teaching as more important than research, the likelihood that these faculty will contribute to a development of shared technical culture.

The third conclusion is related to the second. Subjects' role orientations as teacher education faculty members for themselves and for their students is of a custodial nature. They are guardians of personal traditions, both in their own roles and in their views of successful school programs and public school physical education teachers.

The fourth conclusion worthy of note regards the three waves of socialization originally hypothesized in this study. The relationship between the undergraduate education program, organizational socialization in the school system, and the graduate education program may now be reconceptualized. It appears that a socialization process exists (even earlier than the undergraduate preparation) in the form of exposure to and experiences in sport and physical activity. Consistent with the findings cited earlier by Lortie (1975), biography appears to be more influential than formal education—even for teacher educators.

The fifth conclusion doubles as an important paradox. Although these teacher educators wish to have a major impact on their students in teacher education, their socialization into their roles as teacher and teacher educator is characterized by a lack of impact by formal education programs. Thus, their tacit assumption appears to be "don't do as I do; do as I say." Coupled with their lack of consensus on the substance of and targets for teacher education programs, this assumption is just cause to question whether or not these teacher educators' impact on would-be teachers will be any greater than it was in their own cases. This unfortunate, yet revealing conclusion signals the need for future research and discussion on teacher education faculty in physical education.

References

Alley, L. E. (1982). Two paths to excellence. *Quest, 34* (2), 99-108.

Beam, A. L. (1981). Teacher dropouts: Their process of attraction and adult development including motivating factors in their work life and nonwork life. *Dissertation Abstracts International, 42,* 4209-A.

Hall G. E., & Hord, S. M. (1981). A national agenda for research on teacher education in the 1980's. *Journal of Teacher Education, 32* (2), 4-8.

Kahnweiler, J. B. (1980). So you've been a teacher, now what? Counseling the teacher changing careers. *Vocational Guidance Quarterly, 29* (2), 164-171.

Ladd, E. C., & Lipsett, S. M. (1975). What professors think. *Chronicle of Higher Education, 11* (1), 2; 9.

Locke, L. F. (1982, November). *Research on teacher education for physical education in the U.S.A., Part II: Questions and Conclusions.* Paper presented at the International Symposium on Research in School Physical Education, University of Jyvaskyla, Finland.

Locke, L. F., & Dodds, P. (1981, July). *Research on preservice teacher education for physical education in the U.S.A.* Paper presented at the Third Seminar on the Study of Teaching at the International Conference on the Association International des Ecoles Superieures d'Education Physique, Rio de Janeiro.

Lortie, D. C. (1975). *Schoolteacher: A sociological study.* Chicago: The University of Chicago Press.

Massengale, J. D., & Sage, G. H. (1982). Departmental prestige and career mobility patterns of college physical educators. *Research Quarterly for Exercise and Sport, 53* (4), 305-312.

Rog, J. A. (1979). Faculty attitudes toward teaching: A descriptive interview-based study of three departments of P. E. *Dissertation Abstracts International, 40* (3), 1348-A.

Sarason, S. B. (1977). *Work, aging, and social change.* New York: The Free Press.

Wilson, L. (1942). *The academic man.* New York: Oxford University Press.

Yager, B. (1964). Some characteristics of women who have chosen college teaching in physical education. *Dissertation Abstracts International, 24,* 5182.

PART II

Analysis of Teaching and Coaching

6

Research on Teaching in Physical Education: An Interactive Model in Operation

Beverly J. Yerg
THE FLORIDA STATE UNIVERSITY
TALLAHASSEE, FLORIDA, USA

Research on teacher effectiveness in physical education is beginning to take shape as the amount of research on teaching grows; however, a knowledge base sufficient to support generalizations is still to be realized. Reviews of the state of the art have been presented (Locke, 1979; Siedentop, 1981; Piéron & Graham, 1986) and will not be repeated here.

A Framework for Research on Teaching

Cooley, Leinhardt, and McGrail (1977) presented a framework for identifying effective teaching which has provided guidance for developing our research efforts. The framework lists six components necessary to identify effective teaching:

1. Student outcome measures,
2. Measures of teacher behavior,
3. Measures of other variables thought to effect student outcome measures,
4. Model of classroom process (for selecting, constructing, and organizing the variables),
5. Procedures for data collection, and
6. Data analysis procedures.

This paper will focus on the model phase and will include those components that have impact on the model. Data analysis will not be addressed in this paper. Cooley et al., (1977) state that it is unlikely that all components will be met in early studies, and that results from early studies will suggest refinements in later studies. It was those refinements, as we continued to work through the framework, that led to the development of a descriptive model which is used to guide research efforts in a coordinated, collaborative process.

Probably the most difficult aspect of research on teaching in physical education involves specifying learning outcomes. Consensus on identifying the expected learning outcomes in physical education eludes us as a profession. That is, can we agree on what a second grader, or a fifth or twelfth grader should know and be able to do if he or she is physically educated?

Recently I presented a three-dimensional model, an empty box, in an attempt to stimulate thoughts on how we might organize those learning outcomes. The dimensions included (a) a classification of instructional outcomes, (b) developmental stages of the learner, and (c) learning levels (beginning, intermediate, advanced (Yerg, 1983). That box is still empty. An additional approach that has been used in identifying learning outcomes is the experimental teaching unit (ETU), which was reviewed by Pieron and Graham (1986). The identification of learning outcomes is an aspect of research on teaching in physical education that still needs development and refinement.

Concerning measures of teacher behavior, there is a need to tap into teacher behaviors that occur prior to and during instruction. These behaviors must include those that are thought, by reason or research, to facilitate the learning process and learning outcomes and those that may be detrimental to the learning process. It has been found that some behaviors that inhibit achievement are stronger that those might enhance learning (Yerg, 1980). Identification and measurement are concerns of this facet of the research process.

It has become more and more important to identify other variables that have an impact on student outcomes that are not included in the teacher behavior category. In early process-product studies there were two major areas of concern: teacher behaviors (process) and student learning (product). These are insufficient measures on which to draw conclusions of effective teaching. Student entry behavior is a control. Student in class behaviors are critical factors for enhancing or inhibiting student learning.

Development of a Descriptive Model

With the above components of concern addressed, we turn to the development of a model of classroom processes that will guide the formulation of the research studies. In an early study (Yerg, 1977) a model was used to describe the components addressed in that study. Subsequent research and study indicated that the model was insufficient to describe the teaching-learning process. It stimulated the development of a more comprehensive yet generic model as is presented in Figure 1 (Yerg, 1983). This generic model addressed the factors of presage variables (those that precede the interactive teaching phase) and the interactive teaching phase (the interactive nature of teacher student behaviors during this phase). It was recognized that student behavior during

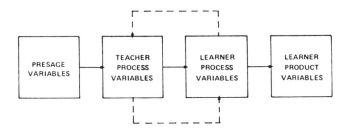

Figure 1. Revised model for RTE in physical education. *Note.* From Re-examining the process-product paradigm for research on teaching effectiveness in physical education By B.J. Yerg, 1983, In Teaching in Physical Education by T.J. Templin and J.K. Olson (Eds). Reprinted with permission.

the interactive teaching phase has a direct impact on student outcomes (Gage, 1978), and therefore there is interest in the teaching behaviors that facilitate the student behaviors that will result in positive learning outcomes. From the generic model, an interim model, as presented in Figure 2, focuses on planning and management (Farmer & Twardy, 1982). The impact of planning on management strategies and instructional strategies resulting in increased Academic Learning Time (ALT-PE) is implied, with the further implication that increased ALT-PE will facilitate motor skill learning.

It should be recognized that ALT-PE alone will not ensure motor skill learning, however, it appears that we may be operating at different levels in considering the effects of ALT-PE. If management is inefficient and/or ineffective and results in decreased ALT-PE, then the impact on learning is detrimental. Planning for instruction requires a knowledge of the learner, of learning, and of the task to be learned. Without planning, the teaching-learning interaction may lack focus and direction and result in considerable trial-and-error, an inefficient mode of learning. However, when planning and management aspects are appropriate, the refinement of the instructional phase is the target for research. ALT-PE alone will not suffice as the measurement of teacher effectiveness. However, the refinement of the teaching-learning interaction may not be possible until the opportunity for such interaction is maximized. The current model

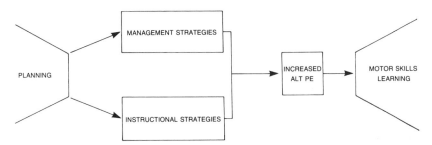

Figure 2. A model of planning and management effects on teaching in physical education. *Note.* From "A model of Planning and Management Effects on Teaching in Physical Education" by J. Farmer and B. Twardy, 1982, Unpublished manuscript. Reprinted with permission.

that serves as the descriptive base for our research on teaching in physical education is presented in Figure 3 (Farmer, Martin, & Twardy, 1984). The model implies presage, process, and product dimensions as described by Dunkin and Biddle (1974) or might be described in the format of input, process, and output.

The components of the model begin with teacher knowledge, the precursor of all that goes into teaching. Research on this facet of the teaching process is very limited, and it appears that it may be the base of all that follows. The knowledge of the teacher directly effects planning for instruction and management. These three components precede the interactive phase of the teaching process.

Initially in the interactive teaching phase, the components of control and rapport must be established. *Control* refers to the establishment of procedures and routines that guide student and teacher behavior throughout the lesson and perhaps throughout subsequent learning encounters. *Rapport* is the interpersonal interactions that build the communication and climate modes. In the instructional phase, the task(s) must be represented in some manner so that learning guidance (Gagne, 1965) and/or practice will be productive. Within the interactive phase a feedback loop includes not only the feedback that is offered but also the perception of the feedback by the learner. This implies that feedback must be appropriate in that the learner is receiving and able to utilize the message that was intended. The product of the interactive teaching phase is the learning outcome.

The idea of a model of classroom processes for selecting, constructing, and organizing variables for study has been expanded to form a descriptive model of teaching in physical education. The model was developed from a simple

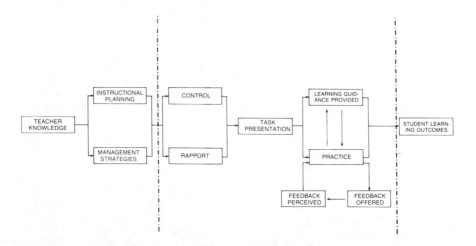

Figure 3. A descriptive model of the antecedent, process, and consequent components of teaching in physical education. *Note.* From "A model describing the antecedent, process, and consequent components of teaching in physical education. by J. Farmer, S. Martin, and B. Twardy, 1984, Unpublished manuscript. Reprinted with permission.

single study paradigm (Yerg, 1977) through the expanded, interactive presage-process-product paradigm (Yerg, 1983) and the planning/management framework (Farmer & Twardy, 1982) to the present model (Farmer et al., 1984). The model is a descriptive framework from which we can develop cooperative research within our existing resources of time and personnel. The components of the model are seen as a whole. Yet they provide a means whereby they can be studied in selected combinations by recognizing the others but not studying the total model within a given research endeavor. Using compatible, if not identical, data collection processes, the resulting research is interdependent and provides support across studies.

Application of the Model

An early process-product study (Yerg, 1977) used the teacher knowledge, task presentation, practice, feedback, and outcome components to examine relationships among the variables. A later study (Yerg & Twardy, 1982) used all of the above except the teacher knowledge component in a similar paradigm. From the results of these two studies it was supported that neither practice nor feedback was the key to student learning if it was not appropriate and not used in the right combination. A study in basketball shooting by Imwold, et al., (1983), using planning, task presentation, and practice components, found that teachers who were in the planning group spent more time giving directions because they had a greater variety of learning activities, were more organized, made better use of equipment and facilities, and provided closure for the instructional episode. Teachers in the nonplanning group used fewer activities, apparently had less organization and fewer activities, used single line/one ball activities, and allowed the class to be terminated by the investigator without closure.

Twardy (1984) studied the components of instructional planning, task presentation, practice, and feedback in the context of teaching the volleyball spike. She found that the planning behaviors of preservice teachers centered on the activities to be taught. She also found that planning behaviors of attention to subject matter and analysis of learning activities were related to task presentation behaviors because those who had planned were actually more precise in their task presentations, and the nonfunctional behaviors in those classes decreased. Twardy also found that task presentation behaviors were related to students receiving information (as opposed to nonreceptive or off-task behavior) and subsequent practice of the task presented. When students were engaged in specific parts of the task at an easy level, off-task behavior was lower. The Twardy study supported the belief that certain planning behaviors were related to teacher in-class behaviors, which in turn were related to learner behaviors that have been shown to be related to achievement (Twardy, 1984, p. 156).

These exploratory studies give rise to additional questions, which are the foundation of additional studies being planned. They include: stages of development/refinement of planning skills intervention as a means of developing planning strategies, and management routines formulated and taught.

Data Collection Concerns

The value of having an overall model which describes the teaching act in physical education in an instructional design format is that it provides a framework for ongoing research with such efforts building with and/or on one another. This framework also involves the data collection process because the utilization of the same or similar instrumentation facilitates comparisons across studies. The Florida Performance Measurement System (FPMS) has provided a framework for data collection across components of the model (Florida Beginning Teacher Program 1982). The FPMS was developed on an extensive research base, and it outlines six domains that are critical in defining teaching:

1. Planning
2. Management of Student Conduct
3. Instructional Organization and Development
4. Presentation of Subject Matter
5. Communication: Verbal and Nonverbal
6. Evaluation of Achievement.

The FPMS provides formative and summative instruments for recording behavioral indicators in the domains. While the system was developed from the research on teaching research base which is classroom oriented, the system provides a framework for modifying data collection techniques that can be used in the physical education setting. Other data collection procedures that have been used across studies include Teacher Behavior Observation System (Yerg, 1977), ALT-PE (Birdwell, 1980), and Anderson's Student Behavior Observation Instrument (1980).

Coordination of data collection processes increases the pool of trained observers for research rather than having to train separately for each study. The data collection process also involves increasingly complex technology. Technological aspects that can be refined and used across studies with increased sophistication include developing film banks which capture the essence of the teaching-learning interaction with sufficient detail to permit meaningful analysis, developing technology for the transmission of voice communications without encumbering the teacher with equipment, and providing recording cues to enhance the reliability of coding procedures. Building on existing technological approaches can enhance the information that is collected in any given situation. This is to be preferred over individual efforts in isolated studies where the researchers must develop all instrumentation and data collection processes for a given study.

Educational Applications

This approach to the study of teacher effectiveness in physical education is only one way. However, it has given us a direction and has stimulated research efforts and results far beyond what would have been possible with a like number of individual efforts. With an ongoing graduate study program in teacher behavior, new students are quickly oriented into a framework that guides their thinking, their review of the literature in a specific area, and their comprehension of the research process. They work as apprentices analyzing existing data banks and asking new questions. And they have a data base from which they can work through these questions and work in ongoing research studies, and they are still relatively free to develop their own interests within the scope of the model. Therefore the model has provided not only a basis for research but also a basis for training researchers in teacher effectiveness in physical education. In addition, the use of the FPMS provides data consistent with the preservice and in-service needs of practitioners in the field. Therefore, as undergraduates work in analyzing their own behaviors and the behaviors of others, they are making a research contribution and are enhancing their own preparation.

Providing a framework for the study of teaching in physical education has permitted the coordination of efforts in research which have implication and application for teacher preparation, in-service education, and staff development.

References

Anderson, W. G. (1980). *Analysis of teaching in physical education.* St. Louis, MO: C. V. Mosby.

Birdwell, D. M. (1980). The effect of modification of teacher behavior on the academic learning time of selected students in physical education. *Dissertation Abstracts International,* **41**, 1472A-1473A. (University Microfilms No. 80-22, 239).

Cooley, W. W., Leinhardt, G., & McGrail, J. (1977). The application of a model for investigating classroom processes. *Anthropology and Education Quarterly,* **8** (2), 119-126.

Dunkin, M. J., & Biddle, B. J. (1974). *The study of teaching.* New York: Holt, Rinehart, and Winston.

Farmer, J., Martin, S., & Twardy, B. (1984). A model describing the antecedent, process, and consequent components of teaching in physical education. Unpublished manuscript, The Florida State University, Tallahassee.

Farmer, J. & Twardy, B. (1982). A model of planning and management effects on teaching in physical education. Unpublished manuscript, The Florida State University, Tallahassee.

Florida Beginning Teacher Program, Coalition for the Development of a Performance Evaluation System. (1982). *Handbook of the Florida performance measurement system.* Tallahassee: Department of Education, Office of Teacher Education, Certification, and Inservice Staff Development.

Gage, N. L. (1978). *The scientific basis of the art of teaching.* New York: Teachers College Press.

Gagne, R. M. (1965). *The conditions of learning.* New York: Holt, Rinehart, and Winston.

Imwold, C. H., Rider, R. A., Twardy, B. M., Oliver, P. S., Giffin, M., & Arsenault, D. N. (1984). The effect of planning on the teaching behavior of preservice physical education teachers. *Journal of Teaching in Physical Education.* **4** (1), pp. 50-56.

Locke, L. F. (1979). Learning from teaching. In J. J. Jackson (Ed.), *Theory into practice* (pp. 133-152). Victoria, British Columbia: Morris Printing Company LTD.

Pieron, M., & Graham, G. (In press). Research on teacher effectiveness: The experimental teaching units. *International Journal of Physical Education.*

Siedentop, D. (1981). State of the art in research on teaching. *Proceedings of the 1981 Convention of the Southern District American Alliance for Health, Physical Education, Recreation, and Dance* (pp. 48-54). Orlando, FL.

Twardy, B. M. (1984). Relationships among teacher planning behaviors and specified teacher and student inclass behaviors in a physical education milieu. (Doctoral dissertation, The Florida State Univeristy).

Yerg, B. J. (1977). Relationships between teacher behaviors and pupil achievement in the psychomotor domain. *Dissertation Abstracts International,* **39,** 1981A. (University Microfilms No. 77-22, 229).

Yerg, B. J. (1980). *Teaching-learning process factors related to pupil achievement in the psychomotor domain.* (ERIC Document Reproduction Service No. Ed 202 815, SP 017 942).

Yerg, B. J. (1983). Re-examining the process-product paradigm for research on teaching effectiveness in physical education. In T. J. Templin & J. K. Olson (Eds.), *Teaching in physical education* (pp. 310-317). Champaign, IL: Human Kinetics.

Yerg, B. J., & Twardy, B. M. (1982). Relationships of specified instructional behaviors to pupil gain on a motor skill task. In M. Pieron & J. Cheffers (Eds.), *Studying the teaching in physical education* (pp. 61-68). Liege, Belgium: AIESEP.

7

The Relationship Between Pupil's Leisure-Time Physical Activity and Motor Behavior During Physical Education Lessons

Risto Telama, Väinö Varstala, Pilvikki Heikinaro-Johansson, and Päivi Paukku
UNIVERSITY OF JYVÄSKYLÄ
JYVÄSKYLÄ, FINLAND

A major goal of school physical education in Finland today is socialization of children into habitual activity, and therefore particular attention should be paid to physically passive children. On the one hand the majority of the pupils have most of their physical activity during leisure time. For instance 73% of 12-year-old girls and 81% of 12-year-old boys participate in physical activities in their leisure time at least twice a week. A large proportion of the pupils also participate in intensive sport training. On the other hand, for a rather large proportion of the pupils, weekly physical activity consists mainly of school lessons. For 5% of the pupils, school physical education is their only physical activity (Telama & Laakso, 1983). From the pedagogical point of view it seems correct to say that school physical education is very important for passive pupils in particular.

According to studies carried out in Finland (Varstala, Telama, & Akkanen, 1981) and in other countries, it seems that in Finland the pupils spend more time on learning tasks and movement than the pupils in other countries do (Pieron, 1983). In all studies variation has been great (e.g., 13-70%, Costello & Laubach, 1978). The crucial question is to what extent school physical education manages to support skill acquisition, fitness training, recreation, and socialization into sport involvement of pupils who are passive during their leisure time.

According to the Pygmalion theory, teacher expectations for pupil behavior influence pupils so that they begin to behave and perform as expected by the teacher (Rosenthal & Jacobson, 1968; Martinek, Growe, & Rejeski, 1982). The teacher gives more opportunities to respond to pupils who are expected to be high achievers than to pupils expected to be low achievers (Martinek & Johnson, 1979; Martinek et al., 1982).

According to Pieron (1982) there is a difference between the high-skilled and low-skilled groups in time-on-tasks, in the amount of specific learning activities, and particularly in successful trials, but there is no remarkable difference in the teacher's behavior and treatment of pupils. In another study by Shute, Dodds, Placek, Rife, and Silverman (1982), the results show no difference in time-on-task (ALT-PE) between high-skilled and low-skilled groups. They conclude that the teacher creates a learning environment where all children find equivalent amounts of success, even though they are performing within a wide range of skill.

It might be expected that pupils who are passive in their leisure time also are more passive than other pupils in physical education lessons. Although leisure time habitual activity is not such a manifest feature as could be supposed in creating teacher expectations for pupil behavior, it may be assumed that teachers have more positive expectations for the behavior of "sport club activists" than for the behavior of other pupils.

As a part of the more extensive Research Project on School Physical Education Classes, the study reported here focuses on the following points: What are the differences in motor behavior in physical education classes between (a) pupils who participate seriously in sport club activities and competitions, (b) those who are active in their leisure time but participate in unorganized physical activity only, and (c) those who are passive in their leisure time; and what are the differences in teacher guidance given to the three groups mentioned?

Methods

The data was collected during 406 physical education lessons mainly in the province of Central Finland from 1981-1983. A total of 812 pupils (2 randomly selected pupils per class) were subjects for the study.

Pupil behavior in physical education classes was observed in terms of a system of 10 categories (reclassified into six categories in this study, see Table 1) using 6-sec time units; at the same time, the intensity of the physical activity was assessed along a five-point scale (1 = does not move....5 = moves a lot). At the end of the lesson the observer also made overall trait ratings (12 traits). The two target pupils also wore a pedometer. After the class, the students were interviewed to find out, for instance, how strenuous they perceived the physical education class to have been, and whether or not they had sweated and become breathless. In the systematic observation of pupil behavior the nominal agreement of two coders reached the level of 78% ($n = 19$ classes).

The correlation between the pedometer readings and the mean heart rate was .70 ($n = 15$). The trait ratings were less reliable, mean $r = .57$.

The leisure time physical activity was measured by means of a questionnaire. The questions were used to divide the pupils into the three activity groups: Group 1, "sport club activists" (SCA), consisted of subjects who participated in leisure time physical activities at least twice a week and who participated regularly in sport club training sessions and in competitions (35% of the boys and 17% of the girls); Group 2, "recreational sport activists" (RSA), included the subjects who participated regularly in leisure time physical activities at least twice a week but not regularly in sport club training and competitions (30% of the boys and 38% of the girls); Group 3, "passive" (PAS), consisted of the subjects who did not participate in leisure time physical activties more often than once a week and who did not participate in sport club training and competition (8% of the boys and 6% of the girls). Only secondary and upper secondary school physical education classes and pupils (193 girls and 172 boys) were included in the final analysis.

Results

There were clear differences between the activity groups of the boys and the girls in terms of their grades in physical education and their own assessments of their skills in physical education. The sport club activists had the best grades and skills, and the passive group had the lowest grades and skills.

A study of the differences between the activity groups did not supply any statistically significant differences from time-on-task or any other activity categories (see Table 1).

There were no differences in the intensity of physical activity, but pedometer readings for the girls correlated with the activity groups; the readings for the sport club activists almost reached the levels of the boys (see Figure 1). The trait ratings by the observers also indicated that sport club activists were assessed as more active and the passive pupils were assessed as less active, but this result is statistically significant for the boys only.

Table 1. Pupil behavior by sex and activity group.

Behavior categories	SCA	Girls RSA	PAS	SCA	Boys RSA	PAS
Organizing	20	21	19	18	17	19
Following teaching	10	13	14	7	8	8
Getting feedback	2	3	2	1	1	1
Time-on-task	48	45	48	54	52	50
Waiting for turn	14	11	12	13	15	13
Other activities	6	7	5	7	7	9
Total %	100	100	100	100	100	100
1) n	50	173	30	92	121	28

1) n = number of observed periods

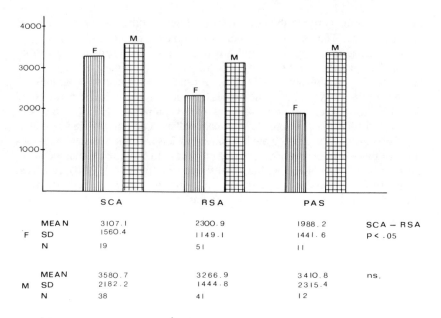

		SCA	RSA	PAS	
	MEAN	3107.1	2300.9	1988.2	SCA — RSA
F	SD	1560.4	1149.1	1441.6	P < .05
	N	19	51	11	
	MEAN	3580.7	3266.9	3410.8	ns.
M	SD	2182.2	1444.8	2315.4	
	N	38	41	12	

Figure 1. Pedometer readings by sex and activity group.

Immediately after the lesson, the pupils were presented with questions to assess, for instance, the physical strain caused by the lesson, loss of breath, and sweating. No differences were found between the activity groups in terms of these assessments.

The differences between activity groups were more pronounced in psychic variables than in physical variables. The sport club activists were the most interested and the passive pupils the least interested in school physical education. There was a similar difference between the groups in pupils' assessment of the pleasantness of the lesson.

According to the observers' overall ratings, the passive pupils were rated as clumsier and more insecure than the more active pupils. The passive girls were also rated as more anxious and the passive boys as having fewer social contacts.

In terms of the teacher-pupil interrelationship, it was found that the pupils belonging to different activity groups received the same amount of feedback (see Table 1). No differences were found among the girls as to how often single pupils were targets of the teacher, while among the boys, the passive ones, more often than the active ones, were target pupils.

Discussion

The study reported here seems to indicate that pupils participate in the activities during physical education lessons actively, irrespective of what they do in leisure time. This was the case despite the fact that the three activity groups were distinguished in terms of skills in physical education as assessed by the pupils themselves and in terms of the grades given by the teachers. There might have been differences in the level of pupils' performances, however, but this variable was not measured.

Although there was no difference in motor behavior, clear differences were found between the three activity groups in the way in which physical education lessons resulted in psychic experiences and in which the pupils felt school physical education was pleasant. It seems that pupils who are not physically active participate in physical education lessons conscientiously, but it does not give them as positive an experience as it gives to pupils who are physically active in their leisure time. This is also reflected in the fact that the observers rated the passive pupils more anxious, more insecure, and less prone to participate in social interaction despite the fact that a tendency towards the average was seen in the ratings.

Physical education in Finland pays due attention also to the most passive pupils. In this respect the results of the study reported here agree with those reported on by Shute et al., (1982). It is clear that passive pupils do not have as positive an attitude toward physical education lessons as active pupils do. Further research is needed on ways in which passive pupils participate in physical education lessons and on the attitudes of the teachers towards such students. In addition to the amount and intensity of physical activity, the level of difficulty of the pupil's performance also ought to be recorded. Attention should also be called to the reasons for negative experiences with physical education lessons.

References

Costello J., & Laubach, S. A. (1978). Student behavior. In W. G. Anderson & G. T. Barrette (Eds.), *What's going on in gym. Motor Skills: Theory into Practice,* (Monograph 1), 11-24.

Martinek, T. J., Growe, P. B., & Rejeski, W. J. (1982). *Pygmalion in the gym: Causes and effects of expectations in teaching and coaching.* West Point, NY: Leisure Press.

Martinek, T. J., & Johnson, S. B. (1979). Teacher expectations: Effects on dyadic interactions and self-concept in elementary age children. *Research Quarterly,* **50** (1), 60-70.

Pieron, M. (1982). Behaviors of low and high achievers in physical education classes. In M. Pieron & J. Cheffers (Eds.), *Studying the teaching in physical education* (pp. 53-60). Liege, Belgium: AIESEP.

Pieron, M. (1983). Teacher and pupil behavior and the interaction process in p.e. classes. In R. Telama, V. Varstala, J. Tiainen, L. Laakso, & T. Haajanen (Eds.), *Research in school physical education,* Reports of Physical Culture and Health 38, (pp. 13-30). Jyväskylä: Gummerus.

Rosenthal, R., & Jacobson, L. (1968). *Pygmalion in the classroom.* New York: Holt, Rinehart, and Winston.

Shute, S., Dodds, P., Placek, J., Rife, F., & Silverman, S. (1982). Academic learning time in elementary school movement education: A descriptive analytic study. *Journal of Teaching in Physical Education,* **1** (2), 3-14.

Telama, R., & Laakso, L. (1983). Leisure-time physical activity. In M. Rimpelä, A. Rimpelä, S. Ahlström, E. Honkala, L. Kannas, L. Laakso, O. Paronen, M. Rajala, & R. Telama (Eds.), *Health habits among Finnish youth, the juvenile health habit study, 1977-79*. Finland: Publications of the National Board of Health **4**, 49-70.

Varstala, V., Telama, R., & Akkanen, O. (1981). Teacher and student activities during physical education lessons. In H. Haag, J. Bielefeld, J. Broeckhoff, J. Falke, K. Feige, P. Kayser, W. Kneyer, E. Krüger, A. Morawietz, & W. Weichert (Eds.), *Physical education and evaluation. Schriftenreihe des Bundesinstituts für Sportwissenschaft*, **36**, 368-374. Schorndorf: Verlag Karl Hoffman.

8

Analysis of a Mastery Learning/Personalized System of Instruction for Teaching Tennis

Michael W. Metzler
VIRGINIA POLYTECHNIC INSTITUTE AND STATE UNIVERSITY
BLACKSBURG, VIRGINIA, USA

While physical education teaching espouses many and varied teaching methods, rarely are those methods tied into some scheme of instructional design. We look to things that can work and not to the kinds of integrated instructional strategies derived from learning models and theories. Furthermore, we tend to teach activity content (volleyball, golf, etc.) in standardized ways; a tennis class of sixth graders does many of the same drills and receives many of the same demonstrations as a class of college freshmen, and thus gets instructed in much the same manner. Such instructional stereotyping has several origins. We generally teach the way we have been taught and look to the abundant, and mostly similar, methods texts and commercial teaching guides for help. Only in rare instances will a physical education teacher look to a different body of literature for instructional schema. Instructional design, the integration of learning theories and models for global teaching strategies, is unfamiliar to many teachers. Some might know what instructional design is, but few incorporate sound, empirically derived design principles into their teaching. Even our own motor learning literature has largely ignored the task of exploring design-derived teaching strategies for physical education, seemingly opting for a more molecular basis of learning inquiry.

Two particular instructional design models seem to have a direct value and easy application for teaching motor play skills. Mastery Learning, first set

63

forth by Benjamin Bloom (1968), is based on the premise that learners must acquire skills in incremental, sequential progressions, with prerequisite skills being learned (mastered) prior to attempting more difficult and complex tasks. Bloom also proposed that time be allowed to vary in Mastery Learning. That is, teachers should hold the amount of content stable, but allow individual learners their own needed time to acquire skills.

Fred Keller developed his Personalized System for Instruction (1968) at the same time. It is based on Mastery Learning principles in that students must progress through the content only after acquiring prerequisite skills. Keller extended this concept to allow individual students to go through a given task sequence at their own learning pace, independent of other learners. The "Keller Method," as it is commonly labeled, has other features. More tutorial time is planned for, and students can proctor each other once they attain mastery of the skills themselves. The teacher is expected to locate learners who need more attention and plan for whatever individual learning activities might be needed.

Description of the ML/PSI Tennis Unit

The ML/PSI tennis unit to be described here was intended to incorporate the best of both designs and to free the instructor from routine managerial and group-dependent instructional functions. It was also decided that students should not progress to playing tennis matches until they had mastered the three basic shots—forehand, backhand, and serve—and were versed in tennis rules. Table 1 shows one of the three skill sequences in the ML/PSI unit. Note that each item has practice directions and a stated criterion for accuracy and consistency. When students complete an item, they initial and date it on their personal skill sheet. To prevent students from progressing without mastery (a polite way to say "cheating"), certain skill items have an asterisk (*) on them, denoting that students must get the instructor to witness their mastery of the item. Furthermore, the first few items in all sequences require a lecture/demonstration from the instructor so no student can begin a new sequence on his or her own.

The ML/PSI tennis unit has other design considerations written into it. Students practice their skills in pairs with someone who works at about the same pace. Partners change every day to reflect individual pacing. Students help each other by being the "tosser" as needed and by collecting balls between practice sets. There is only one whole-class lecture/demonstration, for the forehand, given on the very first day. Immediately after that, students find a partner and begin working on the forehand sequence. All other lecture/demonstrations occur individually or in small groups as students finish one sequence and begin another.

The teacher's role in this unit looks quite different from traditional tennis instruction. There are no management functions: students arrive, stretch on their own, get their skill shett, find a partner for the day, and begin to practice—all without teacher direction. Because the teacher is freed from many routine duties during class time, he or she can circulate more freely around

Table 1. Mastery sequence for forehand (FH)

Task #	Task	Target	Criterion	Date
1*	Lect/Demo from Inst.	The Ready Position The Forehand (FH) Drive	None	
2	FH ready position	On call from instr.	Correct	
3	FH Grip	On call from instr.	Correct	
4*	FH Footwork From ready, w/grip	On call from instr.	Correct	
5	Stand on service line Own bounce Hit FH	Over net, in legal area	6/10 2 sets in row	
6	Stand at service line Partner toss Hit FH	Over net, in legal area	6/10 2 sets in row	
7	Service line Own bounce Hit FH	In legal area Over Power Line (PL) (12' behind opposite baseline)	7/10 2 sets in row	
8*	At service line Partner toss Hit FH	In legal area Over PL	6/10 2 sets in row	
9	At service line Partner toss Hit FH	In legal area Over PL	6/10 2 of 3 sets	
10*	Stand at baseline Partner toss Hit FH	In legal area Over PL	6/10 2 of 3 sets	
11	FH Rally W/partner	All shots to FH Side All shots bounce over service line first	15 consecutive 2 of 3 sets	

*Students must get the instructor's approval of mastering these skills.

the courts to find students who need tutorial help and/or more focused feedback. When students need the instructor to verify a mastery attempt, they ask the instructor to come to their court and keep score. Tennis drills take the shape of the mastery items and are completely student-paced. Occasionally the instructor might suggest a special drill when a student needs help with a skill component that is best worked on outside the sequence. Otherwise, the skill sequence provides most necessary cueing and progressions for the students.

Subjects, Setting, and Data Collection

Students in two intact beginning tennis classes served as subjects for this study. Class 1 was taught with the ML/PSI strategy described above and had 30 students. Class 2 was the "traditional" group, with 35 students. Both were elective basic service classes, taught at Virginia Tech in the summer of 1983. Both met 5 days a week with 22 scheduled classes. Due to weather cancellations, both classes actually met 20 times, for 60 min each time. Males and females were about equal in both classes.

Class 2 in this study had a more traditional tennis class than the ML/PSI students. That is, the instructor began each class with a demonstration and then directed students to practice the day's content. All students practiced the same skill/drill at the same time. Progression through the unit was dictated by the instructor's schedule for covering the content (i.e., a certain number of days for forehand, backhand, serving, and game playing) regardless of whether students demonstrated competence. For lack of a more empirical description of the teaching strategy, Class 2 received the kind of tennis instruction we associate with a beginner's unit in tennis, characterized by teacher demonstration followed by a single drill for the whole period on that skill.

Both classes were observed nine times by a trained observer, about every other day during the term. Three students in each class were chosen randomly to be observed every time. Observations were made only on skill development days. The students were observed with the Academic Learning Time-Physical Education (ALT-PE) interval coding system (Siedentop, Birdwell, & Metzler, 1979). Interobserver reliability was checked once in each class near the middle of the term. With the exception of two categories that had very low frequencies, all agreement percentages were within acceptable ranges.

Student Process Comparisons

Table 2 shows the percentages of occurrence for the ALT-PE coding categories for both classes over the observation period. Students in Class 2 were under more teacher directed instruction than those in Class 1, but not much more. While larger differences might have been expected, neither teacher dominated the instruction; students were given much freedom to initiate their own skill practice responding under both strategies. Students in both classes had similar amounts of PE content, 97.3% for Class 1 and 95.9% for Class 2. However, there were larger differences in how students interacted with the content in each class. For instance, students in Class 1 had more practice intervals and

Table 2. Comparisons between classes on ALT-PE coding categories

		ML/PSI	Traditional
Intervals Observed		1,945	1,824
Direct Instruction		15.8%	19.6%
Task Instruction		84.2%	80.4%
Content General			
Waiting		0.1%	0.5%
Transition		1.8%	2.7%
Management		0.7%	0.5%
	Total	2.6%	3.7%
Content PE			
Skill Practice		88.4%	83.0%
Knowledge		6.4%	11.6%
Fitness		0.8%	0.0%
Social		1.3%	0.0%
Other Motor		0.4%	1.3%
	Total	97.3%	95.9%
Not Engaged			
Interim		26.0%	33.0%
Waiting		3.8%	6.6%
Off Task		1.8%	1.5%
	Total	31.6%	41.4%
Engaged			
Motor Response		48.0%	41.1%
Indirect		11.4%	2.0%
Cognitive		6.3%	11.6%
	Total	65.7%	54.7%
ALT-PE		41.6%	27.2%
Easy Motor Trials		86.4%	65.7%

fewer knowledge content intervals. The ML/PSI strategy planned for individual lectures and demonstration and resulted in nearly half as many knowledge content intervals (6.4%-11.5%). While this is not a large difference, it does reflect a more efficient way to present the same amount of content to students over the traditional approach.

It was in the Learner Moves level of the ALT/PE Coding System that more meaningful process differences began to emerge between classes. Students in Class 1 were more efficient in their use of practice time. They had 26% interim and 48% motor response intervals. Students in Class 2 had 33% and 41.4%, respectively. Students in Class 1 had less waiting time as well. The difference in motor responding might have been due to the use of the task sequence sheets and the pairing of students for practice. Students did not have to wait for more teacher directions or ask questions about how and where to practice items on the sheet. However, students in Class 1 had more indirect intervals, due to periodic assignments as "tossers." Thus, the plan to place students in pairs seemed to bring about a good trade-off.

Two of the expressed benefits of the ML/PSI design emerged in the bottom line process variable comparisons of accrued ALT-PE. ALT-PE was defined as the amount of accrued relevant and easy motor responding only (Metzler, 1983). Students in Class 1 had 41.6% ALT-PE intervals while students in Class 2 had just 27.2%. Part of this difference was due to more motor engagement for Class 1. However, the ML/PSI design resulted in 86.4% success rate in motor trials for Class 1, compared to just 65.7% for Class 2. In other words, Class 1 practiced more motor tasks, and with much more success, than their counterparts. The Mastery Learning feature of basing progression on prerequisite skill acquisition clearly had an impact on Class 1 and the Personalized System of Instruction feature ensured that all students progressed according to their own learning pace.

ALT-PE Over the Length of the Units

It is helpful to visualize the stability of ALT-PE across time for both classes. Figure 1 shows the percentage of ALT-PE intervals for the target students in both classes on the 9 observation days. The horizontal lines represent the mean percentage of ALT-PE intervals across all observation days for each class. The ML/PSI class had substantial and consistently higher ALT- PE accrual patterns during the term.

Progression Through the ML/PSI Unit

The task sequence sheets used by the ML/PSI students provided a good record of just how they did in the unit relative to the three-skill sequence. Table 3

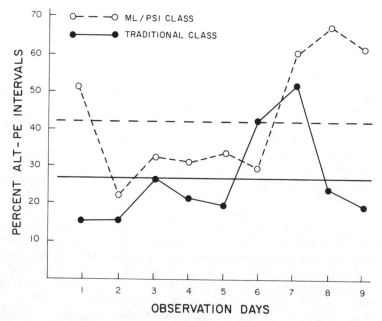

Figure 1. ALT-PE Percentages over the term

Table 3. Student Progressions through the three-skill task sequence, ML/PSI unit

										Class Days									
	1	2	3	4	5	6	7	8	9	10	11	12	13	14	15	16	17	18	19
Forehand																			
1-4	100																		
5	38	77	92	100															
6	38	77	85	100															
7	8	31	77	92	100														
8				54	77	100													
9				54	77	100													
10				39	70	85	100												
Backhand																			
1-4						46	54	69	77	92	92	100							
5						31	39	62	62	85	92	100							
6						23	31	46	54	69	92	100							
7							8	8	31	69	85	100							
8							8	8	16	31	46	54							
Serves																			
1-2													54	54	69	92	100		
3											23	31	32	39	54	62	85	100	
4											8	16	23	31	54	62	85	100	
5														23	46	46	69	100	
6														23	38	46	69	100	
7														23	31	31	62	92	100
8														15	23	23	31	69	100
9														7	15	15	23	62	100

shows the instructional days across the top and the task sequence items on the left. At the intersection of each row and column is the percentage of students who had completed that item by the end of the class. All students who stayed in the class to the end completed the sequence (bottom right), some in the nick of time! The first students to finish the sequence took 15 days, while most finished with 1 or 2 days left to play games. This table illustrates that on some days, students were spread across as many as eight skill items! This certainly attests to the ability of the PSI design to allow for maximum individualization of learning.

Final Thoughts

While these results offer support for the implementation of instructional design-based teaching strategies for physical education, they cannot answer the most critical question, Do students learn more with an ML/PSI design? Bloom (1984) suggests that Mastery Learning can solve the *two sigma* problem. That is, he predicts that Mastery Learning is capable of producing achievement scores greater than two standard deviations above those attainable with other instructional methods, except direct tutoring. While still unable to answer that important question about achievement differences, this study shows a combined Mastery Learning/Personalized System of Instruction strategy that clearly results in better student process measures during tennis teaching.

References

Bloom, B. (1968). Learning for Mastery. *Evaluation Comment,* **1** (2). Los Angeles: University of California, Center for the Study of Evaluation.

Bloom, B. (1984, April). Methods of instruction which are as effective as one-to-one tutoring. Invited informal discussion at the Annual meeting of the American Education Research Association, New Orleans.

Keller, F. (1968). Good-bye, teacher. *Journal of Applied Behavior Analysis,* **1**, 79-84.

Metzler, M. (1983). ALT-PE for inservice teachers: Questions and insights. In P. Dodds, & F. Rife (Eds.), Time to learn in Physical Education: History, completed research, and potential future for Academic Learning Time in physical education. *Journal of Teaching in Physical Education Summer Monograph I,* 17-21.

Siedentop, D., Birdwell, D., & Metzler, M. (1979, March). *A process approach to measuring teaching effectiveness in physical education.* Paper presented at the National AAHPERD Convention, New Orleans.

9

Comparison of Teacher Behavior and Criterion Process Variables in an Experimental Teaching Unit (ETU) Taught by Preservice Physical Education Majors at the Entrance and Exit Levels

Paul C. Paese
SOUTHWEST TEXAS STATE UNIVERSITY
SAN MARCOS, TEXAS, USA

There is a need in pedagogical research to further investigate the effectiveness of early field experiences prior to student teaching and its influence on the teaching effectiveness of student teachers. Further research is also needed on the effect of teacher verbal feedback on student achievement. Some research completed has questioned the importance of feedback and did not find this variables relationship with student achievement significant (Graham, Soares, & Harrington, 1983; Yerg, 1977). Other research studies have concluded that teacher feedback is an important link to student achievement (Yerg & Twardy, 1982), with another reporting a significant relationship with achievement (Pieron, 1982). Also some conflicting conclusions have been made on the use of feedback by more effective teachers during experimental teaching units (Graham et al., 1983; Pieron, 1980; Yerg & Twardy, 1982).

The purposes of this study were as follows: (a) to assess the differences between student teachers and field experience interns during an experimental teaching unit on a novel golf skill with fifth grade children; (b) to determine

71

if a significant change occurred within each group when comparing pretest and posttest results; (c) to evaluate the correlation and level of significance for each criterion process variable on student achievement (posttest scores); and (d) to determine the correlation and level of significance of teacher feedback on Academic Learning Time (ALT-PE) and posttest results.

Methods and Procedures

Subjects and Setting

Five preservice physical education majors (Group 2) and 5 student teachers in physical education (Group 1) were used as teachers in this study. There were 4 females and 1 male teacher in each group. Each early field experience teacher had been involved in observing, aiding, and teaching his or her class during the experience for approximately 3 weeks (9 to 10 hours) at the time of data collection. For all preservice interns in the early field experience group, it was their first experience in teaching an elementary class. All student teachers had already completed an early field experience in the public schools during a methods class. At the time data collection began, student teachers were approximately two thirds of the way through an 8-week student teaching experience. All teachers taught in elementary schools in the central Texas area. Public school students involved in the teachers' classes were all fifth graders and classes were coed. Class size ranged from 20 to 26 per class, with each group of teacher's classes averaging approximately 22 per class.

Experimental Teaching Unit

The modified experimental teaching unit (ETU) used for this study was from the Georgia Physical Education Teaching Unit Project (Graham et al., 1983). The objective was to hit a tennis ball with a hockey stick into a hoop which was set up 30 yards away. Students involved in this task attempted to hit the ball into the hoop area in as few strokes as possible. Further rules and guidelines for conducting the test and the ETU can be obtained from the Georgia project.

Observations and Data Collection

Each teacher in both groups pretested his or her students on the novel golf task. After all students were tested, one 20-min lesson followed. All teachers and their classes were videotaped during their lesson. Each teacher was given a 3-day notice that they were to be involved in this project. The teachers were told that they could teach the 20-min lesson any way they wanted to. In order to minimize subject reactivity, teachers did not know that fellow preservice teachers would be involved in the project. All teachers were also told that they would have 16 hockey sticks and two dozen tennis balls with which to work. After the 20-min lesson was conducted, all students in the class were given a posttest on the novel golf skill. In both pre- and posttests, students were given two attempts at the task. Students were split among testers and were only allowed to go one at a time, with the teacher keeping count of each stroke.

Each teacher's 20-min lesson was coded for amounts of activity time (class time spent in skills/game play), management time, instruction time, motor engagement (individual students doing motor tasks), academic learning time (individual students doing a motor task with success), and teacher verbal feedback. Observations of videotapes were completed by a trained observer using the ALT-PE interval recording system (Siedentop, Tousignant, & Parker, 1982) and the behavioral observation technique of event recording (Siedentop, 1983, chapter 14). Definitions of these categories are included in Siedentop's *Developing Teaching Skills in Physical Education* (1983).

Reliability

Interobserver agreement was checked twice during the coding of videotapes by the scored-interval method of calculation (Hawkins & Dotson, 1975). Techniques used to determine reliability on event recording is described by Siedentop (1983, pp. 264-65). Overall reliabilities were quite acceptable: .86 on the categories in the ALT interval system, and .89 for event recording (feedback).

Analysis

A t-test was computed on all variables to determine if the differences were significant. A t-test was also used to assess differences between the two groups on pre- and posttest results and also to determine if a significant gain in achievement was made within each group on the posttest. A Pearson Product Moment Correlation was used to determine the relationship between each variable and student achievement. Product Moment Correlations were also used to determine relationships between teacher verbal feedback and ALT.

Results

Pretest/Posttest

There were no significant differences between the two groups of teacher's classes on pretest and posttest scores on the novel golf task. Each group of teacher's classes improved its score on the posttest by decreasing the average number of strokes by one. This reduction by both groups was not significant $p > .10$. Table 1 illustrates this data.

Teacher Group

Group 2 (field experience teachers) had lower means in management and instruction time when compared to Group 1 (student teachers). In both cases differences were significant $p < .011$ (management), and $p < .05$ (instruction). Significant differences also occurred between the two groups in favor of the field experience teachers in activity time $p < .014$, motor engagement $p < .008$, and in the amount of teacher verbal feedback $p < .05$. No significant difference occurred between both groups on the amount of ALT-PE $p > .29$. The data on the comparisons between the two groups of teachers is also included in Table 1.

Table 1. Comparison of selected variables between and within teacher groups

Variable[a]	Group	Net gain	r	t	p
Pre to Post	1	−1	−.58	1.93	.160
	2	−1.0	-.48	1.96	.150

Variable[b]	Group	Mean	SD	t	p
Pretest	1	6.2	.6	.223	.820
	2	6.6	.1		
Posttest	1	5.1	.7	.196	.850
	2	5.8	.1		
Management	1	27%	.89	3.35	.011
	2	16.3%	6.6		
Instruction	1	21%	3.5	2.31	.050
	2	16.3%	8.5		
Activity	1	52.5%	9.9	3.06	.014
	2	69%	8.6		
Engaged Motor	1	19%	4.4	4.74	.008
	2	38%	5.4		
ALT	1	13.5%	6.0	1.12	.290
	2	16%	4.4		
Feedback	1	27	8.9	2.30	.050
	2	39	4.4		

[a]Within Groups
[b]Between Groups
$p < .05$

Significance with Achievement/ALT

The final analysis correlated all variables with student achievement and teacher verbal feedback with ALT for all groups of teachers. It must be noted that a negative correlation was the hypothesized direction of relationship between all variable and student achievement because a lower posttest score represents

Table 2. Correlations between selected variable and student achievement

Variable	Achievement	t	p
Instruction	$r = -.22$	0.64	.542
Management	$r = -.43$	1.10	.311
Activity	$r = -.45$	1.30	.223
Feedback	$r = -.49$	1.59	.162
Motor Engagement	$r = -.63$	2.30	.051
ALT	$r = -.56$	1.91	.089
Feedback[a]	$r = -.43$	1.10	.311

[a]Correlation on feedback on ALT other variables correlate with post test results.
$P < .05$

improvement. All variables correlated with achievement (posttest results) were not significant. Motor engagement was the variable closest to a significant relationship with student achievement ($p < .051$). The only other variable that approached an acceptable confidence interval was academic learning time (ALT-PE). Teacher verbal feedbacks' relationship with ALT was not significant, but it also approached an acceptable confidence interval.

Conclusions/Discussion

Even though both teacher groups had overall improvement in student achievement over pretest scores, the results were not significant. Still, significant differences between the two groups of teachers did occur. Early field experience teachers did have lower rates of instruction and management time and higher rates of activity time, motor engagement, and feedback. The differences between groups in ALT were not significant, although a longer ETU lesson might have produced a significant difference. Why did the early field experience teachers do better? One answer might be the fact that methods, techniques, and such are fresher in the minds of early field experience students who have just been involved in methods class. Student teachers have not been involved with much of the pertinent information in a methods class in 6 months to a year because much of their time spent between methods and student teaching was in general education classes.

Another reason for the difference may be that student teachers have not spent substantially longer periods of time with their students than the field experience teachers. Nor have they had substantially more teaching experience than their undergraduate colleagues. Student teachers were around their cooperating teachers for over 125 hrs and were probably affected by them more than the field experience students were by their cooperating teachers. Current research in physical education suggests that the high rates of management time and the low rates of motor engagement, ALT, and feedback are common with many experienced teachers today (Anderson, 1978; Cheffers & Mancini, 1978). This might explain some of the differences between the two groups.

The impact of feedback and selected criterion process variables on student achievement are only partially consistent with previous research in this area. The relationship of motor engagement with achievement was the variable closest to significance, but this variable along with ALT-PE did not warrant the same conclusion as past research (Pieron, 1980; 1982).

Feedback's impact on achievement was not significant and adds to the array of conclusions made in other ETU studies concerning this variable (Graham et al., 1983; Pieron, 1982; Yerg, 1977; 1981; Yerg & Twardy, 1982). As Yerg and Twardy (1982) suggested, it is just possible that the more complex a skill, the less effect feedback has on achievement. Many consider golf tasks to be a very complex skill.

The utility of the ETU for physical education teacher effectiveness research has been demonstrated, but modifications in the paradigm may make it even more useful as a research design. Specifically the 20 min lesson might be lengthened, or two 20-min segments might be included. Differences between the two groups and on the variables' relationship with achievement may have been statistically more significant with longer ETU lessons. Because some of the criterion-process variables (motor engagement and ALT-PE) in this and previous studies (Pieron 1982; Yerg & Twardy, 1982) either correlated significantly with achievement or approached acceptable confidence levels, the need for replication is not as critical today.

The effect of teacher verbal feedback on student achievement, however, is still unresolved. An ETU study could be used to draw some firm conclusions on feedback. If two sets of teachers were to teach a class where everything is controlled, the question on the effect of feedback may be concluded. Two sets of teachers would teach classes with everything similar: equipment, grade level, ratio of boys to girls, organization, management time, activity time, and engaged time. The only difference would be that one group of teachers would give higher rates of specific feedback and the other group of teachers would give no feedback at all. Further research is, of course, warranted in teacher effectiveness research if teacher educators are to ever have firm generalizable conclusions about the teaching/learning process. This is the only way theories of teaching can be generated.

References

Anderson, W. (1978). Introduction. What's going on in gym: Descriptive studies of physical education classes. *Motor Skills: Theory into Practice* (Monograph) **1**, 1-10.

Cheffers, J., & Mancini, V. (1978). Teacher-student interaction. What's going on in gym: Descriptive studies of physical education classes. *Motor Skills: Theory into Practice* (Monograph) **1**, 39-50.

Graham, G., Soares, P., & Harrington, N. (1983). Experienced teachers' effectiveness with intact classes: An ETU study. *Journal of Teaching Physical Education* **2** (2), 3-14.

Hawkins, R., & Dotson, V. (1975). Reliability scores that delude: An Alice in Wonderland trip through the misleading characteristics of interobserver agreement scores in interval recording. In E. Ramp & G. Semb (Eds.), *Behavior analysis: Areas of research and application* (pp. 359-377). New York: Prentice Hall.

Pieron, M. (1980). Analyse de l'enseignement des activities physiques. Liege: Universite de Liege.

Pieron, M. (1982). Effectivenss of teaching a psychomotor task. Study in a micro-teaching setting. In M. Pieron & J. Cheffers (Eds.), *Studying the teaching in physical Education* (pp 79-89). Liege: International Association for Physical Education and Higher Education.

Siedentop, D. (1983). *Developing teaching skills in physical education*. Palo Alto, CA: Mayfield.

Siedentop, D., Tousignant, M., & Parker, M. (1982). *Academic learning time—physical education revised coding manual*. Unpublished manuscript, The Ohio State University.

Yerg, B.J. (1977). Relationships between teacher behaviors and pupil achievement in the psychomotor domain. *Dissertation Abstracts International,* **38**. (University Microfilms No. 77-21-229)

Yerg, B.J. (1981). Reflections on the use of the RTE model in physical education. *Research Quarterly for Exercise and Sport,* **52** (2), 38-47.

Yerg, B.J., & Twardy, B.M. (1982). Relationship of specified instructional teacher behaviors to pupil gain on a motor skill task. In M. Pieron & J. Cheffers, *Studying the teaching of physical education* (pp 61-68). Liege: International Association for Physical Education and Higher Education.

10

Professional Interventions of Physical Education Teachers in Elementary and High Schools

Michel Lirette, Claude Paré, and Fernand Caron
UNIVERSITÉ DU QUÉBEC À TROIS-RIVIÉRES
TROIS-RIVIÉRES, QUÉBEC, CANADA

This study, which was carried out in Québec, focuses on analyzing physical education teachers' in-class intervention at elementary and high school levels. It is a continuation of the work inaugurated by Anderson (1974) and the research of Barrette (1977).

The major point of interest of this study was to assess the types of teacher intervention used in physical education classes. More specifically, each type of intervention was to be identified and categorized, and its duration was to be determined. During the 1970s, under the leadership of Anderson at Columbia University and Cheffers at Boston University, researchers undertook the task of developing multipurpose observation systems to delineate the teachers' and students' behaviors in a physical education environment. Cheffers (1973), Anderson (1974), Hurwitz (1974), Laubach (1975), and Morgenegg (1978), to name a few, were involved in that type of research.

The general assumption supporting those studies was that intervention in physical education teaching is detected not only in guides, educational manuals, or idealistic program descriptions but also in the systematic observation of daily occurrences during the natural course of physical education class in the gymnasium. Therefore, the general goal was to identify as adequately as possible a significant portion of these occurrences in order to better understand the nature of the physical education teacher's intervention.

Objectives

The objectives of the present study were to answer three questions. During an elementary or high school physical education class (a) what types of intervention does the teacher use in his or her interaction with the students? (b) what portion of the total lesson time is devoted to various types of predetermined interventions? and (c) how do the results of the present study compare with those presented by Barrette (1977)?

Methods

Subjects

The sample consisted of students in 36 elementary and 45 high school class periods. It included both male and female students and was divided as follows: 36 kindergarten to Grade 6 classes, totaling 758 students taught by 11 teachers, and 45 Grade 7 to Grade 11 classes, totaling 1,251 students taught by 12 teachers.

Descriptive Behavior Analysis of Teacher Behavior

The observation and systematic codification of recorded behaviors falls into a set of operationally defined categories. It is a multidimensional system and utilizes a natural unit (the function of the teacher) to code teacher interventions according to the following two dimensions:

1. Function: the purpose of the behavior
2. Duration: the actual time elapsed in seconds from the beginning to the end of the unit of behavior

The dimension of the teacher's function is subdivided into 18 identified function categories which are grouped into the following 6 interactive domains:

1. Preparing for Motor Activities, which includes Organizing, Preparatory Instruction, and Providing Equipment or Readying Environment
2. Guiding the Performance of Motor Activities, which takes on Concurrent Instruction, Officiating, Spotting, Leading Exercises, and Intervening Instruction
3. Observing the Performance of Motor Activities
4. Participating in Motor Activities
5. Other Interaction Related to Motor Activities and
6. Other Interactive Behaviors such as Administering, Establishing and Enforcing Codes of Behavior, and Other Interacting

Two other noninteractive categories have also been identified to account for other behaviors or events: Noninteractive Intervals including Dealing with

Equipment and Other Noninteractive Behaviors and Nondiscernable Intervals such as Insufficient Audio/Video and Absence from Gymnasium.

Class Recordings and Data Collections

The recordings and data collections were executed in accordance with the procedure suggested by Barrette (1977). Two cameras, a cordless microphone, an FM receiver, a special effects generator, and a digital clock insert were used. Before being able to code teacher behaviors, competent coders had to be trained so that they could adequately make use of the measuring instrument utilized to analyze interventions in physical education. Four coders translated the data collected from 81 physical education class periods, each lasting 44 min on the average.

Reliability of Measures

To calculate the reliability of the behavior analysis system, three model videotapes were first coded in minute detail by three investigators. These models lasted 5, 9, and 13 min each and represented segments of three teachers' classes. The tapes were then coded by four coders and the average agreement percentage was 90%. To calculate intercoder reliability, three other segments of 5, 9, and 13 min, given by other teachers, were coded by four coders and the average agreement percentage of the coders was 88%.

Results

Table 1 shows how physical education teachers use their class time. It seems that 5 of the 18 intervention categories took up 71.6% of the teacher's time as follows: Organizing—12.6%; Preparatory Instruction—12.2%; Concurrent Instruction—11.2%; Intervening Instruction—13%; and Observing the Performance of Motor Activities—22.8%. Only 4.5% of the total time was devoted to noninteractive intervals.

A closer observation of Table 1 reveals several differences between the grade levels; for instance, the elementary level showed higher percentages in the first two categories as well as in the 4th (Concurrent Instruction) and the 13th (Establishing and Enforcing Codes of Behavior) than did the high school level. On the other hand, the high school level showed a higher percentage in the 5th (Officiating), 8th (Intervening Instruction), and 12th (Administering) categories. Both grade levels showed similar percentages in all other categories.

Similar deductions can be made from the mean frequency per class. The elementary level seems to have a higher percentage level in the Organizing (48), Preparatory Instruction (18.4), Concurrent Instruction (44.3), and Establishing and Enforcing Codes of Behavior (10.6) categories, whereas the high school level dominated the Officiating (28.4), Intervening Instruction (27), and Administering (5.9) categories.

Table 2 deals with a set of categories relating to the comparison of the results of this study and those obtained by Barrette (1977), and permits us to gather more information.

Table 1. Percentages of teaching time devoted to each category of intervention and mean frequency of each category of interventions based upon school level

Categories	Percentage of teaching time			Mean Frequency		
	ES[a]	HS	T	ES	HS	T
1. Organizing	14.6	10.9	12.6	48.0	30.8	38.4
2. Preparatory Instruction	13.6	10.9	12.2	18.4	6.8	11.9
3. Providing Equipment or Readying Environment	3.6	3.8	3.7	9.1	10.5	9.9
4. Concurrent Instruction	16.1	7.1	11.2	44.3	28.3	35.4
5. Officiating	3.0	6.6	5.0	13.0	28.4	21.6
6. Spotting	0.7	0.6	0.6	1.5	0.8	1.1
7. Leading Exercises	0.6	0.0	0.6	1.0	0.0	1.0
8. Intervening Instruction	9.1	16.4	13.0	16.8	27.0	22.4
9. Observing the Performance of Motor Activities	22.4	23.0	22.8	50.5	44.8	47.3
10. Participating in Motor Activities	1.0	1.8	1.5	1.7	1.4	1.5
11. Other Interaction Related to Motor Activities	1.8	2.8	2.3	4.6	2.7	2.3
12. Administering	1.0	3.8	2.5	0.9	5.9	3.6
13. Establishing and Enforcing Codes of Behavior	3.3	1.6	2.4	10.6	5.2	7.6
14. Other Interacting	5.0	6.1	5.6	14.3	14.5	14.4
15. Dealing with Equipment	2.0	1.2	1.6	4.0	1.9	2.8
16. Other Noninteractive Intervals	0.4	1.1	0.7	0.9	2.0	1.5
17. Insufficient Audio/Video	1.0	1.3	1.2	0.9	0.4	0.6
18. Absent from Gymnasium	0.8	1.2	1.0	2.0	2.0	2.0

[a]ES = Elementary School; HS = High School; T = Together.

First of all, this set of categories indicates, among other things, that active instruction accounted for 36.4% of the class time. It also indicates that the teacher spent 22.8% of his or her time observing motor activities and 23.5% of his or her time administering; 10% of the total class time was instruction related.

Discussion

Discussing the results brings us back to the first two questions under investigation in this study, which were: What types of interventions does the teacher use in his or her interactions with the students? and How do the teachers spend their time with respect to the functional categories? Table 1 gave us a global view of the behavior of the teachers who took part in the study. The results indicated that 96% of class time at both the elementary (95.8%) and

Table 2. Percentages of mean class time attributed to the four category groupings for each of the three groups of subjects and for all subjects as a whole

Group	Grouping and categories included in each grouping	ES[a] (%)	HS (%)	T (%)	Barrette (%)
A	Active Instruction Preparatory Instruction (2) Concurrent Instruction (4) Intervening Instruction (8)	38.8	34.4	36.4	36.9
B	Observation (9)	22.4	23.0	22.8	21.2
C	Managing (students and environment) Organizing (1) Providing Equipment (3) Administering (12) Establishing and Enforcing Codes of Behavior (13) Dealing with Equipment (15) Other Noninteractive Intervals (16)	24.9	22.4	23.5	20.4
D	Instruction Related Officiating (5) Spotting (6) Leading Exercises (7) Participating (10) Other Interacting Related to Motor Activities (11)	7.1	11.8	10.0	16.9

[a]ES = Elementary School; HS = High School; T = Together; Barrette = Barrette (1977).

high school (95.4%) levels was devoted to interactive functions. The breakdown of these overall percentages gave us a more precise idea of the utilization of the class time at each grade level. It showed that 81.7% of total class time was designated for the following activities: (a) 28.5% for Preparing for Motor Activities (Categories 1-3); (b) 30.4% for Guiding the Performance of Motor Activities (Categories 4-8); and(c) 22.8% for Observing the Performance of Motor Activities (Category 9). This latter percentage and the frequency of occurrence of that behavior were the highest among the category examined. Generally speaking, intervening functions lasted an average of 11.5 sec, which corresponds to approximately five occurrences per minute. Therefore, it can be concluded that the physical education teacher was highly interactive and that he or she diversified his or her interventions over a relatively short period of time. In regards to the difference between the two grade levels, the teacher spent more time giving organizing instruction on the elementary level than on the high school level. A suggested explanation is that the student's age compelled the teacher to intervene more often in order to organize the group. Another difference was noted in the characteristics of the teachers' feedback.

Teachers seemed to put more emphasis on supplying the students with explanations, initially to direct their behavior and then for demonstration purposes, while the activity was in progress at the elementary level. At the high school level, however, the teachers were more concerned with perfecting each students' performance.

The observation of the Performance of Motor Activities was the same at both levels. Furthermore, in comparing the present results to those found by Barrette (1977), the present study seems to show a certain consistency with regard to this type of behavior. A significant increase in this percentage would probably show evidence of a decrease in the Other Interacting category. Therefore, the following question may be raised: Could the teacher's silent observation be indicative of a lack of involvement on his or her part? Another point of discussion is the teachers' low participation levels in motor activities. The general impression that a physical education teacher is physically active does not seem to be supported by the results of this study (1.5% participation), nor by the results of Barrette's (1977) study (1.1% participation). In fact the teacher seems inclined to view his or her role on a theoretical basis, that is organizing, teaching, observing, and concerning him- or herself with the material content as well as the students' performances. On the other hand, if the teacher overparticipates, he or she risks being accused of not teaching. It is generally accepted that the students like teacher participation for various reasons such as motivation and competition. Teacher behavior in this capacity was apparently underexploited.

The third question mentioned at the beginning of this report dealt with the comparison of the results of this study to those found by Barrette (1977). The set of categories presented in Table 2 indicates that the teachers who took part in the studies displayed approximately the same percentages in three of the four categories. The only possible discrepancy was found in teaching assistance. A more detailed comparison of the data of our study as compared to those of Barrette (1977) indicates that the teachers involved in this study spent less time Officiating (a nonsignificant difference of 2.5%) and on the Other Interacting Related to Motor Activities category (a difference of 4.6%). The latter difference can be explained by the fact that the coders found less interactions directly related to motor activities for which there were no identified categories within the observation system.

In conclusion, videotaping classes and collecting data is a relatively long process. However, in spite of the intrinsic limitations of such a study, it seems that the system developed by Anderson (1974) and Barrette (1977) allowed us to identify exactly what the teachers do during their physical education classes. Also, the percentage of teaching time devoted by elementary level teachers to Concurrent Instructing, and the percentage devoted by secondary level teachers to Intervening Instruction require further investigation. Furthermore, it would be interesting to evaluate the effects of participation or nonparticipation of the teacher upon the classroom climate, the attitudes of the students, and the execution of instruction.

References

Anderson, W.G. (1974). *Teacher behavior in physical education classes. Part I: Development of a descriptive system.* Unpublished paper, Department of Physical Education, Teachers College, Columbia University, New York.

Barrette, G.T. (1977). *A descriptive analysis of teacher behavior in physical education classes.* Unpublished doctoral dissertation, Teachers College, Columbia University, New York.

Cheffers, J.T.F. (1973). *The validation of an instrument designed to expand the Flanders system of interaction analysis to describe nonverbal interaction, different varieties of teacher behaviour and pupil responses.* Unpublished doctoral dissertation, Temple University, Philadelphia.

Hurwitz, R. (1974). *A system to describe certain aspects of physical education teachers role in learning activity selection process.* Unpublished doctoral dissertation, Teachers College, Columbia University, New York.

Laubach, S. (1975). *The development of a system for coding student behavior in physical education classes.* Unpublished doctoral dissertation, Teachers College, Columbia University, New York.

Morgenegg, B.L. (1978). *The pedagogical functions of physical education teachers.* Unpublished doctoral dissertation, Teachers College, Columbia University, New York.

11

Interaction Change as a Function of Grade Level in Physical Education

Paul G. Schempp
KENT STATE UNIVERSITY
KENT, OHIO, USA

Recent studies on teacher interaction and socialization have drawn some interesting conclusions regarding student dispositions and characteristics as manipulators or influencers of teaching behavior. For example, Templin (1981) found physical education students' motor abilities, achievement levels, and compliance with rules all as influencers of the teacher's behavior. Martinek's (1983) classic research on expectancy theory has revealed such student characteristics as physical attractiveness (Martinek, 1981), perceived effort (Martinek & Karper, 1982), physical handicap, and the dynamics of the self-fufilling prophecy (Martinek, 1983) as influential variables in the student/teacher interactional process of the gymnasium.

The common thread uniting the works of Templin and Martinek was the revelation that teaching is not a behavior pattern that lies solely within the domain and determination of the teacher. Students appear to have significant impact on the perceptions and actions of the teacher, but students change. Their characteristics and traits alter as they mature and move through the educational process. This study attempted to determine the consequence of grade level change on the interactional process of the student and teacher in physical education. Will there in fact be a change in the relationship and behavior patterns between teacher and student as a result of grade change? If so, which behaviors change? These questions are not new. Several research efforts have, in part, attempted to address such issues (Cheffers & Mancini, 1978; Godbout, Brunelle, & Tousignant, 1983; Nygaard, 1975). However, previous research has been both limited in number and inconsistent in its findings. Further, previous studies have observed multiple teachers with each teacher represented by only one or two observations. If the question guiding the study is Does the interactional relationship between a teacher and his or her students change as a function of grade level?, it would appear methodologically sound to address the question by studying multiple observations of a single teacher teaching different grade levels. Therefore, this study attempted to extend the body of knowledge by employing a single-subject design to determine the existence of interaction change as a function of grade level in physical education.

Procedures

Subjects

The investigated teacher possessed 12 years of teaching experience and held both the bachelor of science and master of arts degrees in physical education. The teacher had spent the previous 6 years teaching in the same school in which this study was conducted. In general, this teacher was considered outstanding by his colleagues as well as university physical education faculty. The teacher was male and approximately 38 years old. All classes observed were taught by this teacher.

A total of 52 classes provided usable data for this study. In order to address the concerns of this study, these observations consisted of at least 6 physical education sessions from each grade level, kindergarten through sixth grade. Each grade level was represented by at least two intact classrooms. All classes were held in the same school. The school was located in a suburban midwestern univeristy community.

Instrumentation

Observations were made using Cheffer's Adaptation of Flander's Interaction Analysis System (CAFIAS) (Cheffers, Mancini, & Martinek, 1981). This system was specifically designed to systematically record the verbal and nonverbal student-teacher interaction in human movement settings and therefore was considered appropriate for this study. Using "blind-live" techniques, CAFIAS was determined to be a significantly $(p < .05)$ reliable indicator of classroom interaction (Cheffers et al., 1981). For the purposes of this study, the interactional relationship of the teacher and students was defined by the CAFIAS categories recorded for the observations.

Observations

Observations of each grade were made at random points throughout the year. However, no grade was observed more than once per week and no more than 30 schools days lapsed between observations. The first observation for each grade was made within the first 4 weeks of school and the last observation was made within the last 4 weeks of the school year. It was believed these criteria would allow for a representative sample of interaction to be collected for each grade level under investigation.

Reliability

Intra- and interobserver reliability estimates were determined in order to establish the accuracy and consistency of this study's data. Intraobserver reliability was derived by having the investigator code a videotape of the studied teacher twice. The time lag between the first and the second coding was 21 days. Interobserver reliability was established by having the principal investigator code a second videotape of the studied teacher and then having a second person not involved with this study code the same tape. The second coder, Dr. Thomas J. Martinek of the University of North Carolina, Greensboro, had demonstrated competence as a CAFIAS coder through his record of publications (Cheffers et al., 1981). Data from these codings were then applied to separate Spearman Rank Order correlation. Both the intraobserver ($r = 0.77$) and interobserver ($r = 0.78$) reliability estimates were found to be significant at the 0.05 level. It was therefore concluded that the data gathered for this study were significantly reliable for the purposes of interpretation.

Analyses and Results

The hypothesis of this study was tested by applying the CAFIAS codings of the 52 observed classes to a stepwise multiple regression analysis. The predictor variable was grade level and the criterion variables were the 20 CAFIAS categories. Table 1 summarizes the regression analysis.

A significant F ratio indicated that the regression model derived could accurately predict interaction patterns based on grade level. An examination of the regression model revealed the following variables significantly contributed to the model: teacher information giving (verbal), praise (verbal), acceptance (nonverbal), silence, confusion, and predictable student responses (verbal). A mean score analysis by grade level indicated corresponding increases between grade level and teacher information giving (verbal), praise (verbal), acceptance (nonverbal), and confusion (The CAFIAS confusion

Table 1. Stepwise multiple regression of interaction with grade level

| Interaction | | Grade Level | |
Variables	Beta	t	Sig of t
Predictable Student Response	− .43	− 4.13	0.00
Teacher Information Giving	.78	6.38	0.00
Confusion	.69	5.09	0.00
Silence	.49	4.05	0.00
Praise	.33	2.89	0.01
Acceptance	.24	2.33	0.02

$$\text{Multiple } r = .76$$
$$r \text{ Square} = .58$$
$$\text{Adjusted } r \text{ Square} = .53$$
$$F \text{ Ratio (6, 45)} = 10.44^*$$

$^*p < .01$

Table 2. Mean scores of significant interaction variables by grade level

Grade Level Interaction Variables	K $(n = 11)$	1 $(n = 6)$	2 $(n = 8)$	3 $(n = 6)$	4 $(n = 9)$	5 $(n = 6)$	6 $(n = 6)$
Predictable student response	3.58	2.45	1.93	2.88	2.42	2.17	1.67
Teacher information giving	13.21	18.38	16.14	20.20	17.27	26.63	18.72
Confusion	4.06	5.71	4.95	1.43	3.52	11.77	10.27
Silence	6.69	1.02	5.95	8.05	7.10	2.55	3.83
Praise	2.88	2.28	1.74	3.60	2.68	1.43	3.55
Acceptance	1.03	1.27	1.33	0.42	0.97	1.62	2.45

category is indicative of nonverbal student interaction). Corresponding decreases were noted between grade level and student predictable responses (verbal) and silence. Table 2 presents the mean scores of the significant criterion variables by grade level.

Discussion

The results of this study led to the conclusion that the interactional relationship between the teacher and students changed as a function of grade level. It would therefore seem that grade level may serve as an influencer of teaching behavior. This finding supports the research of Martinek (1981, 1983) and Templin (1981), who have concluded that student characteristics possess the potential to modify and influence the behavior of teachers. Grade level appears to be one of those characteristics.

Research by Nygaard (1975) also found that the interaction between students and teacher differed with grade level. The specific interactional changes detected in the present investigation manifested in more information, praise, and acceptance for the student and more confusion, less silence, and fewer predictable responses by the students. Similarities were noted between these findings and those from a study by Godbout et al. (1983). Godbout et al. found higher grade levels spent more time on physical education content. In the present study a similar interpretation could be made from the increase in information, praise, and acceptance. Also Godbout et al. found less time spent on managerial tasks in upper grades. Similarly, this study found more student interaction, fewer student rote responses, and less silence in upper grades. The consistency between the previous research (Nygaard, 1975; Godbout et al., 1983) and the present investigation strengthens the conclusion regarding change as a function of grade level. Additionally, it appears we have some insight into how those changes manifest themselves, that is, the teachers appear to be conveying what it is they want to convey to upper grades, and students interact more with one another and are less silent the longer they are exposed to school.

But what do these changes mean, and why do they occur? The answers to these questions live in the realm of speculation at this point. The present study was an empirically based investigation relying on directly observable behavior. The meanings of those behaviors are beyond the analytic potential of these data. Yet, understanding the meanings of observed behavior appears critical to understanding the teaching process. Perhaps additional research into the meaning of behavioral occurrences and changes will allow such behavior to be set in a context which will in turn deepen our conception of movement pedagogy. With this insight it may then be possible to not only understand the impetus for teaching change, but to consciously guide the direction of that change.

References

Cheffers, J.T.F., & Mancini, V. (1978). Teacher-student interaction. In W.G. Anderson & G.T. Barrette (Eds.), *What's going on in gym: Descriptive studies of physical education classes* (pp. 39—50). Motor Skills: Theory Into Practice, Monograph 1. Newtown, CT.

Cheffers, J.T.F., Mancini, V., & Martinek, T.J. (1981). *Interaction analysis: an application to nonverbal activity* (2nd ed.). Minneapolis: Association for Productive Teaching.

Godbout, P., Brunelle, J., & Tousignant, M. (1983). Academic learning time in elementary and secondary physical education classes. *Research Quarterly for Exercise and Sport,* **54**(1), 11-19.

Martinek, T.J. (1981). Physical attractiveness: effects on teacher expectations and dyadic interactions in elementary children. *Journal of Sport Psychology,* **3**, 196-205.

Martinek, T.J. (1983). Creating Golem and Galatea effects during physical education instruction: a social psychological perspective. In T. Templin & J. Olson (Eds.) *Teaching in Physical Education.* (pp. 59-70). Champaign: Human Kinetics.

Martinek, T.J., & Karper, W. (1982). Canonical relationships among motor ability, expression of effort, teacher expectations and dyadic interactions in elementary age children. *Journal of Teaching in Physical Education,* **1**(2), 26-39.

Nygaard, G. (1975). Interaction analysis in physical education classes. *Research Quarterly,* **46**(3), 351-357.

Templin, T. (1981). Student as socializing agent. *Journal of Teaching in Physical Education,* Introductory Issue, 71-79.

12

Daily Physical Education in Three Brisbane Primary Schools: An Evaluation of the Effectiveness of Programs Implemented by Classroom Teachers

G. I. Peckman, B. E. Tainton, and W. J. Hacker
RESEARCH SERVICES BRANCH
QUEENSLAND, AUSTRALIA

Daily Physical Education (DPE) is a recent innovation in many Queensland primary schools (Tainton, Peckman, & Hacker, in press). Its rise in popularity required an evaluation of current teaching practices and policies. In particular, administrators were concerned with the effectiveness of classroom teachers in implementing a physical education program on a daily basis.

The introduction of the DPE program, like most educational innovations, has not been without problems. Many teachers implementing the DPE program have had little experience in teaching physical education. In addition, preservice and in-service education provisions have been inadequate to meet the current needs of many teachers (Tainton, Peckman, & Hacker, 1984). This paper reports an investigation into the effectiveness of the physical fitness component of the DPE program of three classroom teachers over a 10-month period.

Evaluation Methodology

The project was conducted in three primary schools in Brisbane. At each school one teacher volunteered to implement a DPE program. A second teacher at each school volunteered to act as a control by continuing the conventional physical education program. Classes were at either the Year Five or Six level—aged 10 or 11 years.

The following data was collected from the DPE and control classes: (a) Indicators of physical fitness, that is 1,000 Meter Run, Sit Bend Reach, Vertical Jump, and Agility Run were collected on four occasions throughout the year; (b) Student height, weight and age were collected; (c) Details of every physical education lesson were collected by means of teacher diaries in which the frequency and duration of activities were recorded. The diaries also included the teacher's rating of the intensities of each activity in terms of their demands upon student's muscular and cardiovascular systems; (d) Student's involvement in physical activity during leisure time was collected by periodic student diaries maintained for 1 week on each occasion; and (e) Interviews with the DPE teachers and periodic observations of their lessons were conducted by the research team. Observations by the research team included recording the amount of student activity time, objective measures of work completed by students, and ratings of the intensities of physical activities.

Separate analyses were conducted for each school. The physical fitness data were analyzed using a multivariate analysis of variance with a repeated-measures design (Hull & Nie, 1981) that enabled comparisons among students' performances throughout the program and between the DPE and control classes.

Results

School A

DPE Teacher:
Karen is a dedicated teacher with 4 years of teaching experience. She had not taught DPE previously and had very little experience in teaching physical education or sport. Karen admitted to having a poor knowledge of physical fitness and to failing physical education during her preservice education.

DPE Program:
Her DPE program was based on prepared lesson material provided by the State Education Department. Karen received little assistance in establishing and monitoring the program during the year. An advisory DPE teacher provided one demonstration lesson early in the year. In addition, the school's physical education teacher, who attended the school 1 day per week, provided advice during her physical education lesson with Karen's class.

The most noticeable feature of the DPE program at School A was its adherence to principles of effective physical fitness development. Some significant features of the program were the following:

- During the program, physical activity increased from an initial average of 20 min daily to 30 min.
- Karen participated in many of the activities.
- Of the total time, 52% was spent on physical fitness activities.
- According to the class teacher the intensity of activities promoting endurance and strength rose slightly during the year.

However, the following limitations were noticed:

- The initial intensities of activities promoting strength were low.
- There were insufficient activities which required near maximum performance by the students.
- The time given to running decreased during the year.

Control Program:

The physical education program of the control class was oriented to cardiovascular fitness in which running was the predominant activity. For most of the year the class averaged one 30-minute physical education lesson per week.

Physical Fitness Results:

A comparison of the physical fitness performances of the two classes throughout the year indicated that the DPE boys recorded greater improvements in the 1,000 M Run, Vertical Jump test, and Agility Run. The DPE girls were superior on the Agility Run but recorded similar changes on the remaining tests as the other girls. A closer examination of the students' performances indicated that significant improvements made by the DPE class occurred only during the first period.

Comments:

In spite of Karen's inadequate background in physical education, she implemented an effective program that was characterized by its increasing demands placed upon students throughout the year. Also, Karen provided support and encouragement to her students and was prepared to be a role model when student interest waned.

School B

DPE Teacher:

Jane had been teaching for 5 years and coached the school's netball and softball teams. However, Jane had little experience in teaching physical education or in conducting a physical fitness program.

DPE Program:

Jane also based her lessons on materials provided for her. These were supplemented by other resources from the school's physical education teacher. An advisory DPE teacher visited the school on three occasions during the year and provided demonstration lessons and additional guidance on maintaining a DPE program. In addition, the DPE teachers at the school met to discuss the progress of their classes.

Jane progressed through the year confidently. She established a regular pattern emphasizing physical fitness. The program included circuit training, game and partner activities, distance running, aerobic dancing, and obstacle courses. Significant features were the following:

- Twenty-eight percent of the time was spent on aerobic dance and 23% on the obstacle course.
- Distance running was a relatively minor activity (12%).
- There was a decline in the amount of time spent developing physical fitness during the year.
- The level of intensity of the activities promoting endurance and strength decreased during the year according to the DPE teacher.
- Students' interest in the program slowly declined.

Control Program:
For most of the year the Control class averaged approximately one 30-minute lesson per week. The program was oriented toward games and sport with a minimal emphasis on physical fitness.

Physical Fitness Results:
Examination of the physical fitness profiles of the two classes indicated little variation between them during the year. The exception was the Agility Run in which the boys and girls in the DPE class made greater improvement than their counterparts.

Comments:
The lack of success of the fitness component of the DPE program at School B can be attributed, in part, to the failure of the DPE teacher to maintain student interest. As a response to the decline in the students' attitudes, the teacher decreased the time given to fitness activities and also decreased the physical demands placed on students.

School C

DPE Teacher:
Diane had taught for 10 years. Her understanding of physical fitness and experience in teaching physical education were fairly limited at the beginning of the study. Diane had not attended any in-service programs since graduation. In spite of these problems, Diane was confident of implementing a successful DPE program.

DPE Program:
Diane also based her program on the prepared DPE lesson materials. She received assistance from the DPE advisory teacher on four occasions during the year. However, the physical education teacher who came to the school 2 days per week, provided no help during the year.

There was a moderate emphasis on physical fitness in the DPE program at School C as indicated by the following observations:

- Physical activity averaged 20 min daily.
- Forty-two percent of physical education time during the year was spent on physical fitness activities, but the time given to physical fitness, especially running, substantially decreased later in the year.

- The intensity ratings of the strength and endurance activities maintained moderate levels throughout the year.
- Few activities required near maximum performances from the students.

Control Program:
Although the teacher had volunteered to act as a control, he started a daily fitness program with his class shortly after the study began. The study continued at School C because of the marked contrast between the two programs. The control program was based on calisthenics conducted daily for 10-15 min. By the teacher's own admission, the physical demands of these exercises were relatively low.

Physical Fitness Results:
A comparison of the performances of the two classes during the year indicated few differences. The DPE class recorded greater improvement in flexibility than the control class. It was noticeable that the differential improvement occurred in the early period of the study.

Out of School Activities:
Examination of the boys' recreational behaviors indicated substantial differences between the two classes. Each boy in the control class averaged, per week, 300 min more on activities promoting physical fitness. The effect of this additional time spent on physical fitness activities needs to be taken into consideration when interpreting the boys' results at School C.

Comments:
The different emphasis of the programs at School C were not evident in the physical fitness levels of the students. While the DPE program focused on running and the control class on calisthenics, there were no differences in their performances on the 1,000 M Run or Vertical Jump test. The failure of the DPE class to improve beyond the level of the control class can partly be attributed to inadequacies of the DPE program, especially the failure to apply progressive overload principles. However, the increased flexibility of the DPE class can be traced to its emphasis on aerobic dance and stretching exercises.

Conclusions

The effectiveness of the DPE programs varied across the three schools, with only one considered to be relatively successful. The lack of success at the other schools can be traced to some of the following four factors:

1. The content of programs was not oriented to promoting fitness.
2. The duration of activities and their intensities often remained unchanged all year rather than increasing in line with progressive overload principles. This accounts for the lack of improvement during the latter stages of the programs.
3. Student interest often decreased during the year, which affected commitment to strenuous exercise.
4. The three teachers were inadequately prepared and received insufficient assistance in conducting a daily fitness program and monitoring its progress.

Recommendations

Five major recommendations arising from the study follow:

1. The effectiveness of prepared lesson materials must be carefully evaluated. Special consideration should be given to the progressive nature of the lessons to ensure adherence to the principles of training.
2. The use of prepared lesson materials must be accompanied by intensive instruction.
3. The DPE program needs to be carefully monitored during the year. This ensures that the activity is promoting a training effect and that teachers and students receive feedback on their progress.
4. Many DPE teachers require considerable assistance. They need help designing programs that motivate students throughout the year, systematically increasing students' workloads, and providing feedback to the teachers and the students.
5. Finally, the role of the physical education teacher needs to be reconsidered so he or she can provide consistent and practical assistance to the classroom teacher.

In conclusion, the quality of prepared lesson materials or the good intentions of teachers are insufficient on their own for implementing an effective DPE program. Its effectiveness is determined by the quality of the interaction among the teacher, the student, and physical activity. There must be careful evaluation of this triad at the classroom level, based upon the recognized principles of physical fitness training. Only when our focus is at this level will there be significant improvement in the effectiveness of DPE programs conducted by classroom teachers.

References

Hull, C.W., & Nie, N.H. (1981). *SPSS Update.* New York: McGraw-Hill.

Tainton, B.E., Peckman, G.I., & Hacker, W.J. (1982). Evaluation of the daily physical education program in three Brisbane primary schools: A progress report. In M.L. Howell & J.E. Saunders (Eds.), *Proceedings of the 7th Commonwealth and International Conference on Sport, Physical Education, Recreation and Dance,* **6**, 37-44. Brisbane: Department of Human Movement Studies, University of Queensland, Australia.

Tainton, B.E., Peckman, G.I., & Hacker, W.J. (1984). *Evaluation of physical education in Queensland primary schools.* Brisbane, Australia: State Government Printing Office.

Tainton, B.E., Peckman, G.I., & Hacker, W.J. (in press) *Evaluation of daily physical education in three Brisbane primary schools: A final report.* Brisbane, Australia: State Government Printing Office.

13

The Use of Learner Reports for Exploring Teaching Effectiveness in Physical Education

Bart J. Crum
FREE UNIVERSITY
AMSTERDAM, NETHERLANDS

When considering the politics of education in The Netherlands, the idea of "back to basics" is becoming more popular. One of the consequences of the growing popularity of this idea is that the pressure on the position of physical education as a recognized school subject has increased. Recently, the Minister of Education proposed a drastic reduction in the number of physical education classes at the secondary level. An important argument in this respect was the opinion that school physical education had produced disappointing returns for the amount of time invested.

Against the background of this development we are interested in empirical data concerned with the learning outcomes of school physical education. In addition we ask ourselves whether the learning outcomes are connected with the professional conception of PE teachers. The latter is linked with the fact that in The Netherlands there is no agreement about the identity of physical education as a school subject. For example, there are those who would put the emphasis on an increase in physical fitness whereby the physical educator is seen more as a "trainer" than a "teacher." In another approach it would be the task of the physical education teacher to ensure that the students are engaged in activities which are pleasant and relaxing. Supporters of this latter approach see the physical education teacher rather in the role of an "entertainer."

In attempting to answer the question as to how far physical education classes might contribute to the realization of the intended student competency, we have to cope with the problem that learning effects, as measured by achievement tests, do not embrace all the intended objectives. Objectives in the social, cognitive, and affective domains of learning are especially resistant to adequate operationalization in achievement tests. De Groot (1974) suggested that the problem mentioned above could be solved by means of the "learner report." His starting point is that the task of school education is to help students acquire "repertoires" or "programmes," the use of which is determined by their own intentions. As a result of a good education students will have learned repertoires as dispositions for behavior.

De Groot's second supposition is that students must be assumed able to indicate what they learned from school education. This could be done in a learner report in which students answer whether or not they have acquired the skills, knowledge, and attitudes that belong to the intended repertoires. Each intended objective can be included in the learner report utilizing a standard format "I have learned that...(or, how to...)."

Because students can over- or underestimate their learning results, such a report cannot be considered to be an objective assessment. However, we are inclined to consider the learner report method to be useful in obtaining a global impression of the extent and nature of student learning in physical education.

In light of these considerations, the decision was made to carry out an explorative study for the following reasons:

1. Develop an instrument for measuring physical education learning based on the learner report idea
2. Obtain a general impression of the learning outcomes of physical education in secondary schools
3. Explore the ways in which students perceive the nature of the professional role of their physical education teachers
4. Check whether significant relationships can be found between student perceptions of the professional role of physical education teachers and learning outcomes

Procedures

In the framework of a university student project an initial version of a learner report questionnaire was developed. Twenty-three possible learning effects were included in the forms of sentences such as "I have learned that..." or "I have learned how to... ." In the formulation of these learning-effect sentences a distinction between "technomotoric," "sociomotoric," and "cognitive" domains of learning was assumed. The first version was tried out with students from the top classes of six secondary schools in Amsterdam. On the basis of the experience so gained, a second version was developed which also included items considered to be representative of the "affective" domain of learning.

In this second version 24 items were included. Each item was prefaced by the standard opening sentence "The physical education classes and sport activities in my secondary school have contributed to my learning... ." Six items were considered to be representative for the technomotoric domain of learning, for example to play well-known ball games (basketball, volleyball, soccer, hockey) and to perform on gymnastic apparatus (rings, horizontal bar, etc.).

Eight items were considered to be representative of the sociomotoric domain of learning (e.g., adapting my way of playing and moving to the level of others, involving weaker players in play). Six items were considered to be representative of the cognitive domain of learning (e.g., to be able to apply the basic principles of endurance training, finding out how sport relates to commerce and politics).

Four items were considered to be representative of the affective domain of learning (e.g., how to cope with my sporting potential or lack of it, how to enjoy exercising my body).

Responses were required on a 5-point scale (a score of '1' indicating a very positive learning effect and '5' indicating no learning at all). At the same time, two other questions were included relating to, respectively, the predominant experiences of physical education in the school of the respondent and how the respondent perceived the physical education teacher's concept of his or her subject area. For each of the two questions, one of three answers had to be selected: (a) predominantly as fitness training, (b) predominantly as teaching-learning, or (c) predominantly as recreation.

The questionnaires were completed by the following: (a) 239 university freshmen studying human movement sciences, economics, or psychology, who had completed their secondary school educations 2 months earlier; (b) 113 students who had just begun a course of training in a college of physical education and who also had completed their secondary school educations 2 months earlier; and (c) 139 students from the top class of two secondary schools (A and B).

Results

In the first stage a factor analysis determined the extent to which the 24 learner report items clustered. The clustering was found to conform to the proposed four aspects model. On the basis of the results of the factor analysis, scales were developed. On these scales tests for internal consistency provided satisfactory results. The scale of technomotoric learning had an α value of 0.71; that for sociomotoric learning an α of 0.80; the scale for cognitive learning an α of 0.74; and that for affective learning an α of 0.69. The four subscales were put together to form a learner report overall scale. This scale had an α of 0.74. The subscale scores were computed by summation of the item scores and division by the number of items. The score for the overall scale was computed by summation of the subscale scores and division by the

Table 1. Means and standard deviations (in brackets) of the learner report subscale and overall scores for all respondents and for the subgroups.

Scale	Total group n = 491		PE teacher training n = 113		Human movement sciences n = 98		Economics n = 87		Psychology n = 54		School A n = 88		School B n = 51	
	M	SD	M	SD	M	SD	M	SD	M	SD	M	SD	M	SD
Technomotoric	2.4	(.89)	2.4	(.91)	2.3	(.72)	2.7	(1.10)	2.6	(.96)	2.4	(.64)	1.6	(.56)
Sociomotoric	2.6	(.85)	2.3	(.77)	2.8	(.78)	3.1	(.85)	2.9	(.98)	2.5	(.66)	2.1	(.76)
Cognitive	3.7	(.87)	3.8	(.84)	4.1	(.70)	3.8	(.95)	3.9	(.81)	3.5	(.80)	3.2	(.88)
Affective	2.6	(1.02)	2.4	(.93)	2.8	(.98)	3.1	(1.10)	2.8	(1.09)	2.4	(.87)	2.2	(.95)
Overall	2.9	(.73)	2.9	(.64)	3.1	(.63)	3.3	(.82)	3.1	(.76)	2.7	(.65)	2.4	(.64)

number of subscales. The means for the learner report overall scale, as well as those for the subscales, are given in Table 1. Analysis of variance indicated that the overall differences between the scores of subgroups were significant ($p < .001$).

Bearing in mind that a score of '1' reflects a very positive outcome with respect to the intended learning results, a score of '3' reflects uncertainty with respect to the question "had learning taken place," and a score of '5' reflects that definitely no learning had taken place, it can be concluded that none of the obtained scores provided evidence for a positive appraisal of the learning outcomes. The most positive results were obtained for technomotoric scale. In contrast, cognitive learning with respect to movement, sport, and training was hardly apparent.

Whereas the scores from School A show only little deviation in comparison with the scores of all respondents, the scores from School B show greater deviation in a positive direction. Apparently the one PE teaching team promotes more learning than the other.

In general, it can be concluded that some empirical support is found for the complaint that little is learned in the physical education classes of many Dutch schools.

The question, What is the predominant professional concept of your physical education teacher? indicated that 53% of all respondents were of the opinion that their teachers assume that physical education is primarily concerned with teaching and learning. Nevertheless, the percentage (42%) that considered that their teachers conceived physical education as a pleasant recreational activity was disturbingly high. Only 5% of the respondents ascribed to their teachers a "fitness-trainer" concept.

A one-way analysis of variance was used to assess the relationship between the PE teacher's PE concept (as perceived by the students) and the scores on the learner report subscales and overall scale.

Significant differences between four of the five (sub-) scale scores of the three professional concept groups were found (Table 2). Students who ascribed to their PE teachers a "teaching-learning" concept scored themselves more positively on the subscales for technomotoric and sociomotoric learning as well as on the overall scale. Students who ascribed to their teachers a "training"

Table 2. Means, standard deviations (in brackets), and F ratios for the learner report subscales and the overall scale: Perceptions of PE teacher's professional concept.

Scale	Training ($n = 24$) M	SD	Teaching/ learning ($n = 244$) M	SD	Recreation ($n = 193$) M	SD	F	P
Technomotoric	2.36	(.77)	2.24	(.82)	2.54	(.98)	6.14	.002
Sociomotoric	2.70	(.70)	2.52	(.84)	2.72	(.89)	3.20	.042
Cognitive	3.21	(.72)	3.61	(.86)	3.94	(.84)	13.01	.000
Affective	2.65	(.83)	2.53	(.98)	2.73	(1.08)	2.27	.105
Overall	2.86	(.56)	2.82	(.69)	3.08	(.78)	7.09	.001

concept scored more positively on the subscale for cognitive learning. This deviant finding was probably caused by the fact that three of the six items included in the subscale for cognitive learning were expressly directed to training and fitness.

Differences with respect to the subscale for affective learning were not significant. This finding might be interpreted from the viewpoint that affective learning can take place without explicit teaching needing to be carried out.

Discussion

The results of this pilot investigation give some support to the proposition that the learner report can serve as an instrument to obtain an indication of the extent and nature of learning in physical education programs. Although the construct validity of the instrument has to be pursued further in subsequent work, the satisfactory homogeneity of the subscales together with the significant positive relationships between the perceptions of the profession concept of the teacher and the subscale results are indications in the right direction.

With respect to the links found, caution is recommended because it is not the PE concept of the teacher but the student's perception thereof which constitutes the condition variable. It is possible that an artifact may arise.

In the light of these findings, it is clearly important to try to trace the causes of the poor learning outcomes in physical education programs. The results of this pilot investigation suggest that these poor outcomes are, in some way, related to the professional concept which gives rise to teachers' work. Further research directed to the relationships between the professional theory of physical education teachers, their daily practices, and the learning results of their students is therefore recommended.

References

De Groot, A.D. (1974). To what purpose, to what effect? Some problems of method and theory in the evaluation of higher education. *RITP - Memorandum No. 40.* Amsterdam.

14

Behavioral Studies of Youth Sport Coaches

Michael A. Sherman, and Jamal S. Hassan
UNIVERSITY OF PITTSBURGH
PITTSBURGH, PENNSYLVANIA, USA

Studies of coaches in action have slowly infused the literature since Smith, Smoll, and Hunt (1977) developed the Coaching Behavior Assessment System (CBAS). This instrument has been used to describe how coaches spend their time (Smith, Smoll, & Curtis, 1978), affect player performance (Smoll, Smith, Curtis, & Hunt, 1978), and respond to educational interventions (Smith, Smoll, & Curtis, 1979).

Although CBAS only produces descriptive measures, some of its users (Smoll, Smith, & Curtis, 1978) have transformed descriptions of coaching into guidelines for effectiveness. Such tendencies raise important issues. Do we know enough about the nature and assessment of coaching behavior? Are the available data so powerful that we can prescribe, with certainty, what coaches should say and do?

Motivated by these questions, we conducted five studies of youth sport coaches, with a special concern for learning more about the occurrence, reliability, and validity of coaching behavior as measured by CBAS. The specific research objectives were to: (a) describe coaching behavior in various sports; (b) determine the stability of CBAS measures; and (c) discover whether CBAS differentiates coaches on the basis of experience and success.

Methods

The subjects (see Table 1) were 102 coaches in baseball ($n = 24$), soccer ($n = 66$), and tennis ($n = 12$). The typical United States coach was a 33-year-old

Table 1. Characteristics of coaches in the CBAS studies

Study	Author (Year)	N	Age	Xper	Origin
Baseball	Rapone (1981)	24	45	8	USA
Soccer A	Hassan (1981)	20	37	5	USA
Soccer B	Hassan (1983)	20	29	5	Iraq
Soccer C	Al-Lami (1984)	26	24	4	USA
Tennis	Kadhim (1982)	12	28	6	USA

Note. Coaches were male, except for three females in tennis. Soccer C included one Brazilian and three Polish coaches.

white male with 5.6 years of experience. The typical Iraqi coach was 25 years old with 5.0 years of experience.

Data were collected in youth sport programs for players, aged 5 to 19 years. Baseball coaches were observed during games. Soccer A and B coaches were observed at team practice. Soccer C and tennis coaches were observed at summer camps. On the average, 16 players were present per observation.

Coding was done with original or modified forms of CBAS (Smith et al., 1977). A silent observation category was used when a coach was monitoring players, but the coder could not evaluate their responses. In this paper, Nonreward and Ignoring Mistakes were collapsed in the Silent Observation category. A brief, partially reorganized outline of CBAS appears below.

Sport-Relevant Reactive Behavior

REWARD (R). Positive reaction to desirable performance.
NONREWARD (NR). No reaction to desirable performance.
MISTAKE-CONTINGENT ENCOURAGEMENT (EM). Encouragement after mistake.
MISTAKE-CONTINGENT TECHNICAL INSTRUCTION (TIM). Corrective feedback after mistake.
PUNISHMENT (P). Punitive reaction after mistake.
PUNITIVE MISTAKE-CONTINGENT TECHNICAL INSTRUCTION (TIMP). Corrective and punitive reaction after mistake.
IGNORING MISTAKES (IM). No reaction after mistake.
SILENT OBSERVATION (SO). Silent observation of player performance.

Sport-Relevant Spontaneous Behavior

GENERAL TECHNICAL INSTRUCTION (TIG). Sport-relevant instruction.
GENERAL ENCOURAGEMENT (EG). Encouragement not following a mistake.

Sport-Irrelevant Behavior

KEEPING CONTROL (KC). Reactions to unruly conduct or inattentiveness.
ORGANIZATION (O). Organization and management not intended to influence play.
GENERAL COMMUNICATION (GC). Social interactions unrelated to sport or team matters.

The coders were trained in three ways. They studied the CBAS manual (Smith, et al., 1977), viewed videotapes (Smith, Smoll, Hunt, & Clark, 1976), and practiced extensively in field settings. Criterion-related agreement on video and written tests was 80% or better for all observers.

CBAS codes were written on-the-spot in baseball, Soccer A, and Soccer B. Videotapes were coded in Soccer C and tennis. Time sampled actions were coded every 5 sec (15 sec in baseball) during preselected periods. A grand total of 44,223 behaviors were coded over 91.5 hours.

Soccer A and baseball coaches were observed on two and three occasions, respectively, to permit estimation of stability coefficients. Median splits classified coaches by experience in baseball, tennis, and soccer (A and B) and designated winners and losers in baseball.

Results

The occurrence data in Table 2 indicate that the coaches spent 85% of their time in sport-relevant behaviors such as instructing (TIG = 33%), monitoring (SO = 18%), and offering feedback (30%). Most feedback messages were positive (R = 12%), or corrective (TIM = 12%). Encouraging or punitive statements were rarely made after mistakes.

Sport-irrelevant behaviors consumed 15% of the time. They were relatively low in discipline (KC = 1%), but somewhat higher in the General Communication (6%) and Organization (8%) categories.

Coaches were the primary communicators. They were verbally active four times more than they were silent. Nevertheless, coach-player interactions were six times more positive (R+ EM + EG=18%) than punitive (P + TIMP=3%).

Repeated observations by Hassan (1981) and Rapone (1981) produced no significant differences over occasions. Intraclass correlations (see Table 3) revealed that most CBAS measures had moderate to high stability, especially in the high-occurrence categories of instructing, observing, rewarding, and corrective feedback. Mean R values were .69 for baseball and .64 for soccer. In baseball, the most stable measures were social interactions, general encouragement, and corrective feedback. The highest soccer coefficients were

Table 2. Relative occurrence of CBAS variables

Study	R	EM	TIM	P	TIMP	SO	TIG	EG	KC	O	GC
Baseball	18	10	4	5	1	27	11	8	1	4	12
Soccer A	11	2	12	2	1	16	38	4	1	9	3
Soccer B	8	2	13	2	1	17	47	2	1	6	1
Soccer C	10	0	14	0	0	18	38	1	1	11	3
Tennis	11	3	16	0	1	13	30	2	0	11	12
Mean	12	3	12	2	1	18	33	3	1	8	6
Norm	17	3	4	2	1	8	27	12	2	8	6

Note. Table values rounded to nearest percent. Norm values from youth baseball study by Smith, Smoll, and Curtis (1978). Soccer C includes 4% uncodable behavior.

Table 3. Stability of CBAS variables.

Variables	Intraclass correlations (R) Baseball games (3 occasions)	Soccer A practice (2 occasions)
R	0.68	0.82
EM	0.69	0.74
TIM	0.70	0.83
P	0.70	0.68
TIMP	0.46	0.55
SO	0.61	0.91
TIG	0.78	0.76
EG	0.82	0.45
KC	0.62	0.25
O	0.64	0.35
GC	0.93	0.67

instructing, observing, rewarding, and corrective feedback. Except for P, sport-relevant reactions were more stable in soccer than baseball. The reverse was true in other categories.

Relationships between CBAS and team win-loss records were examined in baseball (see Table 4). Results were only significant in the SO category, where losing coaches (14.3%) ignored mistakes slightly more than did winning coaches (12.6%).

With respect to experience (see Table 4), three studies found significance in various categories. No differences were reported in baseball. The combined high experience (HiEx) sample gave more TIG and TIM, but did less SO. Though consistent over studies, SO and TIM differences were significant on-

Table 4. CBAS related to coaching experience and success

Variables	Experience High (n = 37)	Low (n = 39)	Mean diff.	Success High (n = 12)	Low (n = 12)	Mean diff.
R	12.4	11.9	0.5	17.8	19.1	− 1.3
EM	4.9	3.6	1.3*	10.5	10.4	0.1
TIM	13.1	8.2	4.9**	3.2	3.4	− 0.2
P	1.9	2.3	− 0.4	4.7	4.3	0.4
TIMP	1.2	1.0	0.2*	1.2	1.6	− 0.4
SO	14.4	22.7	− 8.3**	25.6	28.4	− 2.8***
TIG	33.3	29.7	3.6*	11.3	10.5	0.8
EG	4.3	3.7	0.6	8.0	7.2	0.8
KC	0.3	0.6	− 0.3*	0.2	0.0	0.2
O	7.6	7.6	0.0	4.4	3.9	0.5
GC	6.7	7.5	− 0.8*	12.7	11.3	1.4

*Significant univariate t ratio, $p < .05$, in tennis.
**Significant univariate F ratio, $p < .05$, in soccer A and B.
***Significant univariate F ratio, $p < .05$, in baseball.

ly in soccer. Low experience (LoEx) soccer coaches (11.3%) also ignored mistakes more often than HiEx coaches (6.4%).

Five significant findings appeared in tennis. HiEx coaches gave more TIG. LoEx coaches were higher in EM, KC, GC, and TIMP, however, these categories had rather low frequency counts.

Discussion and Recommendations

The frequency data were consistent with previous research (Lombardo, Faraone, & Pothier, 1982; Smoll et al., 1978), suggesting that youth sport coaches rely almost exclusively upon direct styles of teaching. No doubt our coaching sample spent considerable time instructing, observing, and reacting. But while these behaviors are indicators of directness, their high occurrence was not surprising.

One reason for directness relates to the nature of CBAS. The instrument was conceived from a didactic model of coach-player interaction. It does not code indirect acts (e.g., asking questions, accepting ideas, or encouraging self-evaluation). Another reason was that many of our coaches taught young novice players. Under similar conditions in academic classrooms, direct instruction has proven effective for teaching basic skills to beginners (Rosenshine, 1977).

Unlike the position taken by Lombardo et al. (1982), heavy emphasis on direct instruction may not pose serious problems for youngsters. In fact our coaches were quite positive with their players. This supports Rosenshine's (1977) thesis that direct teaching can also be warm, friendly, and supportive. A key issue for researchers is not how often coaches use direct instruction, but whether their behaviors match particular objectives, players, and situations.

Repeated measures from two studies verified that CBAS has acceptable but moderate reliability. While observed behaviors in baseball and soccer were generally stable over time, the soccer results suggest some measurement error in low-frequency categories. By combining, deleting, or modifying such categories, the reliability of CBAS might be enhanced.

Experiential comparisons produced mixed results. Overall, HiEx coaches gave more instruction. LoEx coaches were more observant, but often ignored player responses. Do LoEx coaches offer less sport-relevant instruction because they have less to say? Do they offer less corrective feedback after mistakes because of poor diagnostic skill and/or sparse knowledge of corrective actions? These questions beg research with instruments vastly different from CBAS.

The validity of CBAS as an indicator of coaching effectiveness was not supported. Based on Rapone's (1981) baseball study, CBAS measures were unrelated to coaching effectiveness when the criterion was team success. The lone significant difference was in ignoring mistakes where losers were only 1.7% higher. These results conflict with Smith et al. (1978) who found moderate negative correlations between reactive behaviors and win-loss records among one cluster of baseball coaches.

Two recommendations are offered for improving the concurrent validity of CBAS. First, more meaningful standards of coaching effectiveness are needed, especially in the youth sport context. Measures of residual gain or long-term success should replace single-season records. Second, CBAS categories should be expanded to permit qualitative assessment of coaching. New categories might require higher levels of inference, but could yield more accurate estimates of behavioral appropriateness and proficiency.

References

Al-Lami, A. (1984). *Behaviors of professional player-coaches at youth soccer camps.* Unpublished master's thesis, University of Pittsburgh.

Hassan J.S. (1981). *A behavioral comparison of low and high experience youth soccer coaches.* Unpublished master's thesis, University of Pittsburgh.

Hassan, J.S. (1983). *A behavioral study of low and high experience Iraqi youth soccer coaches.* Unpublished master's thesis, University of Pittsburgh.

Kadhim, A.H.M. (1976). *Behavior patterns of junior tennis coaches with varying levels of experience.* Unpublished master's thesis, University of Pittsburgh.

Lombardo, B.J., Faraone, N., & Pothier, D. (1982). The behavior of youth sport coaches: A preliminary analysis. In M. Pieron & J. Cheffers (Eds.), *Studying the teaching in physical education* (pp. 189-196). Liege, Belgium: International Association for Physical Education in Higher Education.

Rapone, N. (1981). *An analysis of coaching behavior in little league baseball.* Unpublished master's thesis, University of Pittsburgh.

Rosenshine, B. (1977). Review of teaching variables and student achievement. In G.D. Borich (Ed.), *The appraisal of teaching: Concepts and process* (pp. 114-120). Reading, MA: Addison-Wesley.

Smith, R.E., Smoll, F.L., & Curtis, B. (1978). Coaching behaviors in little league baseball. In F.L. Smoll & R.E. Smith (Eds.), *Psychological perspectives in youth sports* (pp. 173-201). Washington, DC: Hemisphere.

Smith, R.E., Smoll, F.L., & Curtis, B. (1979). Coach effectiveness training: A cognitive behavioral approach enhancing relationship skills in youth sports coaches. *Journal of Sport Psychology, 1,* 59-75.

Smith, R.E., Smoll, F.L., & Hunt, E.B. (1977). A system for the behavioral assessment of athletic coaches. *Research Quarterly, 48,* 401-407.

Smith, R. E., Smoll, F.L., & Hunt, E.B. (1977). Training manual for the coaching behavior assessment system. *JSAS Catalog of Selected Documents in Psychology, 7*(2).

Smith, R.E., Smoll, F.L., Hunt, E.B., & Clarke, S.J. (1976). *CBAS audio visual training module* [Film] Seattle: University of Washington.

Smoll, F.L., Smith, R.E., & Curtis, B. (1978). Behavioral guidelines for youth sport coaches. *Journal of Physical Education and Recreation, 49,* 46-47.

Smoll, F.L., Smith, R.E., Curtis, B., & Hunt, E. (1978). Toward a meditational model of coach-player relationships. *Research Quarterly, 49,* 529-541.

15

A Systematic Approach to Teaching Sport

Richard L. Cox

DUNFERMLINE COLLEGE OF PHYSICAL EDUCATION
EDINBURGH, SCOTLAND

The actual business of teaching physical education in Scotland has developed considerably in recent years through the work of Mosston (1972, 1981). He proposed that all conscious teaching behavior is a chain of decision-making and that an analysis of who makes what decisions in any teaching episode enables the social and psychological climate, in which the pupil-teacher interaction takes place, to be identified. In turn this enables the type of objectives set for the episode to be identified and, by implication, the teacher's intention for the longer-term development of the pupils also.

The coach, like the teacher, is constantly having to make decisions. Before any coaching session he or she has to decide upon objectives, subject matter, where and when the session is to take place, how questions will be handled, how to communicate with athletes, and the criteria by which the session will be evaluated. During the session itself the coach has to decide whether or not to keep to his or her preparation decisions in the light of ongoing evaluation. After the session is over he or she has to decide if and when any feedback is to be given to the athletes, the nature of such feedback, and how it will be delivered. This complex array of decisions has to be dealt with effectively if the coaching session that follows is to be worthwhile.

The majority of coaches and teachers make all of these decisions themselves. Indeed, many would deem themselves to be irresponsible if they failed to do so. However, in teaching, Mosston (1981) demonstrated that the responsibility for making many of these decisions can be shifted to the pupils with considerable educational justification and effect. Moreover, he described this shift of decision-making systematically in accordance with a spectrum of eight different

I am extremely grateful to Mr. Iain Whyte and his wife Lesley, both of whom are professional coaches of gymnastics, for their invaluable help in setting up, conducting, and recording the three coaching episodes described in this paper.

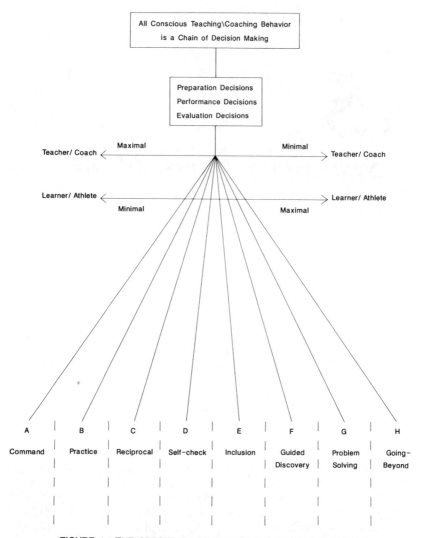

FIGURE 1 : THE SPECTRUM OF TEACHING / COACHING STYLES

teaching styles which is illustrated in Figure 1. Each style is a "landmark" style because it maximizes the assets and minimizes the liabilities of a particular approach to teaching. Clustered around and between the styles are numerous varieties which arise as different decisions are shifted from teacher to pupils or vice versa. Each shift in decision-making establishes a different relationship between teacher and pupils and consequently has implications for a broader range of considerations than simply the pupils' performances.

Most coaches would be identified toward the end of the spectrum where the athlete's involvement is minimal. No criticism is implied in this observation because Mosston emphasizes that no single style is superior in itself to any other style. Rather, each style has its own assets and liabilities, and most likely coaches adopt a Command Style (A) because either they think that is what coaching is about or that it is the best way to achieve competitive success. Obviously, participation in accordance with the spectrum requires involvement in competitive sport to be viewed as a means to an end rather than as an end in itself. Furthermore, it demands of the coach that he or she be more consciously aware of his or her own behavior and the effect that it has on the athlete. What follows is an empirical justification for the development of such awareness.

Coaching Gymnastics in the Reciprocal Style

The investigation about to be described took place in late 1983 in a Scottish Olympic gymnastics club. Gymnastics has remained extremely popular in Great Britain ever since Olga Korbut graced the sport in the Munich Olympic Games. So much so, in fact, that demand has outstripped the supply of qualified coaches and suitable facilities. Thus, most gymnastics coaches in Scotland are faced with one or more of the following problems. First, they may have to share facilities with other sports and therefore be faced with insufficient time to cover as much as would be ideal. Second, there may be insufficient space, apparatus, or coaches available for a group of more than 10 gymnasts to work together at the same time. Therefore, considerable time is lost as gymnasts wait for their turns. Third, with large groups the opportunities for the coach to give qualitative feedback to each gymnast may be limited, and the need to receive feedback immediately upon completion of a task for learning to be maximized is well documented in the psychological literature. Fourth, the gymnasts may vary considerably in their abilities to perform certain movements. When faced with a common task and an authoritarian style of coaching the advancement of the more able gymnast is likely to be retarded, and the less able may feel obliged to attempt movements beyond his or her capabilities.

Because of these problems, each of which pertained to the gymnastics club involved in the present investigation, the coach concerned decided to experiment with Mosston's Reciprocal Style (C) in an attempt to solve some, or all, of the problems. The Reciprocal Style was chosen because, while representing the smallest shift in decision-making from the traditional approach to coaching (a mixture of Command and Practice Styles), it necessitates a radical change in the role of verbal behavior of the coach.

Both knowledge of results and knowledge of performance are vitally important if an athlete is to improve. The former is often obvious to the athlete without the coach's help, but knowledge of performance more often than not requires the presence of an observer. Because the group is divided into pairs, one acting as performer and the other as observer, the Reciprocal Style allows each performer to receive immediate feedback on each and every attempt. The feedback offered by the observer should be in accordance with a 'criteria sheet' drawn up by the coach. The role of the coach also includes being available to the observer for questioning and giving feedback to the observer (only) on his or her role. (For full details see Mosston, 1981, pp. 68-119.)

Four types of behavior were investigated in this study by means of a comparison of a 20-min episode in the Reciprocal Style with two others of equal length in the Command Style (A) and Practice Style (B) respectively. The behaviors were as follows:

1. The number of attempts made at prescribed gymnastic moves within the time allowed.
2. The number of feedback statements offered to performers in each episode.
3. The nature of the feedback statements in terms of whether they were positive and or negative.
4. The number of antisocial behaviors exhibited—these were identified as "inattention," "wandering away," "talking with friends," and "playing/fooling around."

The three coaching episodes, one in each of three consecutive weeks, were recorded by a video camera and four microphones which were strategically positioned so that each of the four types of behavior would be investigated objectively.

Ten gymnasts, 6 male and 4 female, took part in this investigation, none of whom was familiar with its purpose beforehand. Their ages ranged from 9 to 12 years and each was competent at the four gymnastic moves they were asked to perform in each episode. The roles required of them in both Command and Practice Styles were familiar to them through previous exposure (mainly at school) and therefore no prior training was necessary. However, they were unfamiliar with the Reciprocal Style and needed 2 hours of training before this particular experimental episode could be recorded.

Results:

The results, which are recorded in Table 1, revealed that the number of attempted movements differs little from one episode to another. This is somewhat surprising in view of the fact that one of the liabilities of the Reciprocal Style is always described in terms of it being less demanding physically than either the Command or Practice Style—this is because only half of the group is performing the task at any one time. This is true in situations where it is possible for all athletes present to perform the task simultaneously, but in this investigation, the lack of space and apparatus necessitated some queueing regardless of coaching style. The major differences in the results are to be found in the number and nature of feedback statements given and the number of related antisocial behaviors exhibited. The Reciprocal Style resulted in almost three times more feedback statements being offered to performers and 10 times more positive feedback statements than in either the Command or Practice Styles. Little doubt exists that these two findings were largely responsible for the almost total disappearance of any antisocial behavior which is one of the most remarkable results of all.

One observation that should be of interest to all coaches, regardless of their sport, was made only after the video recordings were analyzed and in no way could have been anticipated. The coach concerned judged the quality of

Table 1. The results of coaching the same content in three different styles expressed in terms of four types of behavior.

Behavior	Episode	1 Command Style (A)	2 Practice Style (B)	3 Reciprocal Style (C)
Number of Attempts At Prescribed Movements	Total	386	443	415
	Individ. minimum	32	35	32
	Individ. maximum	41	50	56
	Group M ($N = 10$)	38.6	44.3	41.5
Number of Feedback Statements Offered	Total	146	132	411
	Individ. minimum	10	8	32
	Individ. maximum	24	15	53
	Group M ($n = 10$)	14.6	13.2	41.1
Nature of Feedback Statements	Positive	38	21	374
	Negative	108	111	37
Number of 'Anti-Social' Behaviors		55	39	1

movement performed in the Reciprocal Style episode to be markedly superior to that in either of the two other episodes. One possible explanation for this observation is that, despite only one member of each pair practising at any one time, the other is observing, comparing, contrasting, analyzing, and evaluating the performance in accordance with the prescribed criteria and thereby mentally rehearsing and internalizing the criteria for high-level performance. Thus, when it is his or her turn to practise the task he or she is acutely aware of its requirements. Theoretical justification for this explanation is given by Jones (1974) and Butts (1976) and is supported by recommendations from sport psychologists such as Tutko and Tosi (1976) and Orlick (1980).

Discussion:

The investigation reported here, despite being controlled and carried out carefully, is by no means definitive. Furthermore, it has involved only three of the eight styles described by Mosston. Nevertheless, the results are such as to merit serious consideration by coaches of at least one alternative coaching style to their usual way of operating. Other styles merit equal consideration by coaches for the ways in which they facilitate the achievement of different objectives. For instance, the Inclusion Style (E) allows athletes to make decisions about what levels of work are suitable to their current states of fitness, particularly at the beginning of a season. Pushing athletes too hard or too soon is a sure way of injuring them. Yet many coaches operate in a mixture of styles A and B and thereby insist on their athletes working together on identical schedules.

By contrast, the Divergent Style (G) allows the coach the opportunity to sample a range of possible solutions suggested by the athletes in response to tactical problems. Giving athletes the responsibility for thinking of and testing out a range of solutions of their own making almost invariably results in a higher level of motivation for the task and, in the long term, in athletes who are more independent and versatile in their abilities to cope with tactical changes and ploys during matchplay. (It should be remembered that in several games the coach is not allowed any influence during actual play and, in some, such as rugby football, not even at half-time which is the only 'time-out' as such.) The Divergent Style also facilitates a quality of interaction among team members which the Command and Practice styles preclude, and this, as Yaffé (1975) pointed out, could be an important factor in the effective functioning of the team.

The Reciprocal Style allows injured athletes to take an active part in coaching sessions, and the Guided Discovery Style (F) allows them the opportunity to explore the thinking behind any suggestion made by the coach. This inevitably leads to a higher level of understanding and, subsequently, of internalization. Learning to operate the Self-Check Style (D) effectively is essential for any athlete who wants to practise meaningfully on his or her own. And the level of knowledge and understanding required to operate the Going-Beyond Style (H) is equivalent to a group of high-level coaches in the same sport getting together for a practise session among themselves. The point here is that they would be so knowledgeable and independent in every sense of the word as to render the attentions of a coach unnecessary. Indeed, it should be the long term aim of any coach to render all of his or her athletes independent of his or her coaching in every way. Otherwise the coach runs the risk of basking in the athletes' glory whenever they do well and arguably; this is not what coaching is about.

The main thesis of this paper is that operating in one style only is restrictive by definition, in terms of the objectives that can be reached by the coach. Athletes are individuals, and individuals are likely to have preferred learning styles that are different from one another. The coach who can operate effectively in a range of styles can appeal to more athletes. This is an important consideration for coaches to make if they wish to maximize their success.

References

Butts, D.S. (1976). *Psychology of sport.* New York: Von Nostrand Reinhold.
Jones, R. E. (1974). Notes and comments: Effector mechanisms of co-ordination. *Journal of Motor Behaviour,* **6**(2), 77-79.

Mosston, M. (1972). *From command to discovery*. Belmont, CA: Wadsworth.
Mosston, M. (1981). *Teaching physical education*. Columbus, OH: Merrill Publishers.
Orlick, T. (1980). *In Pursuit of excellence*. Coaching Association of Canada.
Tutko, T., & Tosi, U. (1976). *Sports psyching*. Los Angeles: Tarcher.
Yaffé, M. (1975). Some variables affecting team success in soccer. In H.T.A. Whiting (Ed.), *Readings in sport psychology* **2**. London: Lepus.

16

Analysis of the Practice Behavior of Elite Athletes

Thomas L. McKenzie
SAN DIEGO STATE UNIVERSITY
SAN DIEGO, CALIFORNIA, USA

The performance of athletes during competition, as well as their interactions with teammates and coaches, are directly related to their behaviors during practice sessions. Concerned with conducting high quality practice sessions, athletic coaches take elaborate steps to ensure that the limited time they spend with athletes is productive.

Interest in studying teaching and coaching effectiveness has led increased numbers of researchers to directly observe the behavior of participants in diverse physical activity settings. While the number of studies of learner behavior in physical education and youth sport has increased, the study of the practice behavior of elite athletes has rarely been reported. It is expected that under the direction of elite coaches, world class athletes would be highly motivated and would exhibit high quality practice behavior consistently on a daily basis; hence, upper limits of practice efficiency could be established. Information about how elite performers prepare for competition would add to what is known about how learners behave in physical activity settings, help to provide a frame of reference for evaluating practice sessions, and perhaps eventually lead to the establishment of norms for the efficient conduct of practices.

Recently, many sophisticated observation instruments have been developed to study behavior in physical activity settings (Darst, Mancini, & Zakrajsek, 1983). One of those frequently used to describe how time is spent is the Academic Learning Time-Physical Education (ALT-PE) system (Siedentop, Tousignant, & Parker, 1982). The ALT-PE system typically has been used to study behavior in physical education classes, but occasionally has been used in athletic environments. For example, Rate (1980) compared the practice behavior of high school athletes in five different sports, and Sparks (1982) studied how time was used by junior high school students and athletes in volleyball classes and team practices.

The purpose of this paper is to present descriptive-analytic data on how elite amateur athletes, members of the USA Men's National Volleyball Team, the 1984 Olympic gold medal winners, used time during practice sessions. This research was conducted, not only out of academic curiosity, but also because of the concerns of the team coaches who were preparing for the Olympic Games.

Method

Subjects

Three members of the USA Men's National Volleyball team, who played the same position (middle blocker), had high attendance rates at practices over the previous 2 years, and who were expected to remain on the team throughout the 1984 Olympic Games, were selected for the study.

Data Collection

The Practice Learning Time-Volleyball (PLT) system was used. The PLT system is similar to the ALT-PE system but with category definitions and examples specific to volleyball as follows:

Motor

Appropriate. Player is engaged in a motor skill activity at an appropriate level of intensity and execution.

Inappropriate. Player is engaged in a motor skill activity at an intensity or execution level that does not contribute to team goals.

Supporting. Player is engaged in an appropriate motor activity, the purpose of which is to assist others in learning the activity, such as feeding balls.

Nonmotor

Attending. Player is appropriately attending to an instructional event, such as listening to a coach, watching a demonstration, or participating in a discussion.

Interim. Player is engaged in an ongoing noninstructional activity such as retrieving balls, fixing personal equipment, and changing position on the court.

Maintenance. Player is engaged in a noninstructional task assigned by the coach and not part of the ongoing activity (such as talking to the press or repairing and moving team equipment).

Waiting. Player has completed a task and is awaiting the next instructions or opportunity to respond (such as waiting in line for a turn or waiting for a drill to begin).

Off-task. Player is either not engaged in an activity that he or she should be doing or is engaged in an activity that he or she should not be doing. The latter includes talking when a coach is explaining a skill, misusing equipment, and disrupting a drill through inappropriate behavior.

The PLT system is a hierarchic decision system used by trained observers to code a player's behavior into predetermined Motor (Appropriate, Inappropriate, and Supporting) and Nonmotor (Attending, Interim, Waiting,

Maintenance, and Off-task) categories. Observers, directed in 6-second observe/record intervals by a cassette recorder equipped with an ear jack, monitored the players in a fixed rotational order.

Two observers were trained to use the PLT system. Observer training consisted of studying the coding manual and decision log, coding sample videotapes, and practicing coding in the actual setting. Observer drift was reduced by having observers review observation training tapes periodically throughout the study. Interobserver agreement was checked by having two observers code the same player at the same time during approximately one fourth of the practice sessions. Interobserver agreement scores for the different player behavior categories, computed using the Scored-Interval agreement method (Hawkins & Dotson, 1975), ranged from 88.2 to 96.0%.

Data were collected during regularly scheduled practice sessions at the team's Olympic training site in San Diego during Winter and Spring 1983. Observations were made only during on-court time; time was allocated for skill practice on one or more of the three volleyball courts in the gymnasium. Player behavior during preliminary taping, warm-up, weight training, lengthy lectures, and travel planning periods is not included.

Results

Data for how the team members used their time are presented in Table 1. More than half of their time was spent in Motor activities (55.7%). Most of that time was Motor Appropriate (54.2%). Little movement time was coded as Supporting (1.0%) or Not Appropriate (0.5%).

Of the Non-Motor categories (totaling 44.3%), Waiting constituted the largest amount of time (21.1%) with Interim being the next highest (10.3%). Attending and Maintenance occurred 7.1 and 5.3% of the time, respectively. Off-task behavior occurred rarely (0.5%).

Table 1. Mean percent occurrence of behavior categories for three players

Category		A	B	C	M
			Player		
Motor					
	Appropriate	56.5	53.4	52.5	54.2
	Supporting	0.8	1.5	0.7	1.0
	Not Appropriate	0.0	0.5	1.1	0.5
Non-Motor					
	Attending	7.1	6.1	8.0	7.1
	Interim	8.6	10.9	11.5	10.3
	Waiting	21.2	20.8	21.4	21.1
	Maintenance	5.7	6.5	3.8	5.3
	Off-task	0.1	0.4	1.0	0.5

Note. Data are based on 4,510 observation samples taken during 16 practice sessions.

Discussion

The high rates of Motor Appropriate activity indicated that the athletes had substantial opportunities for active involvement in appropriate tasks. While high levels of Motor Appropriate activity were found, it appears that motor engagement rates in physical activity settings are sport specific, that is, controlled by the nature of the individual activity. For example, in this volleyball setting, substantial amounts of Interim and Waiting time occurred even though expert coaches were working with motivated and highly skilled athletes in relatively ideal practice conditions. The coaches used large numbers of volleyballs (more than 40), systematic ball retrieval procedures, small groups (2 or 3 players) at multiple task stations, and frequently all three coaches instructed simultaneously. Despite these strategies, Interim and Waiting time totaled more than 31% of the observed time, providing the athletes ample rest and recovery time without taking long breaks. Comparison data for other elite teams are not available; however, these Interim and Waiting times were much lower than those for the junior high school volleyball classes and teams reported by Sparks (1982).

Little Attending time was recorded because the coaches used brief demonstrations (rarely longer than 30 seconds) and short, precise, verbal statements to tell the players what to do and how to do it. In this regard, their instructional tactics were similar to those of John Wooden (Tharp & Gallimore, 1976). Lengthy discussions were reserved for team meetings held off the courts outside of practice time.

Low rates of Supporting were found because the coaches arranged drills in such a manner that players in a supporting role practiced appropriate motor skills simultaneously. Furthermore, the Motor Appropriate category on the coding system took precedence over the Supporting category. Because practice contingencies were arranged to promote high intensity involvement, little Not Appropriate motor time occurred.

As can be expected for elite athletes, rates on various categories for these players seemed more favorable than the ALT-PE rates reported for participants in physical education classes and interscholastic practices (Dodds, Rife, & Metzler, 1982; Rate, 1980; Sparks, 1982). Exact comparisons with the results of other studies cannot be made, however, because of differences in the behavioral definitions and in the observational procedures used.

Rate (1980) indicated that considerable variability is apparent in practice time use among teams within the same sport. Data for the present study indicated that there is also wide variability on how time is spent by a single team during different practice sessions. For example, daily team rates for Motor Appropriate ranged from 47.3 to 66.7%. Additionally, engagement rates varied from player to player both from session to session and overall. For example, on Day 6 Player C's Motor Appropriate time was 45% while Players A and B accrued 65 and 67%, respectively.

Some differences in players' rates may have occurred because of the way practice sessions were structured by the coaches. For example, a player might accrue more Motor Appropriate time if he were engaged in individualized instruction with a coach while his teammates were involved in a scrimmage. Rushall (1982) indicated that during training, university coaches in a variety of sports provided more highly skilled athletes with greater opportunities to practice than their less skilled teammates. This skill differential was not evidenced in the present study because Player A, the only nonstarter monitored accrued the highest Motor Appropriate rates. On the other hand, it appeared that much of the interplayer differences resulted from factors controlled by the athletes. The coaches easily detected small changes in players' rates of Motor Appropriate and Off-task behavior, and in an effort to intensify work performance they frequently reacted by providing encouragement and reprimands.

The present paper is one of the first to present descriptive-analytic data on the practice behavior of elite athletes. It extends the data base for what is known about how learners spend their time in physical activity environments, and it may serve as a frame of reference for evaluating time usage in other settings. Because the practices of elite athletes are likely to approach the upper limits of efficiency and productivity, information about these limits may help coaches of less skilled athletes evaluate their practices.

The systematic and objective analysis of practice engagement rates of these elite athletes seemed to be a worthwhile exercise. The coaches and players were interested in the various category definitions and the rates they emitted under practice conditions. Additional studies of elite athletes and of coaches in different sports are recommended so that the information may lead to increased knowledge about teaching and coaching effectiveness.

References

Darst, P., Mancini, V., & Zakrajsek, D. (Eds.). (1983). *Systematic observation instrumentation of physical education.* West Point, NY: Leisure Press.

Dodds, P., Rife, F., & Metzler, M. (1982). Academic learning time in physical education: Data collection, completed research, and future directions. In M. Pieron & J. Cheffers (Eds.), *Studying the teaching in physical education* (pp. 37-51). Liege, Belgium: AIESEP.

Hawkins, R., & Dotson, V. (1975). Reliability scores that delude: An Alice in Wonderland trip through misleading characteristics of interobserver agreement scores in interval recording. In E. Ramp & G. Semb (Eds.), *Behavior analysis: Areas of research and application* (pp. 359-376). Englewood Cliffs, NJ: Prentice Hall.

Rate, R. (1980). *A descriptive analysis of Academic Learning Time and coaching behavior in interscholastic athletic practices.* Unpublished doctoral dissertation, The Ohio State University, Columbus.

Rushall, B. S. (1982). What coaches do: Behavioral evidence of coaching effectiveness. In L. Wankel & R. Wilberg (Eds.), *Psychology of sport and motor behavior: Research and practice. Proceedings of the CSPLSP Annual Meeting* (pp. 185-202). Edmonton, Alberta: CSPLSP.

Siedentop, D., Tousignant, M., & Parker, M. (1982). *Academic learning time--Physical education: Coding manual, 1982 revision.* Columbus: The Ohio State University, School of Health, Physical Education, and Recreation.

Sparks, J. (1982). *A comparison of Academic Learning Time and teacher/coach behavior during volleyball classes and interscholastic volleyball practices.* Unpublished master's thesis, California State University, Long Beach.

Tharp, R., & Gallmore, R. (1976). Basketball's John Wooden: What a coach can teach a teacher. *Psychology Today, 9*(8), 75-78.

17

The Academic Learning Time-Physical Education of High-, Average-, and Low-Skilled Female Intercollegiate Volleyball Players

Deborah A. Wuest, and Victor H. Mancini
ITHACA COLLEGE
ITHACA, NEW YORK, USA
Hans van der Mars
UNIVERSITY OF MAINE AT ORONO
ORONO, MAINE, USA
Kristine Terrillion
LAFAYETTE HIGH SCHOOL
LAFAYETTE, NEW YORK, USA

During the 5 years since the Academic Learning Time-Physical Education (ALT-PE) observation instrument's development (Metzler, 1983; Siedentop, Birdwell, & Metzler, 1979) many researchers have used it extensively to answer a variety of questions. ALT-PE is defined as the amount of time a student is engaged in a relevant motor task with a high degree of success (Siedentop et al., 1979). Conceptualized from the findings of the Beginning Teacher Evaluation Studies (Fisher et al., 1972), which sought to identify correlates of teacher effectiveness and student achievement, the ALT-PE instrument has been used to provide researchers with information about how students spend their time in the gym and as a measure of student time-on-task; it has also been used to provide an indicator of teacher effectiveness.

Both the original (Siedentop et al., 1979) and the revised (Siedentop, Tousignant, & Parker, 1982) ALT-PE instrument had been used extensively to describe students' behavior in physical education classes and increasingly to describe the amount of ALT-PE accrued by different subgroups within these classes, such as males and females, mainstreamed and nonmainstreamed students, and students of different ability levels. Particularly germane to this investigation are studies which have investigated the amount of ALT-PE accrued by students of different ability levels. Research findings differed as to whether high and low ability students achieved different amounts of ALT-PE during classes. Placek, Silverman, Shute, Dodds, and Rife (1982) found no significant differences in the ALT-PE accrued by male and female students of high-, medium-, and low-skill ability in traditional elementary physical education classes. Similarly, Shute, Dodds, Placek, Rife, and Silverman (1982) reported that equal opportunities to learn were provided to male and female students and to students of different ability levels by the teacher of elementary movement education classes. On the other hand, Pieron (1983) and Wuest, Mancini, and Smith (1984) reported that students who were classified as high-skilled or high-achievers had more opportunities to actively participate in physical education classes and accrued more ALT-PE than their low-skilled counterparts. Pieron (1983) also commented that because high-achievers had higher rates of productive behavior the gap between low- and high-achievers was expected to widen.

While the use of the ALT-PE instrument to investigate athletes' opportunities and success in the athletic environment has become increasingly frequent, few studies have investigated the differences in the ALT-PE accrued by athletes of different ability levels. Van der Mars, Mancini, Wuest, and Galli (1984) used the original ALT-PE system (Siedentop et al., 1979) to compare the behaviors of a high-skilled basketball player and low-skilled basketball player throughout the interscholastic season. They found that the players spent about 85% of practice time in Content-PE. The high-skilled player experienced more game play during practice, spent less time waiting, and engaged in more Content-PE than his low-skilled teammate; however, the low-skilled player received more knowledge during practices from the coach. Slightly more ALT-PE was accrued by the high skilled player, 33.4% versus 30.9%, but the amount of ALT-PE(M) accrued was equal 9.4%.

Thomas, Mancini, and Wuest (1984) used the revised ALT-PE instrument (Siedentop et al., 1982) to compare the amount of ALT-PE accrued by low- and high-skilled male and female intercollegiate lacrosse players. A male and a female lacrosse coach and 10 high-skilled and 10 low-skilled players from each team were subjects and were observed 10 times during the season. While little difference was found between the teams and between the players of different abilities at the context level, several differences were observed at the learner involvement level. High-skilled male and female players were motor engaged more often, had to wait less, were less frequently inappropriately engaged, and accrued more ALT-PE than their low-skilled teammates (high-skilled males, 33.4%; high-skilled females, 33.6%; low-skilled males, 24.3%; low−skilled females 21.4%). The purpose of this investigation was to compare the ALT-PE accrued by low−, average−, and high-skilled female intercollegiate volleyball players during the season.

Methods and Procedures

Subjects

A female intercollegiate volleyball coach, who had 8 years of coaching experience, and her 12-player team were the subjects. During the year in which this investigation was conducted the team finished among the top 20 Division III teams in the United States.

Instrument

The revised ALT-PE observation instrument (Siedentop et al., 1982) was used to describe how the coach organized practices and how the players spent their time during these practice sessions. The ALT-PE instrument consisted of two levels: a group-focused context level and an individually-focused learner involvement level. There were three major subdivisions at the context level—General Content, Subject Matter Knowledge, and Subject Matter Motor—and 13 categories within these subdivisions that described the time devoted to various activities during practice. Two major subdivisions at the learner involvement level—Not Motor Engaged and Motor Engaged—and the eight categories within them described the nature of the involvement of individual players during practice.

Procedures

The coach, wearing a wireless microphone, and the volleyball team were videotaped throughout the season for a total of 18 entire practice sessions. At the conclusion of the season the coach was requested to assess each player's overall playing ability and then rank the players on a continuum from high to low ability. The top four players were classified as high-skilled, the next four players as average-skilled, and the remaining four players as low-skilled.

The videotapes were coded by two observers using the revised ALT-PE instrument (Siedentop et al., 1982). Three target students were selected, one from each group, and were observed alternately using a 6-second observe, 6-second record format. The observers used a programmed cassette to provide cues to observe and to record.

To obtain interobserver agreement (IOA) four videotapes were randomly selected and coded simultaneously and independently by the two observers, paced by the programmed cassette. The scored-interval method was used to compute IOA. The mean IOA was .91.

Percentages were calculated for each ALT-PE category. Visual comparisons were made between the data for each group.

Results

Visual comparison of the data at the context level revealed virtually no difference between the low-, average-, and high-skilled players (see Table 1).

The players spent 21.6% of their time in general, noninstructional activities. This time was largely devoted to transition activities (11%), such as moving from place to place, and to warm-up activities (about 8%).

The coach spent approximately 14% of her time providing her players with information. Approximately 5% of the time was devoted to relating information about volleyball techniques, and approximately 9% of the time was spent discussing various strategies with the team.

The coach planned practice so that over three-fifths of the practice time could be spent actively practicing volleyball skills. Slightly more than half of this time (about 34%) was spent in executing volleyball drills focusing on specific skills. Scrimmages, in which players primarily rehearsed various offenses and defenses while receiving feedback from their coach, occurred slightly more than 10% of the time. Actual game play accounted for close to 17% of the time. Little time was devoted to development of fitness.

Comparison of the percentages for the learner involvement level categories (see Table 1) revealed several differences between the players. The low-skilled players spent more time (57.1%) not actively engaged in motor activity than

Table 1. Percent occurrence of ALT-PE categories for low – , average – , and high – skilled players.

Categories	Low – Skilled	Average – Skilled	High – Skilled
General Content (Total)	21.6	21.6	21.6
Transition	10.9	10.8	11.0
Management	1.4	1.4	1.3
Break	1.0	1.0	1.0
Warm-up	8.3	8.4	8.3
Subject Matter Knowledge (Total)	14.5	14.8	14.5
Technique	4.8	4.8	4.7
Strategy	8.6	9.0	8.8
Rules	----	----	----
Social Behavior	----	----	----
Background	1.1	1.0	1.0
Subject Matter Motor (Total)	63.9	63.6	63.9
Skill Practice	33.6	33.7	34.0
Scrimmage	11.2	10.5	10.3
Game	16.8	17.1	17.3
Fitness	2.3	2.3	2.3
Not Motor Engaged (Total)	57.1	55.2	52.6
Interim	2.3	2.5	2.4
Waiting	18.1	15.0	14.4
Off-task	1.6	2.5	1.7
On-task	15.3	15.2	15.2
Cognitive	19.8	20.0	18.9
Motor Engaged (Total)	42.8	44.8	47.4
Motor Appropriate	23.4	25.8	32.7
Motor Inappropriate	16.6	15.7	11.5
Motor Supporting	2.8	3.3	3.2

their average-skilled (55.2%) and high-skilled (52.6%) teammates. Most of this difference was due to the longer time they spent waiting. For all players, close to 20% of the time was devoted to performing transitional, managerial, and warm-up tasks in the prescribed manner (on-task). The players spent little time performing interim activities and engaging in off-task behaviors.

Compared to their teammates, the high-skilled players spent more time actively engaged in performing motor skills (Motor Engaged). During this time they experienced more success and accrued more ALT-PE (Motor Appropriate) (32.7%) than their average skilled (25.8%) and a low-skilled (23.4%) teammates. The low- and average-skilled players experienced similar amounts of inappropriate motor activity, about 16%. The high-skilled players were involved in inappropriate motor activity less often; they found the activities too easy or they were unsuccessful in their performance only 11.5% of the time.

Discussion

The findings from this investigation suggest that disparities existed in the opportunities provided for the low-, average-, and high-skilled players during volleyball practices. Low- and average- skilled players had fewer opportunities to actively participate during practices than the high-skilled players. Much of this difference was accounted for by the time these lesser skilled players spent waiting. During the time the high-skilled players were involved, they experienced greater success performing volleyball skills and accrued more ALT-PE than the low- and average-skilled players. The findings of this investigation were congruent with the findings of Thomas et al., (1984) who found that high-skilled female as well as high-skilled male intercollegiate lacrosse player accrued more ALT-PE than their low-skilled teammates. While van der Mars et al. (1984) reported no differences in the amount of ALT-PE accrued by male high- and low-skilled interscholastic basketball players, the researchers did find, similar to this investigation, differences in how the high- and low-skilled players spent their time during practices. The findings of this investigation were also congruent with the findings of Pieron (1983) and Wuest et al. (1984); these researchers found disparities in the amount of ALT-PE accrued by low- and high-skilled students in physical education classes. Pieron (1983) suggested that the gap in performance between students of different abilities was sure to widen because the high-skilled students were more productively engaged in activities during class. It seems likely that the gap in performance between low- and high-skilled players would similarly be affected. Thus, to reduce the gap coaches need to design their practices to include progressions to allow the lesser skilled players to experience success and to improve their skills to the level of their high-skilled teammates.

The use of systematic observation instruments, such as ALT-PE, can assist the coach not only in designing practices to maximize players' development but to effectively use the time allocated for practice. For example, as shown in Table 1, one-fifth of practice time was spent in noninstructional activities. The coach may want to reorganize activities to reduce the time spent in transition or employ hustle behaviors to urge the athletes to move more quickly from drill to drill. Reduction of time spent in noninstructional activities would increase the time available to actively practice volleyball skills.

It would also appear desirable for the coach to reduce the time the athletes were inactive during practice (nonengaged). The coach may accomplish this by reducing the time the athletes spend waiting to participate either through the use of smaller drill groups and/or by providing activity stations. Finally, strategies to maximize the amount of ALT-PE accrued by different players should be considered. Strategies could include designing different tasks for athletes of different abilities or using different progressions for each group.

In conclusion, the ALT-PE data from this investigation provided information about the actions and achievements of different ability players within the intercollegiate volleyball setting. Hopefully, additional descriptive analyses of different sport settings, perhaps in conjunction with the use of standardized performance tests and/or game statistics, can provide researchers with further information about the science of the art of coaching, much as how it has provided us with information about the art of teaching.

References

Fisher, C., Filby, N., Marliave, R., Cahen, L., Dishaw, M., Moor, J., & Berliner, D. (1972). *Teaching behaviors, academic learning time, and student achievement: Final report.* San Francisco: Far West Laboratory for Educational Research and Development.

Metzler, M. (1983). An interval recording system for measuring academic learning time in physical education. In P.W. Darst, V.H. Mancini, & D.B. Zakrajsek (Eds.), *Systematic observation instrumentation for physical education* (pp. 181-195). West Point, NY: Leisure Press.

Pieron, M. (1983). Teacher and pupil behavior and the interaction process in P.E. class. In R. Telama et al. (Eds.), *Research in school physical education* (pp. 13-30). Jyvaskyla, Finland: The Foundation for Promotion of Physical Culture and Health.

Placek, J., Silverman, S., Shute, S., Dodds, P., & Rife, F. (1982). Academic Learning Time (ALT-PE) in a traditional elementary physical education setting: A descriptive analysis. *Journal of Classroom Interaction, 17*(2), 41-47.

Shute, S., Dodds, P., Placek, J., Rife, F., & Silverman, S. (1982). Academic learning time (ALT-PE) in elementary school movement education: A descriptive analytic study. *Journal of Teaching in Physical Education, 1*(2), 3-14.

Siedentop, D., Birdwell, D., & Metzler, M. (1979, March). *A process approach to measuring teaching effectiveness in physical education.* Paper presented at the American Alliance for Health, Physical Education, Recreation, and Dance National Convention, New Orleans.

Siedentop, D., Tousignant, M., & Parker, M. (1982). *ALT-PE coding manual* (rev. ed.). Columbus, OH: School of Health, Physical Education, and Recreation of The Ohio State University.

Thomas, J.T., Mancini, V.H., & Wuest, D.A. (1984, April). *A comparison of the academic learning time-physical education of high- and low- skilled male and female collegiate lacrosse players.* Paper presented at the American Alliance for Health, Physical Education, Recreation, and Dance National Convention, Anaheim, CA.

Van der Mars, H., Mancini, V.H., Wuest, D.A., & Galli, G.L. (1984, July). *A comparison of the academic learning time of a high-skilled basketball player and a low-skilled basketball player.* Paper presented at the 1984 Olympic Scientific Congress, Eugene, OR.

Wuest, D.A., Mancini, V.H., & Smith, D.B. (1984, April). *A comparison of the academic learning time - physical education of secondary male and female low— and high-skilled students during a unit of instruction.* Paper presented at the American Alliance for Health, Physical Education, Recreation, and Dance National Convention, Anaheim CA.

18

Coaches' Use of Nonliteral Language: Metaphor as a Means of Effective Teaching

David C. Griffey
THE UNIVERSITY OF WYOMING
LARAMIE, WYOMING, USA
Lynn D. Housner
NEW MEXICO STATE UNIVERSITY
LAS CRUCES, NEW MEXICO, USA
Darrell Williams
UNIVERSITY OF TEXAS
AUSTIN, TEXAS, USA

Over the last decade those who have studied human performance have embraced more complex theories about the use of language in communication and thought. A particularly fascinating body of inquiry centers on the uses of nonliteral language in conveyance and representation of thought. How humans employ similes, idioms, adages, anomalies, and metaphors reveals much about the way we learn and manipulate information.

It has been estimated that people utter about four figures of speech per minute in free discourse (Pollio, Barlow, Fine, & Pollio, 1977). As Hoffman and Honeck (1980) point out, this works out to about 21 million figures of speech per lifetime. There is a great deal of speculation that metaphor forms the basis of all human cognition (Lakoff & Johnson, 1980) and learning (Petrie, 1979).

It is becoming increasingly apparent that thought and memory are not at all like the discursive processes traditionally used to convey them. Rather it appears that human cognition is more metaphorical in character. Thinking is not only discursive but also holistic; characterized by calling up and comparing metaphors that encapsulate all experiences related to the matter at hand.

This allows one to think about issues without sequentially addressing their parts while holistically considering the complexity.

Learning has also been characterized by having metaphor as its single salient characteristic. It has been argued (Petrie, 1979) that learning is the result of resolving the ambiguity between two apparently disparate things. And that is precisely what a metaphor begs the hearer to do: wrestle with the incongruous literal meaning of a statement while uncovering the real ground, or intended meaning, that is being presented. This resolution brings the person to a new understanding of a phenomenon. The matter is summed up in the famous paradox of the Memo as posed by Plato:

> You argue that a man cannot enquire either about that which he knows or about that which he does not know; for if he knows, he has no need to enquire; and if not, he cannot; for he does not know the very subject about which he is to enquire. (Plato, Jowett translation, 1937)

As a modern day example, consider looking up a word in a dictionary when the correct spelling is not known.

How can one learn really new knowledge if one does not already know it? The resolution of metaphor's ambiguity seems to be the most plausible explanation. It has been posited (Petrie, 1979) that such a learning process has four parts:

1. Perceiving a disturbance between what is being said and the context that it is being presented in
2. Attempting to apply the metaphorical conception literally
3. Conducting a series of active mental operations in an effort to eliminate the anomaly
4. Final accommodation to the ground, or nonliteral meaning, of a metaphor

If such a process forms the basis of cognition, then it must also be operational in the learning of human movements and sport skills. During informal listening to coaches' dialogues, it has become apparent to us that expert coaches do rely on metaphor and other nonliteral forms for communicating information about skill performance to athletes.

The purpose of this study was to document and categorize the nonliteral uses of language employed in coaching high-level athletes. To that end, video and audio tapes of practice and contest sessions of six nationally and internationally ranked coaches were collected over the course of their season. Examples of nonliteral language were transcribed and analyzed using the scheme proposed by Richards (1936) and refined by Perrine (1971). It was intended that such a study would be an initial step at making the coaches' use of language in pedagogical interactions more efficient and effective.

Method

Six nationally known college coaches were followed during the course of their seasons. Coaches were periodically fitted with wireless microphones. The transmissions were tape recorded and subsequently transcribed. The sports represented by these coaches included basketball, swimming, diving, and gymnastics.

The focus of the recording was simply the verbal utterances of the coach. No attempt was made to record the comments of athletes. The Richards-Perrine Scheme for studying nonliteral language attends to four attributes of a nonliteral phrase: metaphor, topic, vehicle, and ground. For example, the phrase "the optimist has congenital anaesthesia," is a metaphorical statement; any attempt at a literal interpretation of its meaning proves anomalous. The topic of phrase is the attitudes of optimists. The vehicle for expressing this topic is congenital anaesthesia. The ground is that the optimist is ignorant or unaware. This general scheme was employed in deciding when an utterance was a metaphor. The critical element in selecting verbalizations for study was verifying that the statement could not be literally interpreted. That is, the statement had to be anomalous in the literal context where it was used. Once a coach's comment was selected, it was analyzed with the Richards-Perrine Scheme to resolve the anomaly and understand the ground, or intended meaning, of the phrase. In cases where the ground was not evident to the transcriber or when the statement was an idiomatic expression, coaches were asked to clarify their intent by explaining what they meant by the statement.

After gathering and verifying uses of nonliteral language, statements were classified by general intent: improvement of form, motivating athletes, directing attention to kinesthesis or other physical sensation, or overall focusing of athletes' attention during performance. It was hoped that the substantive outcome of the analysis would be to understand when and for what purposes coaches use nonliteral language when working with athletes.

Findings

Four hundred and fifty-seven utterances were selected from the transcripts as nonliteral. The frequency of use of nonliteral language varied among coaches. It was most often used by gymnastics and diving coaches, accounting for as much as 60% of their utterances. It was used less often by basketball coaches (30%) and rarely by swimming coaches (9%) (see Figure 1).

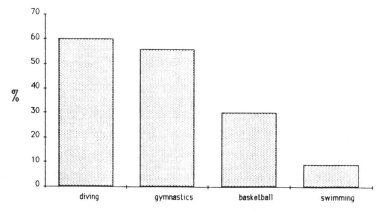

Figure 1. Percent of nonliteral language use

Some examples of nonliteral language use by coaches are shown in Table 1. It can be seen that coaches use nonliteral language to a number of ends and in response to different exigencies. The examples seem to have been spoken for four general reasons, in terms of the kind of focusing of attention that the coach wished to engender in the athlete. Examples 1, 2, and 3 appear to address concerns about the form of a performance in a kinematic sense. That is, a communication from the coach to the athlete about the coach's perception of the appearance of some part of the performance. These seemed to be statements aimed at the fine-tuning of a performance, accomplished by addressing some body part or segment. It seemed common for coaches of gymnastics and diving, sports that are judged by nuance of movement, to give comments about subtle positions of some body part.

Table 1. Types of Metaphor

Metaphor	Topic	Vehicle	Ground
1. You're cutting the arms off a little	Use of arms during sommersault	Cutting arms off	Use arms more emphatically
2. A little heavy on the shoulders	Form of shoulders while in the air	A little heavy	Lower your shoulders during the flight
3. Pull the rings right into your hip	Final location of rings	Pull into your hip	Motion of arms during kip-up
4. Way to get home	Amount of effort used	Home	Good effort at finish of race
5. Paul, you need to quit playing like a freshman	Amount of effort and concentration	Like a freshman	You are not thinking or trying enough
6. Don't lose any water	Maximum propulsion	Lose water	Pay attention to the feeling in your hands
7. You muscled it	Rotation off diving board	Muscled it	Relying too much on strength off the board and not form in tuck
8. Sam, I want pressure on the back side	Defensive position	Back side pressure	Move to the side away from the ball to stop pass
9. Ride the board	Getting energy for the dive	Ride	Stay on the board as long as possible

Examples 4 and 5 can be interpreted as appeals to athletes to become more involved or motivated about what they are doing. These examples do not give any specific instructions nor do they address any specific part of the athlete's performance. They are general chides of encouragement.

Examples 6 and 7 also seem to fall in a different category, sensation or kinesthetic perception. They can be interpreted as efforts by the coach to cue athletes to feelings and sensations within their bodies. Implicit in this is the feeling on the part of the coach that by cueing athletes to these feelings, athletes will perceive them and adjust their performances accordingly.

Examples 8 and 9 are nonliteral utterances that speak to global aspects of performance. Coaches in every sport, other than swimming, had a high percentage of this kind of nonliteral language use. These phrases appear to be efforts by the coach to focus athletes' attention on the overall quality of their performances. They are comments that have the purpose of focusing athletes' attention on a general sensation, strategy, or gestalt for their performances. These comments appear to be aimed at calling up large amounts of information in the athletes' minds about the character/style of their performances. It must be noted that the actual interpretation of the ground of a metaphor is an individual matter, and the examples given could be construed to have ground other than those presented.

The relative usage of these categories of nonliteral language varied according to the sport (see Figure 2). The swimming and basketball coaches used nonliteral language primarily to motivate their athletes. This did not occur among the gymnastics and diving coaches, who relied on metaphor to give athletes information about form, sensation, or overall performance. Basketball coaches, in particular, often used metaphor and simile to cajole, frighten, or even shame athletes into more enthusiastic and careful performance.

Diving, swimming, and basketball coaches used many general metaphors—ones aimed at the overall quality or character of a performance. These

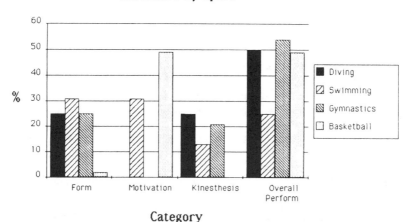

Figure 2. Percentage of purpose for utterance by sport

comments were like compact word packages that contained large amounts of meaning.

In sum, coaches made frequent use of nonliteral language. Semantically, coaches appeared to use metaphor to communicate information about form, level or arousal (motivation), kinesthesis (physical sensations), and general focus for athletes' attention during performance. Syntactically, coaches used nonliteral language as a means of expressing things that were literally inexpressible in normal language, as a compact way of expressing ideas, and as a way of conveying vivid images or other representational structures that otherwise might be inexpressible.

Discussion

When nonliteral language and metaphor are used in conversation, they set up a tension in the mind of the listener. Because such language forms cannot be construed to be literally true in the context that they are spoken, they demand that the hearer eliminate the tension that results from the anomaly. Nonliteral forms beg the hearer to construct a rational bridge between what is known and what is unknown and decipher the intent of the speaker. By constructing such a bridge, the hearer is brought to new understanding and knowledge.

Pedagogically, the use of metaphor holds great potential for making the development of sport performers more efficient. By choosing metaphors that are vivid and that result in athletes actively resolving the tension of an anomalous statement, coaches can be of great assistance to their charges.

Coaches use nonliteral language for three main purposes. First, coaches use metaphor and other nonliteral forms to express things that are literally inexpressible with language. In this way coaches could address an athletes' perception, sensation, and overall focus of attention. These are things that are very difficult, if not impossible, to describe in any direct way. Second, metaphors have compactness and can contain a message much more economically than discursive language could. Athletic competition often takes place under the constraint of time, and this requires that communications be compact yet complete. Skilled use of metaphor is the most likely candidate for accomplishing this task. Third, metaphor and other nonliteral forms are often more vivid than discursive language. Phenomenologically and psychologically, metaphors are more image evoking and more vivid than even their best literal equivalents (if any exist). In this vein metaphors can be, and seemingly are, used to evoke emotion and other complex representation in athletes.

Language use can be a powerful tool in teaching sport performance, as evidenced by the prevalence of such language among these expert coaches. The study of nonliteral language holds the potential for improving the efficacy of sport pedagogy. Obviously, metaphor can make coaching more vivid, direct, and efficient. Continued study of nonliteral language use by coaches holds the potential for improving the effectiveness of sport pedagogy. Many questions demand investigation:

1. How do coaches make decisions about how they convey information to athletes?

2. What meanings do these forms of expression have to the athletes?
3. How consistent are certain metaphors at engendering accurate resolution of anomalous information in athletes?
4. Can coaches be trained to use verbal forms that are effective for developing skilled performance in athletes? and
5. What kinds of experiences should coaches have had to insure that they can form the kinds of metaphors that will lead their athletes to the understandings and perceptions that truly lead to success in their athletes' performances?

Continued study of language use by coaches holds the potential of answering these questions.

References

Hoffman, R.R., & Honeck, R.P. (1980). A peacock looks at its legs: Cognitive science and figurative language. In R.R. Hoffman and R.P. Honeck (Eds.), *Cognition and figurative language* (pp. 3-24). Hillsdale, NJ: Lawrence Erlbaum Associates.

Lakoff, G., & Johnson M. (1980). *Metaphors we live by.* Chicago: University of Chicago Press.

Perrine, L. (1971). Four forms of metaphor. *College English, 33,* 125-138.

Petrie, H.G. (1979). Metaphor and learning. In A. Ortony (Eds.), *Metaphor and thought* (pp. 438-461). Cambridge, England: Cambridge University Press.

Plato. (1937). Memo. In B. Jowett (Ed. and Trans.), *The dialogues of Plato.* New York: Random House.

Pollio, H.R., Barlow, J.M., Fine, H.J., & Pollio, M.R. (1977). *Psychology and the poetics of growth: Figurative language in psychology, psychotherapy, and education.* Hillsdale, NJ: Lawrence Erlbaum Associates.

Richards, I.A. (1936). *The philosophy of rhetoric.* London: Oxford University Press.

PART III

Curriculum: Theory & Practice

19

Stamp Out the Ugly "Isms" in Your Gym

Patt Dodds
UNIVERSITY OF MASSACHUSETTS
AMHERST, MASSACHUSETTS, USA

"Ellis" ... "Paul" ... "Eric" ... "Cindy" ... . A pudgy third-grade boy stood fidgeting from one foot to another, scuffing his sneakers in the sand. His fingers curled into and out of fists, and his palms were slightly sweaty. "John" ... "Barbie" ... "David" ... "Sam". Benjamin edged closer to the dwindling groups, as if for comfort or protection. "Susan" ... "Eddie" ... "Jamie" ... "Bobbie" ... A slight frown appeared on the boy's face, his lips began to quiver a bit, his eyes looked only at the toes of his shoes. "Kim" ... "Marie" ... (longer pause between names) "Jonathan" ... and at last! "Benjamin." He slowly trudged to the end of his team line.

And so it goes, day after day, in physical education classes around the United States—the public choosing of teams by children for game play. Too few of us give any thought to the feelings engendered by this practice, especially in the children who are always chosen last, those who die many deaths as they stand waiting, seemingly endlessly, for others to pick them in some relentless hierarchy. This pecking order is based on any of several possible factors: how proficient at the game children are, whether one is a best friend or not, if one is a boy or girl, what race a child belongs to, which socioeconomic class one is a member of, and many other features of which we are less aware. Each feature exemplifies an "ugly ism," the major ones being sexism, racism, motor elitism, and socioeconomic classism, which appear in every gym once in a while, but in many gyms far too frequently.

Research on Training Teachers for Equity

In the United States the "isms" each in turn have constituted the focal point for fairly substantial volumes of educational writing and research: In the '60s the topic was racism, in the '70s sexism, and in the '80s motor elitism or "isms" in general. What follow are brief generalizations about the equity training literature and some recommendations for faster progress.

Equity training literature is partially research on teaching (RT), as when teachers use curriculum materials to teach their own students about sex stereotyping or racial discrimination, and partially research on teacher education (RTE), as when teachers are the subjects who learn about sexism, racism, or motor elitism (Locke & Dodds, 1981). Roughly two categories of writing are represented: (a) prescriptions for making changes (i.e., "how to" training manuals, curriculum units, and evaluation checklists), and (b) research reports which evaluate the effects of specific training packages or treatments.

Space does not permit an extensive review of the studies in which either teachers, students, or both were the recipients of training. Readers are instead directed to the author's currently updated version of a comprehensive working bibliography (Dodds, 1983) compiled from sources including *Resources in Education, Current Index to Journals in Education, Dissertation Abstracts International,* the ERIC microfiche system, and the journals themselves. No claims are made for total inclusion of all relevant studies, for one characteristic of this literature is that papers are widely scattered and frequently difficult to access, particularly final reports of federally funded projects. Included are examples of government-funded research, independent research (not funded by agencies), and graduate student research. While general features of the body of literature are simply outlined below, readers are urged to consult the earlier paper for specific reference citations (Dodds, 1983).

This outline is based on the questions: (a) Who was trained (subjects)? (b) How was the training carried out (interventions)? (c) What were the research/evaluation designs used? and (d) What was discovered (results)?

I. Subjects
   A. Teachers: in-service, preservice, preschool through college (RTE)
   B. Students: preschool through college (RT)
   C. Teachers and students (RT & RTE yoked)
II. Methodologies
   A. Experimental, quasi-experimental, Solomon 4 group
      1. Pre-and posttests
      2. Experimental treatment and control (no treatment) groups
   B. Correlational
   C. Descriptive-analytic
   D. Qualitative: case study, ethnography
   E. Data source triangulation
   F. Research review
III. Interventions (independent variables)
   A. For teachers
      1. Courses, workshops, minicourses (many)
      2. Written materials, PSI modules (some)
      3. Theory-based model (one)
      4. Pre-and posttraining observations (few)
   B. For students
      1. Modeling techniques

        2. AV materials, curriculum unit packages
        3. Simulation games
IV. Results
        A. Dependent variables: awareness, attitudes, and/or actions
        B. Most popular target: attitude changes
        C. Least popular target: overt behavior changes
        D. Success rate: mixed for all DVs, positive to unclear outcomes

Recommendations for Future Research

The first caution to researchers interested in equity questions is to replicate, replicate, replicate (Sidman, 1960). Until training procedures, research designs, or results are consistent across several studies, there is no guarantee that positive results are not simply a function of chance. The clear and persistent demonstration of functional relationships between X treatment package for teacher training and Y results in the awareness, attitudes, or actions of teachers or their students is crucial for progress in equity training research.

The stringent verification of treatment variables is just as important as replication. When training packages are only alleged to have occurred, it is unlikely that alert readers will believe the results produced. When levels of treatment are clearly indicated, findings are easier to interpret, and it is then possible to determine what the functional relationships are. Helping teachers to exhibit equitable behaviors in the training setting is far different from checking in their own classrooms to see if those behaviors persist under actual teaching conditions.

For "improvement" studies (Doyle, 1978), it is essential to yoke more RT/RTE dimensions together, in tightly controlled design conditions, with triangulated data sources. Training teachers who then help their own students learn to be more fair in their treatment of others and thorough measuring of the RT and RTE dimensions can help researchers be efficient, orderly, and wise in their use of time, and will contribute to the economy of those research efforts.

For "understanding" studies (Doyle, 1978), more qualitative strategies could help answer some research questions which we now can address only indirectly. The early descriptive work at Teachers College, Columbia, was the first step toward embellishing the purely quantitative views we formerly held about the events happening in the gymnasium (Anderson & Barrette, 1978). But qualitative research methodologies can open our eyes to richer perceptions of the complicated interactions between teacher and students in the learning environment (cf. Griffin, 1983).

The maintenance issue has been addressed by those concerned with long-term effects of behavior changes, but not even the radical behavior analysts have demonstrated continuations of positive behavior changes once achieved. Particularly with issues like equity, where teachers must work over long periods of time, it is essential for teacher developers serving as consultants to build a workable system for maintaining the good changes that happen. Whether this involves training administrators or peer teachers to support those making changes or making substantial alterations in the student grading system or setting yearly goals with teachers committed to becoming more fair in their teaching or whatever, definite attention to this much neglected aspect of equity training can do much to assure that good behavior changes do not attenuate.

The final caution is simply to ask important questions, not trivial ones. The best designed study in the world can only find trivial answers for trivial questions, and conversely, poorly designed research on good questions will be of little value. Thinking carefully about the issues to be addressed, consulting the research literature available, and conferring with trusted colleagues in the design stage are all good strategies for avoiding insignificant research.

In summary, if equity training research is to contribute significantly to our knowledge about what really goes on in the gym, it must exhibit at least several of these characteristics: replication, maintenance strategies, more liberal use of qualitative methodologies, verification of treatment variables, yoked RT/RTE studies, and the right, important questions. Researchers attending to these issues with care can do much to improve the credibility and real significance of this body of work.

Elements of Equity

Building physical education curricula that are fair to all students means that teachers must be sensitive to the operations of the "isms" in their classes. Then the teachers can plan carefully to avoid the "isms," interact with students in ways to exemplify and encourage fairness and sensitivity to others and appreciation of differences, and devise learning environments where each person can enjoy the most opportunities to learn all of the skills needed to play well with others.

One purpose of this paper is to encourage teachers and teacher developers to think about issues of equity (i.e., being fair to all students as individuals regardless of the groups to which each belongs) and to consider how each of us can address those issues in our own work. Being an equitable teacher is not as easy as learning a simple set of behaviors to mix and emphasize at will in much the same way as an orchestra conductor calls for more woodwinds or less brass. *Equity* is a way of looking at the world, an outlook, a cosmology, more akin to the overall tone of a symphony, a concerto, a string quartet, or to the idiosyncratic style of the conductor. As such, equity (or inequity) frames every aspect of one's teaching. It is an underlying thread or theme, a ground bass easily recognizable in daily lessons, in activity units, in a year of skill themes work, or in entire elementary or secondary programs of physical education. Equity is sometimes subtle, sometimes distinctly obvious. It builds and fades, gradually or suddenly it is always woven among the other elements of a lesson.

Why should physical educators be concerned about equity in the gym? While the answers are to some extent culturebound, and therefore may differ along some dimensions from country to country, all teachers whose intention is to help students learn would probably agree that they want those students to learn as much as possible. In the United States our rhetoric about education holds that free, public schooling for all children has the underlying purpose of providing opportunities for each student to make the most of his or her individual potential. The idealized function of teachers is to set up optimal conditions for their clients to learn—from them, from other adults, from each other, and from the educational environment (the classroom, the school, and the immediate community).

Part of maximizing each person's opportunity to learn, however, is working to minimize the restrictions and barriers to learning. When bias, prejudice, stereotyping, or discrimination operate in schools, they result in all of the ugly "isms" (sexism, racism, classism, motor elitism) which create unfairness for some students. Each instance of bias, every incident of prejudice, and all of the events of stereotyping create barriers which prevent children from working at their greatest potentials. Some limitations are imposed by others in the school (teachers, administrators, fellow students), while some are self-imposed, as when prejudice triggers a destructive cycle of the self-fulfilling prophecy.

A variety of inequitable limitations may restrict learning, and teachers need to understand each type of inequity if they are to assess correctly the extent to which "isms" influence events in their classrooms. *Bias* or *prejudice* is the use of predetermined judgments about a person by virtue of her or his membership in a particular subgroup of society. In the gym, such bias may take the form of sexism (judging that a girl cannot excel at upper body strength activities simply because she is female), racism (automatically expecting high performance from black students in track and field or basketball while holding lower expectations in tennis, gymnastics, or swimming), or motor elitism (using only one learning task for a whole class when it is obvious that some students will be unable to perform the task at all).

Stereotyping serves to ..."bang people into shape with a cultural sledgehammer ..." (Pogrebin, 1980, p. 29). Biased attitudes are based not on knowing an individual person, but upon knowing only the particular group into which the individual falls. Expecting a person to exhibit certain behaviors because she is a girl, he is a black, she is Hispanic, or he is small, quiet, and bespectacled demands that each person act in accord with some mythical norm for a wider group. Out of the careless demands of such attitudes, teachers can create or sustain inequity of opportunity. Counseling all the girls into field hockey units rather than football, placing all black students in the low-skilled swimming section, or being totally surprised when the smallest boy in the class gets the best score on the fitness obstacle course are illustrations of ways teachers may perpetuate stereotypes in the physical education setting.

Discrimination is the restriction or denial of rights, privileges, or choices because of membership in a given subgroup. In the U.S.A., women, blacks, Hispanics, and poorly skilled participants have been frequent victims. Even federal legislation has been unequal to the task of eliminating discrimination in the gymnasium. Title IX's first 10 years resulted in tremendous, but insufficient, advances in equal opportunities for girls and women in athletics. More varsity teams were established, more money was given to balance the financial inequities between men's and women's sports, and more women began to coach girls' teams. Today, however, the teeth have been drawn from this law through political manipulations, and sex discrimination may once again increase. And finally, no law protects students with less motor ability against the implacable "law of nature" which guarantees that in the gym, as in the wider world, the rich simply get richer and the poor get poorer.

The common element is unfairness to some students, either from expectations too high, too low, or too different from the socially accepted norms for their group membership. Equity in the gym maximizes fairness to all students, regardless of the groups in which they hold membership. Teachers who want kids to learn as much as they can will want to work toward being maximally fair to everyone. Equitable physical education is nothing more or less than quality physical education.

It should be recognized that the previous discussion was focused on conditions as they are in the U.S. Although prejudices, biases, stereotypes, and the exact nature of discrimination will have different faces in different countries, all teachers everywhere are confronted with the same kinds of battles against inequities in the educational arena, even though the particulars will differ with the specific cultural context.

Problems: Why It's Not So Easy to Become Fair to All

The list of problems teachers face when they decide to work on equity issues in the gym is long. None of these is insoluble, but each requires great and sustained effort, and some must be solved in conjunction with others. Teachers concerned with equity must realize that they have a significant battle ahead, just as they would have if they tried to change any teaching behaviors. What follows is based loosely on findings from research studies and federal training projects, but specific citations are not included here (see Dodds, 1983, for those). The points made are taken from the collective experience of many researchers and trainers, and therefore do not limit readers to the specific context of any single effort.

Problem 1: Teaching is multidimensional

Teaching is never a single task attended by a teacher at a single moment. It is an ever-changing web of relationships which vary from one instant to the next, a complex set of activities requiring the teacher to be an orchestra conductor rather than a solo performer.

Teachers cannot totally concentrate on one behavior pattern called "fairness to all" as a single dimension of their work. They must interweave their focus on equity issues in and out of concerns for class management and organization, presentation, and monitoring of work tasks for groups of students, social and task-related verbal interactions with individuals, and the constant flow of decisions that must shape the fabric of each class session. Because physical educators and their students live in an incredibly complex environment where they must simultaneously attend to multiple events (Locke, 1975), asking teachers to put on equity lenses imposes on them a brand new framework for viewing the controlled chaos of classes in the movement environment. In essence, such action requires adopting a whole new system for making sense out of their world. Teachers trying to manage 30 children, distribute equipment, provide workspace for all, monitor safety, keep track of individual progress, and solve discipline problems may not believe that they can really keep the lid on everything else and still do equity, too.

In addition, equity work means far more than minor alterations in a few isolated teaching behaviors. Being fair to all may require major changes in a number of teaching behaviors (as well as attitudes and beliefs). No simple cure exists for inequity. The issue involved in working toward being fair to all students may seem like another "extra" to squeeze into a 45-minute class session. Many teachers fear that they would lose control if one more thing were added to think about while performing their daily juggling acts. Putting attention on equity means taking it away from some other aspect of a class. Continuous attention and effort are required to maintain a delicate balance between equity concerns and other critical aspects of teaching. Even given the good advice to start small and try one tiny step at a time, realizing that equity is a long term investment, may in the end leave many teachers believing they are being asked to do too much.

Problem 2: Where to start?

Teachers who are aware of equity problems and who may possess a reasonable level of knowledge about combatting the "isms" in the gym, may still be puzzled about where or how to begin. Should they start revising the program of activities for students, reviewing their grading standards, working on interactive teaching behaviors within a chosen activity unit, rethinking their purposes for administering fitness tests, being careful about addressing all students the same way, ... or what?

One relatively benign place to start, which requires only persistent self-monitoring over an extended period of time, is the use of language. In both written and verbal communications, teachers can see or hear themselves often. It is easy to tell if you constantly bite your tongue when "you guys" rolls out, or use inclusive pronouns or plural structures to avoid the "he's" and "she's", or label sport terms generically rather than by gender (first base player instead of man, or one-on-one defense instead of man-to-man). Beginning with language patterns allows teachers to practice frequently, self-monitor their progress, obtain feedback from others if they wish, and get at least one equity issue under control.

Lest changing one's language patterns be considered too trivial an effort to count as a blow struck for equity, it might be remembered that many linguists take the position that language patterns shape thought patterns, not the other way round. And if working on language patterns is not a teacher's first choice, anyplace that seems reasonable to the person committed to improving equality of opportunity in the gym is an adequate place to start. The energy required to make changes in teaching behavior is considerable, so the choice of focus is an individual matter.

Problem 3: How long must I go on?

The institutional nature of schools and the social unit characteristics of a class dictate that significant changes in teaching strategies will not be either quick or easy, particularly when the issue is as complex as creating equitable learning environments. Educational change for teachers means not only adjusting one's own actions, but also convincing 30 other people to act in different ways as well, and doing so with six different groups a day. Getting students to understand the reasons why teachers want them to operate more affirmatively is both difficult and time-consuming. Complicating this process is the fact that teachers committed to equity often face the Herculean task of contradicting deeply ingrained social interaction patterns that students have learned literally from the moment of birth. It is not easy to overcome clusters of attitudes and behaviors that are reinforced daily by TV commercials, adult messages, family values, or peers' actions.

An additional problem is that when teachers stop working on becoming more fair to all their students, any progress made will soon disappear. Without maintenance, no behavior patterns will long remain in effect because of competing contingencies for their alternatives. Thus the question "How long must I go on?" is answered with a plaintive "forever" if teachers are truly committed to providing equality of opportunity for their students.

Problem 4: What's in it for me? (the question of reinforcements for teachers).

Promoting the idea that teachers ought to want to be more fair to all students is like convincing teachers that they ought to do anything differently. A payoff or reward must be offered for their practice. Physical educators are among the most socially conservative groups in the educational community, and they require powerful persuasion if they are to make changes in traditional behaviors. Motivation thus becomes the critical factor in trying to induce changes toward more equitable practices in the teaching of physical education.

Too often teacher developers assume automatically that all teachers are highly committed to their own professional development. All too frequently, however, teachers are interested only in preserving the status quo in their classes. In one federal teacher training project in which the specific focus was eliminating race and sex inequities in public schools (Sweeney & Girard, 1983), the majority of teachers who completed the training workshops and on site practical activities were already fine teachers eager for any new skills. The real question of how to attract ineffective teachers, those considered "dead wood," proved much more intractable.

Further, equity is a sensitive issue for many teachers who believe that they may experience real losses of power if they acknowledge the need for improvements in their classes. Whites, males, and the highly skilled (i.e., the dominant groups in American society) may consider being more equitable as giving up something significant when the subordinate/minority groups are treated better than before.

In order to lure teachers into equity training experiences, some aspect of the present reward system for teachers must be changed. No financial reinforcers are available for being especially good at teaching: Rewards coming from students are too few, too infrequent, and too weak; administrative support for acquiring an expanded repertoire of teaching skills is lacking; and often other teachers punish rather than reward those who are trying to do things better (through setting up self-reinforcement support systems). And the bad ones continue to teach the very first days over and over again.

Problem 5: Who's teaching today, anyway?

The last problem for teachers trying to be fairer to all students is that they alone do not control all of the significant events in the class. Children learn from each other, multiplied by the number of others in the class, as well as from the teacher. It is impossible to determine how much variance in learning is due to which of the many "teachers" is interacting with each student. Both congruent and dissonant messages are sent to students from their many "teachers" at the same time, and each "teacher" may send conflicting signals at different times.

If the teacher works intensely to help students treat each other fairly while the students continue to limit and discourage each other, mixed unclear signals received from these multiple sources wash out the effects of those clearly advocated by the teacher. Eventually, enough students must support the teacher's equitable efforts so that group-level changes can occur. If not, the teacher will have a long lonely battle because intermittent schedules of reinforcement, when only a few students continue unfair behaviors towards others, are among the strongest in maintaining behaviors. In effect, the equitable gym cannot easily be set up or maintained.

The roles of students helping students have not been studied much. The complex process of building equitable learning environments and the necessity for full participation by both teacher and students require detailed analysis of how students affect each other in order to help teachers work best in these situations. While teachers who are vigilantly aware may catch the blatantly unfair interactions among students, it is much tougher to confront the less apparent, subtle interactions that add up to inequity. Unless teachers can learn to discriminate such events, their efforts toward more fairness may be doomed.

The five problems outlined offer some explanation of why more teachers may not be framing their work in terms of equity for all students. These difficulties may partially explain the relative scarcity of highly successful training projects devised to help teachers improve their sensitivity toward students of different genders, racial and ethnic groups, socioeconomic classes, and levels of motor skill.

Conclusion

Creating physical education classes where all children join a team without being subjected to humiliation or stress; where Blacks, Hispanics, Asians, and Whites play together peacefully; where the norms are cooperation, sensitivity to others, and appreciation of differences; and where each individual can learn in an atmosphere of encouragement and joy for every achievement is a vision held up for every teacher willing to pay the price to be fair and affirmative to all students. Equity in every gym may be only a fantasy today, but every teacher who tries to stamp out the "isms" moves all of us one step closer to the dream.

References

Anderson, W., & Barrette, G. (1978). What's going on in gym: Descriptive studies of physical education classes. Monograph 1, *Motor Skills: Theory Into Practice.*

Dodds, P. (1983, April). Sex equity in schools: A research review of developmental and training studies (A working bibliography). Resource made available at AAHPERD annual meeting, Minneapolis, MN.

Doyle, W. (1978). *Research on the realities of the classroom. Who needs it?* Paper delivered at the annual meeting of the American Educational Research Association, Toronto, Canada.

Griffin, P. (1983). Gymnastics is a girl's thing: Student participation and interaction patterns in a middle school gymnastics unit. In T. Templin & J. Olson (Eds.), *CIC Big Ten symposium research on teaching in physical education* (pp. 71-85). Champaign, IL: Human Kinetics.

Locke, L. (1975). The ecology of the gymnasium: What the tourists never see. *Proceedings of SAPECW,* 38-50.

Locke, L, & Dodds, P. (1981, September 11). Research on teacher education for physical education. *Revista de educacao fisica* e Desportos, pp. 60-67 (English version, Artus).

Pogrebin, L. (1980). *Growing up free: Raising your child in the 80's.* New York: McGraw-Hill.

Sidman, M. (1960). *Tactics of scientific research.* New York: Basic Books.

Sweeney, J., & Girard, K. (1983). *Meeting the challenge: Project TEAM—Sex and race equity in physical education.* Washington, DC: Women's Education Equity Act Program.

20

Relationships of Curriculum and Instruction Theory as Major Aspects of Sport Pedagogy

Herbert Haag
UNIVERSITY OF KIEL,
FEDERAL REPUBLIC OF GERMANY

This investigation intends to make a contribution to further develop the self-understanding and status of sport sciences in general, and sport pedagogy specifically. The structure of the 1984 Olympic Scientific Congress was divided into four sport sciences categories: physical sciences, neurobehavioral sciences, sociocultural disciplines, and management sciences. Sport pedagogy is explicitly a subsection of the sociocultural discipline together with "anthropology of play," "sport and history," "sport philosophy," and "sport sociology."

Even if the word pedagogy, meaning teaching and learning processes, is not too common in the English language, it is becoming used more and more, especially in connection with sport. The word *sport* is not used in this context in the narrow sense of athletics or competitive sport; rather, it means the sum of physical activities of formal and informal nature realized mostly in sport disciplines but also in fundamental forms like calisthenics, fitness-training, or aerobics. *Curriculum* and *instruction theory* are well established terms also on the international level, of course with variations in meaning.

The analysis of the given topic will be realized in five steps. First of all, the foundations of the investigation have to be explained. Next, sport pedagogy will be explained in a second part as theory field of sport sciences and as applied field of educational sciences. The following two parts will clarify the major aspects of curriculum theory and sport and instruction theory and sport. Within the final part the curriculum-instruction-integration-theory (CIIT) will be explained in terms of this investigation to present the relationships of curriculum and instruction theory as major aspects of sport pedagogy.

Foundations of the Investigation

The procedure employed in this investigation can be characterized as theory grounded research (Willimczik, 1968). The purpose of the study was to develop a theoretical framework to analyze the relationship of curriculum and instruction theory. In spite of the fact that both areas of research are well established, it is often difficult to clearly see the relationship as well as the mutual connection and distinction of both aspects. This in turn is important in order to contribute to further conceptualization of sport pedagogy as one theory field of sport sciences. Because sport sciences by themselves are a young scientific discipline, it took some time until sport pedagogy started to develop as a theory field of research process (Haag, 1978). It is important to follow this line and hopefully see sport pedagogy as a recognized theory field of sport science ("Sportwissenschaften") (Grupe, 1975).

Procedures

The procedures of this investigation were based on the descriptive method (status quo design) because it is neither a historical nor an experimental study (Haag, 1982). Because available literature has been analyzed in a systematic way, content analysis was the major technique of data collection. Thus the character of the investigation is hermeneutic and not phenomenological or empirical. The technique of data treatment consequently is following hermeneutic strategies; this means deductive logical reasoning, interpreting, and drawing of conclusions. Also this investigation has the character of the so-called theory-grounded research because a theoretical concept and model was developed (Bain, 1982). It is a contribution in the line of the so-called fundamental research as opposed to applied research. In this type of research my own reasoning, reflections, and considerations played a major role because some new ideas, models, and constructs had to be found (Haag, 1982).

Sport Pedagogy as Theory Field of Sport Sciences and as Applied Field of Educational Sciences

A basic hypothesis is that the consideration of intra- and interrelationships of theory fields of sport sciences and relation sciences are necessary for the understanding and constant development of sport sciences as an academic field. Interrelationship means the relation of the different theory fields of sport sciences with each other, which is important for the so called interdisciplinary approach in sport sciences (Singer, Lamb, Loy, Malina, Kleinman, 1972). For example, sport pedagogy has very close relationships to sport psychology and sport sociology.

Intrarelationships exist from sport pedagogy to pedagogy (education) in general; this means from sport pedagogy as theory field of sport sciences to the respective "mother," or related science. Sport pedagogy, therefore, is often also called an applied science as opposed to a basic science. This mentioned inter- and intrarelationship paradigm also serves for the following distinction of two subchapters.

Interrelationship

To describe the body of knowledge of sport sciences, three major possibilities were given: organization-oriented approach (Grupe, 1971), theme-oriented approach, and theory-field-oriented approach. The last approach has to be seen in connection with the interrelationship paradigm, in which a certain number of theory fields are derived from already established scientific fields. These theory fields have an applied character and are not clearly limited to a certain number (Baitsch, Grupe, & Lotz, 1972).

The so-called 7-theory-field-model, developed by the author within the department of sport pedagogy of Kiel-University, seems to provide a good rationale for the perception of sport sciences. This model can be seen in the following way (Haag, 1979). The sequence in which the seven theory fields are listed in Figure 1 is indicative of the kinds of interrelationships among them. In order to conceptualize sport pedagogy, these interrelationships have to be considered.

Intrarelationships

The relationship of sport pedagogy to the respective "mother", or "relation" science is necessary in order to engage in high quality scientific thinking and research results on a broad scale. The intrarelationships have to be seen in both directions because it is also interesting for the relation science to see the

```
a. Anatomical-Physiological-Mechanical Foundations
   Sport Medicine
   Sport Biomechanics

b. Social and Behavioral Foundations
   Sport Psychology
   Sport Pedagogy
   Sport Sociology

c. Historical-Philosophical Foundations
   Sport History
   Sport Philosophy
```

Figure 1. Theory-field-model for sport sciences.

application level for example, in sport pedagogy. In this regard it has to be mentioned that the scientific consolidation of educational sciences took place in three directions (Wehle, 1973):

- Establishment of education as a science in clear distinction to the neighboring discipline of psychology and sociology.
- Development of a study curriculum of educational sciences as opposed to practical teaching.
- Interpretation of education as one social and behavioral science with hermeneutic and empirical research concepts.

This also has consequences for the conceptualization of sport pedagogy as in this analysis, because the scientific developments in the relation science have a direct impact on the applied field (Grupe, 1975; Widmer, 1977; Haag, 1978).

Curriculum Theory of Sport

Curriculum research and the "new" curriculum approach have a much longer tradition in North America than in Central Europe. Robinsohn (1971) introduced this concept in 1967 in the discussion of educational sciences in the Federal Republic of Germany. This general background of curriculum theory is important in order to present sport specific aspects of curriculum theory.

General Aspects

The first incentives for curriculum thinking given by Robinsohn were further developed in the Federal Republic of Germany by experts like Blankertz, Flechsig, and Frey. Just recently, an excellent handbook was published by Hameyer, Frey, and Haft (1983) summarizing curriculum research for the years 1970-1981.

A key term in this area is *curriculum theory* . In general they deal with normative questions and basic categories of education, especially under the aspect of social genesis. Other terms are constitutive for curriculum theory, namely *curriculum methodology/strategy, curriculum construction/development, and curriculum structure/elements.* These six terms stand for three major concerns of curriculum theory, namely foundations of scientific and research approaches, fundamentals of the process of making a curriculum in a scientific way, and the content basis of a curriculum.

Curriculum theory is a relatively general construct and it is partly doubtful, if the general curriculum theory is even available. Hameyer (Hameyer, Frey, & Haft, 1983, see pp. 57-60) has developed a framework for curriculum theories comprised of five areas of curricular articulation:

1. Theories dealing with curriculum relation systems; this means mainly the respective starting situation.
2. Theories of legitimation for engaging in the curriculum process as well as for educational aims/objectives, and content.
3. Theories for curriculum process; this means the aspects of a curriculum development system.
4. Theories for structuring the curriculum as it relates to time, subject matter, and learning.

5. Theories for curriculum implementation; this implies in detail planning, teaching, learning, counseling, and evaluating on the basis of the developed curriculum.

Curriculum is understood in this context on one hand as a medium and on the other hand as a process. This process can be summarized in different phases of a curriculum development system as: (a) Deriving aims and objectives, (b) Planning the curriculum, (c) Performing a trial run/field testing of the curriculum, (d) Realizing the curriculum on a broad scale, and (e) Controlling overall quality.

Curriculum theory implies all of the theories behind a process from the analysis of the starting situation up to the evaluation of the results from implementing a certain curriculum as a medium within the education field.

Sport Specific Aspects

Within the theory field of sport pedagogy a step by step reception of ideas and models from general curriculum theory has taken place. During the first years the Robinsohn model (situation, qualification, curriculum element), taxonomies, and the operation of objectives were the major issues in sport specific curriculum development. Unfortunately, evaluation, as an important aspect of the new curriculum approach, was and still is considered only slightly relevant in Central Europe as opposed, for example, to North America. However, step by step this deficit is taken away (Haag, 1981). The first enthusiasm with the curriculum approach, at least in the Federal Republic of Germany, was decreasing quite rapidly. Curriculum development for different school levels, if it would have been realized according to the available theories, would have been much too complicated and time consuming. Nevertheless, many innovations have been realized through the new curriculum approach including a sport specific adaptation of the taxonomies in cognitive, affective, and psychomotor domains. A more decentralized approach for curriculum development seems more practical (Kurz, 1979). If curricula are developed for smaller units, eventually the same curriculum theories can be applied as in larger projects.

Haag (in Denk & Hecker, 1985) has developed a model of curriculum theory of sport following a process structure of curriculum development. The following steps are distinguished (IKIOR-model):

1. Input evaluation (socio-cultural and anthropological preconditions).
2. Construction (definition of aims, conceptualization of learning situations, sequencing of content, and developing of instructional material, teaching devices, and evaluation instruments).
3. Implementation (pilot-trial, corrections, and field-trial).
4. Output evaluation (process and product).
5. Revision (part aspects and total curriculum).

If a relatively solid curriculum development can take place after following these steps no matter on what level of generality, this curriculum development process still is relatively complex. This is mainly due to the structure of the field of sport and physical education with a cognitive, affective, and psychomotor domain.

Instruction Theory of Sport

General aspects have to be considered as foundation for sport specific considerations in instruction theory as well as curriculum theory. Instruction in sport and physical education is quite complex as compared to instruction in so called theoretical subjects. Thus many instruction theories are available that deal with various aspects of teaching and learning processes (partial theories) and imply different levels of abstraction.

General Aspects

Theory of instruction in the German language is identical with models of didactics. A traditional understanding of instructional theory was based on the "Triad" teacher-pupil-subject matter. Today some more factors are considered within the context of instruction theory as indicated in Figure 2.

Especially because of Blankertz's work (1971), different models of didactics or instruction theory are described. The so-called "learning theory model of instruction" offers a very comprehensive view of teaching and learning processes on the basis of the six factors: sociocultural preconditions, anthropological preconditions, aims/objectives, content, methods, and media (compare Figure 3).

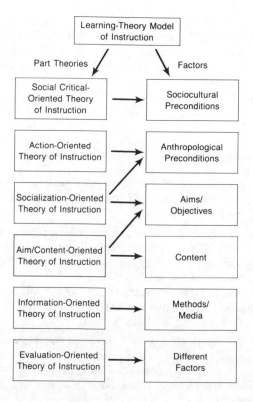

Figure 2. Framework of instruction theory.

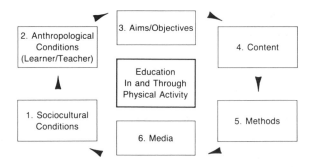

Figure 3. Learning theory model as factor-static explanation of teaching-learning processes.

Many partial theories of instruction are available with some of the following orientations: social-critical, action, socialization, aim/content ('Bildungs-theorie'), information, and evaluation (Haag, 1981). In Figure 2 an attempt is made to indicate which factors have a major relationship to what kind of partial theory of instruction. Thus it is possible to apply the large amount of instruction knowledge to a general framework, namely the learning theory model, which is also a solid basis for the very complex instruction in sport and physical education.

Sport Specific Aspects

Within the field of sport and physical education many different instructional theories or didactic models are available. Grössing (1979) has edited a reader, including a "spectrum of sport didactics." The most important models of didactics or instruction theories are:

- Learning-theory model of instruction: S. Grössing and H. Haag
- Social critical-oriented theory of instruction: J. Jensen
- Socialization-oriented theory of instruction: H.W. Ehni
- Aim/content-oriented theory of instruction: J.N. Schmitz and O. Grupe
- Information-oriented theory of instruction: D. Ungerer
- Evaluation-oriented theory of instruction: H. Haag

The learning-theory model of instruction is the most comprehensive model. It has been used by the author to develop an instruction realization system based on two models with factor-static and process-dynamic characters:

- learning-theory model as factor-static explanation of teaching-learning processes (compare Figure 3), and
- A-P-R-E model as a process dynamic explanation of teaching-learning process as presented in Figure 4.

This dual approach allows a very thorough explanation of instruction, which considers process-dynamic and factor-static aspects as presented in its mutual relationship in Figure 5.

This model for an instruction realization system, therefore, can serve as a guideline to adequately understand the very complex structure of instruction

A — Analyzing Preconditions of

P — Planning Elements of   Teaching and
                                    Learning Processes
R — Realizing Phases of   in Physical Activity

E — Evaluating Results of

Figure 4. A-P-R-E model as process-dynamic explanation of teaching-learning processes.

Process-Dynamic	Factor-Static
A — Analyzing	1. Sociocultural Preconditions
	2. Anthropological Preconditions
P — Planning	3. Aims/Objectives
	4. Content
R — Realizing	5. Methods
	6. Media
E — Evaluating	3./4. (Product)
	5./6. (Process) Related to 2

Figure 5. Phases of an instruction realization system.

in sport and physical education. This has just recently become a preferred research topic in the Federal Republic of Germany (Kayser & Preising, 1982).

Curriculum-Instruction-Integration-Theory (CIIT)

After the explanation of curriculum and instruction theories in their general and sport specific dimensions, the relationship of both theories can be investigated. On the basis of both the curriculum and the instruction theory of sport, a new theoretical framework has been developed with the name of CIIT, standing for curriculum-instruction-integration-theory.

Fundamentals of CIIT

Tanner and Tanner (1975) pretend that there is a "doctrine of dualism" and that curriculum and instruction are essentially two separate action contexts: one (curriculum) producing plans for further action and the other (instruction) putting plans into action" (see p. 5). Macdonald and Leeper (1965) in contrast, suggest that not enough distinction has been made between curriculum and instruction, two distinct realms of relevant operation (compare Eisner, 1971, see p. 126). Tanner and Tanner (1975, see pp. 36-42) argue against this dualism that leads to educational discontinuity and isolation. This also would violate John Dewey's thesis of the intrinsic continuity of ends and means.

The solution is neither keeping up a rigid dualism nor maintaining an undifferentiated perception of curriculum and instruction. The approach should be of a dialectic nature; this means that distinction is necessary and at the same time related. Basically the same factors are of relevance for curriculum and instruction theory, namely the factors important for planning, realizing, and evaluating teaching and learning processes.

The world famous Tyler Rationale (1950), considered the foundation for developing curriculum and instruction after World War II, indicates common interest in both the curriculum and the instruction theory. It proposes four major steps for the two theories: (a) stating objectives, (b) selecting experiences, (c) organizing experiences, and (d) evaluating results.

In some more detail, the model of curriculum construction by Taba (1962) can be taken as proof of the common interest of the curriculum and instruction theories. The seven actions, taken step by step as a sequence, apply in the same way for a curriculum development system as for an instruction realization system. The seven actions are (a) diagnosis of needs and expectation, (b) determination of objectives, (c) selection of learning aim relevant contents, (d) structure of contents, (e) selection of learning experiences, (f) structure of learning experiences, and (g) evaluation of results.

Another witness for dialectic and integrated thinking was Beauchamp (1968), who has developed within this curriculum theory the concept of the "Dynamic Cycle of Schooling" as expressed in the following three major steps:

1. First, goals are set for curriculum and instruction.
2. Afterwards, means can be applied in realizing curriculum and instruction.
3. Finally, the curriculum and the instruction are evaluated.

Two classes of means are indicated for schools: curriculum and instruction that takes place in response to the curriculum. The processes of evaluation help us to determine the adequacy of the two means in producing the desired results—the achievement of the goals. The results of evaluation help us to redefine the goals and replan the means for achieving them. Thus a dynamic cycle is established for schooling (Beauchamp, 1968).

Tyler, Taba, and Beauchamp provide good arguments for dialectic-integrative thinking when dealing with curriculum theory and instruction theory. This will be explained in some more detail in a so-called "Curriculum-Instruction-Integration-Theory (CIIT)," which can be applied within sport pedagogy.

Application for Sport Pedagogy

In developing the CIIT a model from Johnson (1977, see p.10) was used as a starting point and was modified for an application in regard to sport pedagogy as shown in Figure 6: By help of this CIIT the importance of theories for teaching and learning processes in sport and physical education can be clarified.

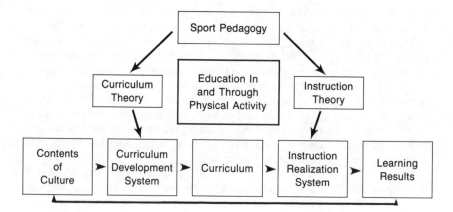

Figure 6. Curriculum-instruction-integration theory (CIIT) as basis of sport pedagogy.

Curriculum theories are providing the necessary framework for the development of curricula (construction, implementation, evaluation, and, if necessary, revision). As a result of this development, curricula for sport and physical education are available.

Instruction theories are providing the framework for the realization of instruction, which is made concrete in sport specific teaching and learning processes, on the basis of the curriculum. The curriculum development system and the instruction realization system are related on one hand to the factors that are important for teaching and learning in sport such as sociocultural preconditions, anthropological preconditions, aims and objectives, content, methods, and media. On the other hand, they are related to the central action dimensions of a physical education teacher or coach, namely to analyze preconditions, to plan, to realize, and to evaluate in regard to sport instruction.

With CIIT, both the curriculum and the instruction theories are seen in their specific role as governing a certain process, namely developing a curriculum and realizing instruction. The link between both theories can be seen threefold:

- Curriculum can be seen as a medium to write guidelines, regulations, and proposals.
- The feedback function of learning can be seen in relationship to culture as the basis for possible curriculum revision or change.
- Factors that have to be considered in both theories are noticeable. (compare Figure 3).

The answer therefore is integrative which implies dialectic approaches.

Concluding Remarks

In five steps I tried to analyze the relationships of the curriculum and instruction theories: Foundations of the investigation, sport pedagogy as a theory field of sport sciences and as an applied field of educational sciences, curriculum theory of sport, instruction theory of sport, and-"Curriculum-Instruction-Integration-Theory (CIIT)". This CIIT is a constructive answer to the topic "Relationships of Curriculum and Instruction Theory." A theoretical framework based on integration and on dialectic, dynamic, and alternative thinking is also very important for the further development of the theory field of sport pedagogy. Scholars working in curriculum or instruction research need mutual relationships and should not follow two separate lines. Curriculum and instruction, including the respective theories, are two sides of the same coin and cannot be separated.

A final conclusion may be that theoretical frameworks like CIIT are necessary so that the nature of different theory fields of sport sciences, in this case sport pedagogy, is clarified. This in turn is important for the planning of teaching and research in sport pedagogy.

References

Bain, L. (1982). Future directions for research in physical education curriculum. *International Journal of Physical Education, XIX* **3**, 10-13.

Baitsch, H., Grupe, O., & Lotz, F. (Eds.). (1972). *Sport im Blickpunkt der Wissenschaften.* Berlin/Heidelberg/New York: Springer.

Beauchamp, G.A. (1968). *Curriculum theory* (2nd ed.). Wilmette, IL: the Kagg Press.

Blankertz, H. (1971). *Theorien und Modelle der Didaktik.* 5. Aufl. München: Juventa.

Denk, H., & Hecker, G. (1985). *Texte zur Sportspädagogik.* Teil II. Schorndorf: Hofmann.

Eisner, E.W. (Eds.). (1971). *Confronting curriculum reform.* Boston: Little Brown and Company.

Grössing, S. (Hrsg.). (1979). *Spektrum der Sportsdidaktik.* Bad Homburg: Limpert.

Grupe, O. (1971). Einleitung in die Sportwissenschaft. *Sportwissenschaft,* **1**, 3-9.

Grupe, O. (1975). Grundlagen der Sportpädagogik. Schorndorf: Hofmann.

Haag, H. (1978). *Sport pedagogy: Content and methodology.* Baltimore: University Park Press.

Haag, H. (1979). Development and structure of a theoretical framework for sport science ("Sportwissenschaft"). *Quest* **31**(1), 25-35.

Haag, H. (Ed.). (1981). *Physical education and evaluation.* Schorndorf: Hofmann.

Haag, H. (1982). Research methodology in sport science. Implication for the Comparative Research Approach. In J. Pooley & C.A. Pooley (Eds.), *Proceedings of the 3rd international symposium for comparative physical education and sport,* 89-110. Halifax: Dalhousie University.

Hameyer, U., Frey, K., & Haft, H. (1983). Handbuch der Curriculumforschung. Erste Ausgabe. Übersichten zur Forschung 1970-1981. Weinheim/Basel: Beltz.

Johnson, J. Jr. (1977). Definition and model in curriculum theory. In A.A. Bellack & H.M. Kliebard (Eds.), *Curriculum and evaluation* (pp. 3-19). Berkeley: McCutchon Publishers.

Kayser, D., & Preising, W. (1982). *Aspekte der Unterrichtsforschung im Sport.* Schorndorf: Hoffmann.

Kurz, D. (1979). Elemente des Schulsports. Grundlagen einer pragmatischen Fachdidaktik. Schorndorf: Hofmann.

Macdonald, J.B., & Leeper, R.R. (Eds.). (1965). *Theories of instruction.* Washington, D.C.: Association for Supervision of Curriculum Development.

Robinsohn, S.B. (1971). *Bildungsreform als Revision des Curriculum und ein Strukturmodell für die Curriculum entwicklung.* Neuwied: Luchterhand.

Singer, R.N., Lamb, D.R., Loy, Jr., J.W., Malina, R.M., & Kleinman, S. (1972). *Physical education. An interdisciplinary approach.* New York: MacMillan Comp.

Taba, H. (1962). *Curriculum development. Theory and practice.* New York.

Tanner, D., & Tanner, L.N. (1975). *Curriculum development. Theory into practice.* New York: MacMillan Publishing Company.

Tyler, R. (1950). *Basic principles of curriculum and instruction.* Chicago: University of Chicago.

Wehle, J. (Ed.). (1973). Pädagogik aktuell. Lexikon pädagogischer Schlagworte und Begriffe. Müchen: Kösel.

Widmer, K. (1977). Sportpädagogik. Prolegomena zur theoretischen Begründung der Sportpädagogik als Wisenschaft. Schorndorf: Hofman.

Willimczik, K. (1968). *Wissenschaftstheoretische Aspekte einer Sportwissenschaft.* Frankfurt: Limpert.

21

A Change in Focus for the Teaching of Games

Rod D. Thorpe, David J. Bunker, and Len Almond
LOUGHBOROUGH UNIVERSITY OF TECHNOLOGY
LOUGHBOROUGH, LEICESTERSHIRE, ENGLAND

In England, games tend to take up about 65% of the total time available to young people in Physical Education curriculum (Hill, 1984). In the last 10 years or so, the staff and research students at Loughborough University, in recognition of the time being devoted to games and their dissatisfaction with traditional methods of teaching them, have developed an approach to games that places greater emphasis on developing a child's tactical awareness of playing games and less emphasis on the acquistion of techniques. Technical requirements were not neglected, instead it was argued that in order to play games it is necessary to reduce the limiting factor of technique. In the sense that children are helped to recognize the problems posed by games and think about solutions to the problems, the approach has been called "teaching for understanding."

Previous papers (Bunker and Thorpe, 1982; Thorpe and Bunker, 1982) have outlined the approach and discussed the probable shortcomings of more traditional methods. The first of these papers, and other articles published in the *Bulletin of Physical Education* (Spring 1982), led to most local education authorities in England running courses for their teachers or setting up working parties to examine the practicalities of teaching for understanding. As a result of these, teachers requested specific examples of how to teach in this way; papers were published subsequently in the Spring issue of the *Bulletin of Physical Education* (1983).

Once one accepts an understanding approach it becomes difficult to separate games into discrete elements because the principles that are used to solve tactical problems are common. For example, the teacher recognizes that what he or she says in basketball may well be useful in soccer and he or she begins to view the games curriculum in a different light.

The Games Curriculum

If games represent an important and unique aspect of physical education with a potential and richness all of their own, we should do something more than present them in isolation from each other. If this is to be avoided it is necessary to frame a set of fundamentals to guide our practice in developing the games curriculum. At this stage of our thinking four fundamentals have emerged:

1. Sampling
2. Modification - Representation
3. Modification - Exaggeration
4. Tactical Complexity.

Although these will be discussed one by one, it needs to be noted that they are not discrete entities; for example, it may only be possible for less able children to sample a wide variety of games if modifications to equipment are made.

Sampling

By sampling from different types of games the focus of the games curriculum takes on a radically different perspective. Instead of selecting games because they have always been taught or because the facilities are available, one should select games for their possibilities. Not only can a variety of experiences be offered, but possibilities exist that can show similarities between apparently dissimilar games and differences between apparently similar games, all leading to a much better understanding of games in general.

To assist the sampling procedure we might use any one of a number of games classifications. We would draw attention to one presented by Ellis (1983), which is based on the physical properties of games, for example, territory (invasion) with a line target (American Football or Rugby Football), which will determine the tactics to be decided:

1. Target	(a) opposed	
	(b) unopposed	
2. Court	(a) divided	
	(b) shared	
3. Field	(a) fan shaped	
	(b) oval shaped	
4. Territory (invasion)	(a) goal	
	(b) line	

(Ellis, 1983)

To give an example of sampling the curriculum in English schools, where territorial type games receive the lion's share of time, there would be a need to rethink the allocation and provide more time (and resources) for other types of games.

Modification - Representation

Implict in an understanding approach is that children will be able to play a game, although we recognize, of course, that "the game" is beyond the reach of many children. Thus we support the notion of game representation, by which we mean that games are developed that contain the same tactical structures of the adult game but are played with adaptations to suit the children's size, age, and ability. In games in which the number of players represent a problem, the essential characters of the game are identified and retained in game representation; thus softball might require that six players are on each side to allow for all tactical considerations of fielding to be invoked. In a game such as tennis, in which the equipment that is used presents a problem to all but a few, sponge ball, plastic bat, and a badminton-size court may be adopted to allow children to play a game that represents the adult game of tennis from a tactical point of view.

In so far as "mini games" (Sleap, 1981) are designed to represent the adult games, these should contain most of the problems to be encountered in the adult games. Therefore players involved in "mini basketball" should be deciding when to mark one-on-one and when to retreat into the zone, when to run the fast break and when to set up play. In this way children will be exposed to a situation in which we can reasonably expect them to develop tactical awareness, to make appropriate decisions, and to practice skills. But is this the best way to arrive at "games" understanding? We think not.

Modification - Exaggeration

The fact that most adult games have evolved to allow for alternative strategies of playing a game, for example, zone or one-on-one defense, adds much to their interest. The trouble is that if mini-games truly represent the adult game then the solutions to the problems posed may be difficult to arrive at for the learner—who is to say whether it is better to go to the net or stay on the baseline in tennis?

If a specific game is being played some primary rules are necessary to give the game its essential form (Brackenridge, 1979). For example, the fact that soccer players (except the goalkeeper) cannot handle the ball and must score by directing the ball between two markers enables us to label the game soccer. While the primary rules will always be present, it will be necessary to think carefully about the introduction of secondary rules when the game breaks down and when there is a need to exaggerate a tactical point to be explored. For example, the pattern of play in badminton includes shots which are directed to the front and back of the court—the beginner must be led into this pattern of play by a modification of the shape of the court. Playing on a long and thin court only leaves spaces for drop shots and clears—the modification exaggerates those elements of the game thought to be important at a particular moment in time. In fielding games it may necessary to dispense with some of the rules that state the ways in which a batsman/striker can be dismissed so that the problem for fielders of stopping runs can be looked at, for example, a batsman/striker will have a predetermined number of hits from a cooperative feeder as he or she attemps to pierce the field. In a 5v5 territorial/invasion type game, using a skittle as the target, a zone defense is highly effective because the goal is completely screened from view. But if the same game is played with a wide line to attack, some form of one-on-one marking is required because there it too much space for zone defenders to cover. In this example the targets are being exaggerated to make important points of a tactical nature.

The skill of the teacher lies in his or her ability to select a suitable game modification to exaggerate tactical considerations and to build these modifications into something with resembles the full game. These modifications are illustrated in Figure 1.

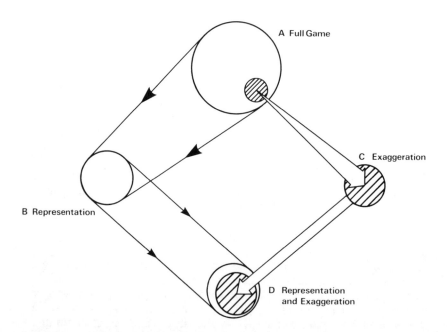

Figure 1. Stages in game modification
A. Full game—the game played by adults with all the inherent techniques and tactics, for example doubles tennis.
B. Representation—a game that maintains most of the tactical complexity of the adult game but reduces the problems posed by the technical and physical limitations of youngsters, for example, short tennis, doubles.
C. Exaggeration—a game that maintains the primary rules of the full game but is modified to exaggerate the tactical problem in question, for example singles on the doubles court exaggerates the necessity to gain lateral balance.
D. In most cases where young people are being introduced to a game both B and C would seem to operate; technical limitations must be recognized and tactical problems simplified; for example, making the short tennis court wide exaggerates the same problem as C.

Tactical Complexity

If understanding games is to be of prime importance to the physical education teacher then the game must be built up carefully, as indeed many teachers do. Therefore, it is surprising that in the United Kingdom at least, programs start with games that are tactically complex, like soccer (for boys) and hockey (for girls), whereas a game like badminton, often presented as a game option in the later years of the secondary program (ninth and tenth grades) is relatively simple.

If the intention is to help children to understand games—and suitable game forms exist which allow the vast majority to play a game—then it would seem sensible to base sampling on tactical complexity. Referring to the classification proposed by Ellis (1983), a starting point may well be games that are "target-unopposed," followed by those that are played on a "court divided," and moving on through "fielding fan-shaped" games to "fielding in oval shaped" areas and finally to territoral/invasion games. Of course the teacher must make the decision about complexity; is a court-shared game more or less complex than a fielding game when the striker can hit through 360°?

The simple decision to base the order of game sampling on the tactical complexity of the games presents a radically different conception of the games program. In addition the teacher may want to shift from one game to another as a result of the tactics being developed. This is particularly true when working with elementary children or when the specific game is less important than the principle of play involved. The following example, using the basic skills of throwing and catching, shows how children can be led through a variety of game types to bring about an understanding of the concept of space. If a child can throw a ball, the first step might be to throw at a target on the floor (target unopposed), he or she might then try to hit the target as well as getting the ball past a defending fielder: the questions posed are where to field, where to throw the ball, and why. If both players have a target area and a net is placed between them, they will have to attack their opponent's court and defend their own court (court-divided). The problem now is where to throw to win a point or where to throw to make space to win the point on the next throw. Take away the net and let them invade each other's territory to score points or goals (and to stop points or goals from being scored) by hitting a target (territory-goal). The lessons learned from creating space and denying space transfer from one game situation to the next; the only techniques required are to throw and catch—if this proves to be difficult then the teacher must represent the games using a more appropriate kind of ball.

Accepting that children can move in and out of types of games which are presented in an order that recognizes their complexity, again forces us to recognize that a completely different set of criteria are operating in developing our games curriculum. It should now be obvious that a very strong link exists between tactical complexity and exaggeration; a game which, in its full form, is complex but can be made tactically simple.

Implications for Teachers

The idea of a games curriculum and the fundamentals for selecting what we teach can lead to a basic foundation course that samples the richness and potential of games. From this foundation course the games curriculum could have a number of lines of development. One might be the development of a particular game such as soccer, that has significance within a community. Another might be to continue the foundation course into more complex forms, or follow a path along which young people devise games for themselves. It seems that at last progress is being made in the direction of a *games education*. However, a games education presents a real challenge to our games teaching because it raises doubts about what teachers know about games. A teacher's understanding of games is different from a practical knowledge of the playing of games, the technical requirements of games, or how to teach games. Yet this feature of understanding games represents a major problem for teachers because they do not appear to have had the opportunity of acquiring this understanding in their training. As a result it is difficult for them to conceptualize games and translate them into forms that can bring out their key properties (Almond, 1983).

If this paper presents a new approach in thinking about games then it needs to take into account the reality of innovations in the teachers world. It is our experience that anyone involved in creating change in the games curriculum will need to be aware that:

1. When new ideas are presented the method of presentation is important, because teachers need to be challenged to think critically about their existing practices. They need to stand outside their perspectives of what and how to teach in order to adopt a reflective and critical stance.
2. The presentation of new ideas needs to be through the experience of a practical session: lectures or even seminars on their own are inappropriate media for gaining access to an idea.
3. When trying out new ideas experienced teachers require support from:
   (a) clearly defined guidelines with practical samples;
   (b) supportive colleagues in a local area who will discuss the teacher's work; and
   (c) examples of case studies by teachers who have tried out the ideas.
4. guidelines need to involve the teacher in exploring a new idea so that he or she feels like part of the development. The exploration could take the form of monitoring one's teaching of an idea.

The understanding of games teaching has been developed through the reflective practice of teachers in using these ideas and the resulting critical dialogue. This is an important process for the development of ideas, therefore the reader is encouraged to enter into further dialogue on games teaching.

References

Almond, L. (1983). *Teaching games through action research.* Paper presented to International AIESEP Congress Teaching Team Sports, Rome.

Brackenridge, C. (1979). *Game: Classification and analysis.* Unpublished mimeograph, Sheffield City Polytechnic, South Yorkshire, England.

Bunker, D., & Thorpe, R. (1982). A model for teaching of games in secondary schools. *Bulletin of Physical Education,* **18,** 5-8.

Bunker, D., and Thorpe, R. (Eds). (1983). *Games teaching revisited.* Bulletin of Physical Education, **19**(1).

Ellis, M. (1983). *Similarities and differences in games: a system for classification.* Paper presented to International AIESEP Congress, Teaching Team Sports, Rome.

Hill, C. (1984). *An analysis of the physical education curriculum in a local education authority.* Unpublished M. Phil. thesis, Loughborough University of Technology, Loughborough, England

Sleap, M. (1981). *Mini-sport.* London: Heinemann Educational

Thorpe, R., & Bunker, D. (1982). From theory to practice: two examples of an "understanding approach" to the teaching of games. *Bulletin of Physical Education,* **18**, 9-16.

22

Curriculum Theory and Practice in Physical Education in Secondary Schools in England and Wales

Gordon L. Underwood
NONINGTON COLLEGE
NONINGTON, ENGLAND

The relationship between theory and practice in the planning and implementation of the physical education curriculum in secondary schools in England and Wales has always been rather tenuous. Physical education teachers in these countries may be placing a great deal of emphasis on the actual teaching of activities and less emphasis on the planning stages of the total curriculum. If this is the case, then it may be losing some of its effectiveness; without a sound and progressive foundation program throughout the several years that children are in secondary school, from 11 to 18 years, attempts to produce excellence will be more difficult.

In the construction of any curriculum the teacher should normally give consideration to the aims and objectives of the subject, the selection of subject matter considered to be appropriate for the teaching methods and learning experience to be used, and some aspects of evaluation. Some of the earlier models, for example Tyler (1949), suggested that a linear relationship may exist among these four components, whereas some of the later models, for example Taba (1962) and Nicholls and Nicholls (1972), indicated that a more cyclical relationship might be more appropriate. A further development by Eraut, Goad, and Smith (1975) suggested a much more flexible approach in which the main components could be arranged in any order. All of the stated models incorporated aims and objectives, content, method, and evaluation, although the order and emphasis varied considerably. The extent that these components are used in the planning of the physical education curriculum in England and Wales is the subject of this paper and is based on a larger study by Underwood (1983).

Procedures

The research strategy adopted an eclectic approach that involved interviewing teachers, examining documentary sources, and mailing a questionnaire. This enabled information to be collected from a variety of sources using different methods. Accordingly, eight male teachers and eight female teachers who were all heads of physical education departments agreed to be interviewed. Each of the groups comprised four teachers over and four teachers under 40 years of age.

A partly structured interview technique with prepared questions was used. The technique focused on the main areas of planning, namely: courses, aims and objectives, content, method, and evaluation. All interviews were tape recorded. The documentary sources comprised 71 syllabuses and these were examined in relation to planning procedures. Two analyses were conducted. The first was carried out by three independent judges and involved ascertaining the weight given to aims and objectives, content, method, and evaluation in each syllabus. The second analysis examined the format, presentation, and major sections of the syllabus, and identified those areas considered to be important by practicing teachers. The third research strategy involved the construction of a 13-page questionnaire, which widened the range and scope of the study and examined some of the issues that had been identified earlier. The sample consisted of approximately 800 schools in England and Wales, and a return rate of 77% was achieved.

Results and Discussion

The extent to which physical education teachers considered aims and objectives, content, method, and evaluation to be important was ascertained through an analysis of the 71 syllabuses by three independent judges and through a self-rating by 572 respondents in the national questionnaire. A clear pattern seemed to emerge as shown in Table 1.

Table 1. Comparison of percentage allocated by judges and teachers (self-rating) to four aspects of planning.

	Aims & objectives %	Content %	Method %	Evaluation %
Independent judges	15	61	19	5
Teachers- (self-rating)	25	36	24	15

Taking the scores given by the independent judges first, the largest proportion was allocated to content and the least weight was given to evaluation techniques. This supported the notion that evaluation was the least sophisticated and articulated part of planning; over half of the syllabuses made no reference to this aspect. The aims and objectives were stated in some detail in a number of syllabuses and received an average weight of 15%, but approximately one third of the syllabuses made no statement concerning these aspects. Teaching methods received a proportion of 19%, but one quarter of the syllabuses made no reference to this area of planning.

In comparing the results of the two groups in Table 1, both allocated the highest proportion to content, but a significantly higher percentage was recorded by the independent judges. In contrast, the teachers gave more emphasis than the judges to aims and objectives, method, and evaluation. The results support the notion that an uneven emphasis exists in physical education curriculum planning, and that content received the most attention and evaluation received the least. However, a much more even distribution occurred among the four components in the ratings given by teachers about their own syllabuses. The implication here is that the emphasis that teachers place on their own syllabuses may be interpreted differently by outside observers. This suggests the need for greater clarity and structure in the presentation.

In the analysis of the 71 syllabuses no consistent pattern was noticed in the overall presentation, and each one was presented differently. It is interesting to record that not one used aims and objectives, content, methods, and evaluation, which are the four most commonly identified aspects of curriculum planning. Quite often, major areas of planning, for example the financial, resource, and time-table allocations, extracurricular activities, and the internal and external competitive programs were omitted. Thus the documentation was not a true reflection of the work of the department and consequently left something to be desired.

The importance and nature of the aims and objectives of physical education were the subject of a more detailed investigation. During the courses of the interview, the heads of department were asked, "What are the main aims you hope physical education achieves in your school?" The five most frequently mentioned aims are set out in Table 2 according to sex and age variables.

The two most frequently mentioned aims were the acquisition of skill and recreation for leisure. In each case these aims were referred to by 12 teachers. Perhaps the most surprising fact is that one quarter of the sample made no reference to these important aspects.

Seven male and three female teachers included the development of health and fitness. Whereas the male interpretation was mainly related to strength, endurance, and flexibility, the female teachers referred to posture, jogging, keeping fit, and proper diet. There would not only appear to be a difference in defining this area of "fitness," but there is also a difference in the importance it is given by male and female teachers.

The social benefit of physical education was given greater importance by female teachers and also by those teachers in the younger category. It is interesting that no man in the over 40 category referred to socialization as an aim. It may perhaps indicate that some of the more recent humanistic trends in education are affecting philosophical ideals in physical education.

Table 2. Aims of physical education: Teachers' recordings according to sex and age variables.

Aims	Men 40 +	Men 40 –	Women 40 +	Women 40 –	Total (n = 16)
Skill Acquisition	XX X	XXX	XX	XXXX	12
Recreation for Leisure	XXXX	X XX	x XX	XX	12
Health and Fitness	XXX X	XXXX	X	XX	10
Socialization		X X	XX	XXXX	8
Enjoyment	X X	X	XXXX	X	8

The importance of enjoyment by the children was stated by eight teachers, six of whom were in the older age bracket. While it would be difficult to substantiate the inclusion of a subject in the school curriculum solely on the grounds of enjoyment, undoubtedly this aspect was rated highly by both male and female teachers.

Eighteen other aims were named by the teachers (mainly by female teachers under 40 years of age) during the course of the interviews. The aims were very broad and far ranging and included areas such as fair play, body awareness, helping to pass examinations, and expression. However, none of these aims was referred to more than three times and the majority were named only once.

While recognizing the smallness of the sample, two points are tentatively made. The first is that the aims as stated by theorists, for example Kane (1974), may not all be given the same importance as those by the practicing teacher. This is evidenced by the fact that only a small minority referred to aims such as self-realization, emotional stability, moral development, cognitive development, and aesthetic appreciation. The second observation is that when discussing the aims of physical education some teachers may exclude aims of the utmost importance, for example skill acquisition, recreation for leisure, and organic development.

The extent to which teachers communicated to children the long-term aims of physical education and the short-term objectives of a course were questions that were asked. In the interviews most teachers stated that they did not deliberately communicate the aims of the subject to the children and gave the impression that when this did happen it was done infrequently and incidentally. However, a greater likelihood was that the children would be told the short-term objectives of a block of work. This finding was also evident from the national questionnaire. Clearly, the fact that many teachers are haphazard in communicating the aims of the subject to the children can only result in some uncertainty about the true purposes of physical education in the minds of the pupils. There was, however, a greater likelihood that the children would be told the short-term objectives of a course, and this could have been due to their more tangible nature. Although many teachers do communicate their aims and objectives to children, a substantial number do not. While it may not always be possible, or indeed advisable, to specify aims and objectives, an initial statement about the intended learning outcomes can provide a sense of direction and be a source of motivation for the pupils. A failure to provide the underlying purposes of courses of study may result in haphazard and possibly ineffective learning taking place.

Most teachers attempted to achieve progression within the first 3 years when all children followed a common core of activities. However, from the fourth year onward the major part of the curriculum was devoted to optional activities, and less planning was evident. The questionnaire response revealed that over three quarters of the teachers gave more thought and planning to the common core of work, which suggested a greater commitment to planning and preparation in the early stages of the curriculum. This may have been at the expense of planning the optional activities program where a less diligent approach was apparent.

As indicated in Table 1, evaluation did not receive a great deal of emphasis. Nevertheless, the teachers were asked to rate the importance of a number of methods that are used to judge the success of curriculum planning. The six highest ranked items were development of good attitudes, enjoyment, working atmosphere, skill levels, participation in postschool recreation, and extra curricular participation. Although the development of motor skills and participation in extracurricular and postschool recreation figured prominently, the results suggested that the greatest importance was attached to areas in the affective domain concerned with the development of good attitudes, enjoyment, and the acquisition of skill in a good working atmosphere. Affective outcomes are not usually in the forefront of teachers' thinking, but they figured prominently in this study.

In relation to the theoretical models of curriculum planning, no evidence suggested that teachers use the models to guide the planning of the physical education curriculum. The fact that many syllabuses made no reference to aims and objectives or to evaluation procedures indicates that models are not a significant influencing factor. Indeed, in a factor analysis based on the intercorrelations between 572 teachers' ratings of 23 items that influenced their planning, the largest factor was named "school climate" and related to the attitudes of the school staff, the traditions of the school, and the help offered by nonphysical education staff, particularly male colleagues, in the development of the subject. The lack of emphasis on the prespecification of objectives and methods of evaluation clearly indicated that teachers were not adopting an objectives approach in the pursuit of accountability.

Conclusions

The following statements can tentatively be made about physical education planning in secondary school in England and Wales:

1. Most emphasis is placed on the content of programs, while less emphasis is placed on aims and objectives and methods, with evaluation procedures being rarely included.
2. Not all of the aims of physical education as proposed by the theorists are considered to be important by practicing teachers.
3. Teachers are more likely to communicate the short-term objectives of a course to their students than the long-term aims of the subject.
4. Almost all schools insist on a common core of work during the first 3 years, and this is followed by a progressively increased choice in a range of activities.
5. Greater thought is given to the planning of the progressions for the common core of work than for the optional activities.
6. Many teachers judge the success of their courses through the affective domain.
7. Teachers are not adopting an objectives approach in pursuit of accountability.
8. Most teachers do not follow the theoretical models of curriculum planning in their physical education planning procedures.

References

Eraut, M., Goad, L., & Smith, G. (1975). The analysis of curriculum materials. University of Sussex Education Area. Occasional Paper No. 2.

Kane, J.E. (1974). *Physical education in secondary schools.* London: Macmillan.

Nicholls, A., & Nicholls, H. (1972). *Developing a curriculum: A practical guide.* London: Allen & Unwin.

Taba, H. (1962). *Curriculum development: Theory and practice.* New York: Harcourt Brace Jovanovich.

Tyler, R.W. (1949). *Basic principles of curriculum and instruction.* Chicago: University of Chicago Press.

Underwood, G.L. (1983). *The physical education curriculum in the secondary school: Planning and implementation.* Lewes: Falmer Press.

23

Physical Education Curriculum Congruence of Illinois Secondary Schools with Selected Recommended Procedures

Marian E. Kneer
UNIVERSITY OF ILLINOIS AT CHICAGO
CHICAGO, ILLINOIS, USA

The gap between theory and practice has been widely decried by theorists and practitioners. Curriculum theorists often claim that their role is as stated by Bain (1978), to "provide program planners with a description of the alternatives available in the selection and organization of content" (p.25). Practitioners lament that the recommended procedures are only theory and will not work in the real world. It is difficult, if not impossible, to find much research that describes the extent to which theory is practiced.

Curriculum theory and/or recommended practices relate to administrative structure, program structure, decision making, content selection, and organization. In addition curriculum components that respond to cultural and pluralist demands relating to provisions for the handicapped and sex integration are advocated. Melograno (1978) identifies five curriculum components: organizing centers, learning objectives, content, learning experiences, and evaluative process. Much has been written about the failure of the physical education curriculum to reflect changes as a result of research, theoretical ideas, or cultural pressure (Siedentop, 1980; Anderson, 1973). Little systematic research has been conducted to verify that belief. Ross (1981) defines theory as a "body of established hypotheses that have been confirmed to a reliable degree" (p.42). The term *theory* will be used in this paper to denote recommended practices or procedures based on tested and untested ideas and opinions that represent several curriculum theories.

The purpose of this investigation was to determine the extent to which the physical education curriculum was congruent with recommended procedures and the reasons for the perceived failure of the physical education curriculum to reflect practices based on research, theoretical ideas, or cultural pressure. Curriculum design components of (a) organization, (b) content selection, and (c) evaluation procedures were investigated.

Procedures

Information to meet the purpose of this study immediately is beset by the usual methodology problems confronting curriculum and instruction research relative to the validity of the research, especially in field research. Curriculum documents were studied, and the physical education program leaders and faculty were interviewed to obtain information concerning recommended curriculum practices from a random sample of 20 secondary schools. A questionnaire was designed to serve as a controlled means to obtain the data.

Questionnaire Development

After reviewing the literature on curriculum theory in physical education, a list of usually recommended procedures based on tested and untested theory was developed. This list was sent with the proposed questionnaire to five nationally known physical education curriculum experts who conduct research and study curriculum theory. They were to determine the validity of these practices as recommended and suggest any usually recommended procedures that were not included. In addition, the panel was asked to assess the appropriateness of the procedures, the clarity of the questions and responses, and the objectivity of the statement.

Any item receiving less than 80% agreement on appropriateness was eliminated. A questionnaire was designed to serve as a controlled means to obtain data. The panel rated the entire questionnaire for the content format on a 5-point scale, 5 being high. All items received a rating of 4 or better. The questionnaire was pilot tested as a means of collecting data based on an interview.

Curriculum Congruence

A curriculum index was constructed and based on a 20-point scale weighted to reflect the proportion of items included. Points were given if the procedure was utilized or present. The scale was as follows: organization = 10 points; content selection = 5 points; evaluation = 5 points.

Sample

Twenty schools were selected at random from the Illinois School Directory for field study. Selection was not based on school size or geographic location.

Data Collection

The field visits were planned to permit a minimum of one half of one date at each site. Each department head or designee was personally interviewed using the curriculum questionnaire as a guide. Curricular guides and materials were personally studied. Administrators were requested to review the recorded data for accuracy. Frequencies and percentage of responses were obtained for the following procedures: organizational components of guide contents, program provisions, content selection, and evaluation components.

Results

Organization

Curriculum Guide

Even though it would seem that every school would have a physical education curriculum guide because it is required by most state and accrediting agencies, only 75% had a curriculum guide. Of those who had none, two schools stated that they did not believe in them and two blamed the lack of a guide on teacher apathy. The existing curriculum guides were relatively current. Only 13% had not been revised within the past 5 years. Eight percent of those schools that did not have a curriculum guide had enrollments of less than 500 students.

The curriculum guides were studied to determine the nature of the contents (Table 1). Most guides contained a goals statement (75%) and a philosophy statement (70%). Almost two-thirds of the schools had determined the scope and sequence of their curriculum. The gap between recommended practice and application is, thus, about one third. However, the disparity grows much larger in other usually recommended content items, ranging from activity objectives (50%) to references for each activity (25%). Seventy percent of the schools provide no plan for evaluating their curriculum.

Table 1. Curriculum Guide Content

Content items	n	Percent providing
Philosophy Statement	14	70.0
Goals Statement	15	75.0
Scope and Sequence	13	65.0
Objectives per Activity	10	50.0
Scope and Sequence per Activity	9	45.0
Unit Teaching Strategies	7	35.0
Unit Management Plan	9	45.0
Unit Evaluation Plan	9	45.0
Evaluation Plan	6	30.0
Unit Learning Experiences	7	35.0
Unit References	5	25.0

Program Provisions

The overall gap between recommended procedures and practice in program provision is approximately 55-60% (Table 2). Seventy percent of the schools stated that they mainstreamed the handicappped in their program. However, 50% offer special programs for the temporarily and permanently handicapped. The reason most often given for not providing mainstreaming is that the faculty is believed not "adequately trained" to manage such provisions (80%). All of the schools not offering programs for the temporarily handicapped indicated that they did not believe in the need to offer such programs. Safety (60%) and disbelief in the need (40%) were given as reasons for not providing programs for the permanently handicapped.

Sex integrated physical education in the secondary schools has been required in the United States since 1976; yet 30% of the schools offer programs that are less than 24% sex integrated (Table 2). Reasons for not offering programs that have at least 50% sex integrated classes are: concern for staff ability to teach them (83.3%), safety (50%), ability differences (33%), and disbelief in the idea (33%). Forty-five percent of the schools offer no student choice. Only 10% always provide student choice. Reasons for not providing student program choice were not sought.

Content Selection

No one theoretical basis seemed to guide content selection. Content for the curriculum was selected primarily to provide a variety of activities (95%). However, 85% of the schools also selected content to primarily provide for physical development and to satisfy perceived student motives (70%). Sixty-five percent of the schools stated that student "fun" was a major consideration in satisfying student motives. The least mentioned basis for content selection was disciplinary knowledge (5%) and developmental stages (20%).

Decision Making

It would appear that faculty have considerable opportunity to participate in curriculum decision making (75%) and to make final decisions (55%). However, participation by others such as parents and student occurs in only 30% of the schools sampled. Forty-five percent of the administrators and 20% of the department heads participate in curriculum decision making and the final decision.

Curriculum Evaluation

The gap between theory and practice in the area of curriculum evaluation practices is easily the largest found (see Table 3). Fitness testing was meager. Only 25% used the AAHPERD Fitness Tests, and none used the new Health Related Fitness Tests. Reasons for not giving the fitness tests were "don't believe in" (40%) and "takes too much time" (26.7%). Fifty percent of the schools were unaware of the AAHPERD Health Related Fitness Test.

Skill was evaluated by 70% of the schools. Both skill tests and subjective skill ratings were used by 70% of the schools to measure skill. Student attitude was assessed by 30% of the schools. Reasons for not evaluating attitude were 50% "other" (usually indicated that they did not know how) and 36% "don't believe in." Forty-five percent of the schools do not use written knowledge

Table 2. Program provisions: Percent of reasons for not offering

Provisions	n	Percent	Don't believe in	Too costly	Staff not trained	Safety	Not required	Ability differences	Student choice	Other
Handicapped										
Mainstreamed	14	70.0	0.00	20.0	80.0	20.0	0.0			80.0
Temporary	10	50.0	100.0	0.0	0.0	0.0	60.0			10.0
Permanent	10	50.0	40.0	0.0	20.0	60.0	20.0			60.0
Sex Integrated										
− 24%	6	30.0	33.0	16.67	83.33	50.0		33.0	16.7	50.0
+ 24-50%	0	0.0								
+ 50-75%	5	25.0								
+ 75-99%	3	15.0								
100%	6	30.0								
Student Choices										
None	9	45.0								
Occasionally	3	15.0								
Considerably	6	30.0								
Always	2	50.0								
Knowledge of Movement	10	50.0								

Table 3. Curriculum evaluation practices: Reasons for not using

Procedure	n	Percent	Don't believe in	Staff inability	Staff won't use	Too much time	Other
Fitness							
AAHPERD P. Test	5	25.0	40.0	0.0	13.3	26.6	26.6
AAHPERD H.R.	0	0.0	25.0	0.0	10.0	15.0	50.0
Test							
Skill							
Tests	14	70.0	17.0	0.0	0.0	66.6	17.0
Subjective Ratings	14	70.0	66.6	0.0	0.0	33.3	0.0
Attitude	6	30.0	36.0	0.0	0.0	14.0	50.0
Written Tests	11	55.0	33.3	0.0	0.0	44.4	23.0
Annual Goal							
Assessment	14	70.0	17.0	0.0	17.0	16.0	50.0
Grades							
Based on Learning	15	75.0	80.0	0.0	0.0	20.0	0.0
Based on Participation	20	100.0	0.0	0.0	0.0	0.0	0.0

tests. The reasons most often given for not giving written tests was that it "took too much time" (44.4%) and "don't believe in" (33.3%).

Only 30% of the schools did not annually assess goal attainment. Most schools indicated, however, that the assessment was basically nondata based. Grades were given by all schools and all included participation as a major component. Thirty-five percent of the schools did not use learning as a basis for the grade.

Curriculum Congruence

A curriculum congruence with theory rating was given to each school in the sample. Fifty-five percent of the schools received ratings in the lower third of the 20-point scale, 35% were in the middle third, and only 10% placed in the upper third or were highly congruent with recommended practices.

Discussion

Results would indicate a gap of about 50% exists between curriculum recommended procedures and practice. Twenty-five percent of the schools did not have written curriculum guides, and of those that did only 65% included a scope and sequence for their program. Content was selected to provide a variety of activities that would aid in physical development and satisfy student motives. Program provisions such as handicapped programs, sex integrated classes, student program choice, and knowledge concepts were provided by about 50% of the schools. Systematic evaluation of the curriculum was practiced by about half of the schools. Fitness and skill testing was rarely offered. These findings support the research of Imwold, Rider, and Johnson (1982). They found that skill tests were given 76.9% in secondary schools. It would appear that the gap is the smallest in decision making because 75% of the school include faculty in curriculum decision making and 55% permit their participation in final decisions. Only 10% of the school ranked high in congruence with recommended curricula practices.

Reasons for the discrepancy between theory and practice vary. However, it may be said that the lack of program provisions for the handicapped and sex integrated classes are the result of concern for the lack of faculty training to teach them and concern for the safety of students involved. The large gap in evaluation practices is attributed to many reasons; but a surprisingly large percentage of schools that do not evaluate their programs indicate that they do not believe in the need for evaluating.

Given the results of the study it would appear that the theory/practice gap exists. Since the data was of a self-report nature, any errors in reporting would probably be toward over-statement of the use of the practices rather than an understatement.

References

Anderson, W. (1973). Cues to Reading (Review of Physical Education: An Introductory Analysis). *Quest, 19,* 133-135.

Bain, L. (1978). Status of curriculum theory in physical education. *Journal of Physical Education and Recreation.* **49**(3), 25-26.

Imwold, L., Rider, R., & Johnson, D. (1982). The use of evaluation in public school physical education program. *Journal of Teaching Physical Education* **2(1)**, 13-18.

Melograno, V. (1978). Status of curriculum practice. *Journal of Physical Education and Recreation,* **49**(3), 27-28.

Ross, S. (1981). The epistemic geography of physical education: Addressing the problem of theory and practice. *Quest,* **33**, 42-84.

Siedentop, D. (1980). Physical education curriculum: An analysis of the past. *Journal of Physical Education and Recreation,* **51**(7), 40-41.

24

Fitness in the Curriculum

Ann E. Jewett
UNIVERSITY OF GEORGIA
ATHENS, GEORGIA, USA

A lot is known about the development of health-related fitness. Less is known about maintaining fitness over the life span. Unfortunately, very little is known about effective fitness education that will actually result in adult self-directed health-related fitness. Ample documentation exists that the majority of United States citizens do *not* maintain active, healthy lifestyles. A main argument for physical education in schools and colleges is that self-directed adult fitness is important. Yet little evidence exists that formal educational programs in health and physical education are, in fact, achieving excellence in respect to the desired long-term results.

Selected findings of three recent studies completed at the University of Georgia are reported in this paper. The intent is to focus on educational objectives and curricular outcomes with the specific focus on health-related fitness. The University of Georgia (UGA) has a five quarter hour credit physical education requirement. The stated desired outcomes are health-related fitness, performance skill, and creative/aesthetic outcomes. By any of the usual standards or evaluative criteria it is a good basic physical education activity program. Still, no convincing evidence of long-term results exists as reflected in the active lifestyles of our graduates. Going (1984) investigated the current physical recreation participation levels of 492 University of Georgia alumni, who had graduated in 1974, 1977, and 1981, using a stratified random sample of 1,000 UGA graduates. Although the primary reason for participation among the sampled population was to improve and maintain physical fitness levels, 54.5% of the respondents indicated that the required physical education experience had had no influence on their current levels of participation.

A three credit Fitness for Life course was initiated in 1977. The student may or may not choose to take the Fitness for Life course to meet the UGA physical education requirement. Fitness for Life is a daily 10 week course taught by a team of four to six instructors. A key feature is a major activity selected by the student (jogging, running, cycling, or swimming). Participation in the major activity for 3 days per week is supplemented by strength and flexibility activities, mini lectures, and testing.

The three studies to be reported used Fitness for Life students as subjects and were designed to provide information to assist curriculum designers in planning for more effective fitness education. Each researcher investigated the impact of physical education on adult participation in fitness activities from a different perspective. Tiburzi (1979) validated a model for testing the major components of physiological fitness for use in designing the fitness curriculum. Norton (1982) studied the personalized fitness curriculum from the perspective of participant purposes for engaging in fitness activities. Gorman (1983) focused directly on fitness program variables associated with adherence to a personalized fitness program. These investigations used, respectively, 162, 197, and 266 subjects who were student participants in the Fitness for Life classes.

A Model for Planning Components of the Fitness Curriculum

Tiburzi (1979) investigated the structure of the domain of physiological fitness using factor analysis. The assessment of fitness has been complicated by the inability to agree on the components of fitness. To a considerable extent this has resulted from the fact that fitness has been operationally defined by the tests used to measure it. Tiburzi developed a theoretical model to clarify the components of physiological fitness. Her specific purpose was to investigate fitness as a curriculum area and a focus of instruction in terms of the types of tests that physical education teachers are actually administering in the school. She hypothesized a theoretical model comprised of 12 factors: upper-body strength and endurance, trunk strength and endurance, leg explosive strength and endurance, arm explosive strength and endurance, sprinting speed, controlled speed, balance on an object, static and dynamic balance, upper body flexibility, leg and trunk flexibility, circulorespiratory endurance, and body fatness.

Twenty-four experimental tests were selected to represent the 12 theorized dimensions of physiological fitness. The tests were administered to 162 undergraduate student volunteers enrolled in the Fitness for Life course. Intraclass reliability coefficients ranged from .598 to .994. The correlation matrix for all 24 test items was subjected to four different models of factor analysis: incomplete principal components, alpha factor analysis, canonical factor analysis, and incomplete image analysis. Each initial solution was rotated by orthogonal and oblique rotations. Only those factors found to be robust across solutions were considered useful. Analysis of the results of the eight derived solutions suggested that the 24 tests could be essentially represented by five robust factors for the female data and seven robust factors for the male data.

Tiburzi concluded that the domain of physiological fitness is multidimensional and can be explained by the following factors for coeducational groups: balance, body fatness, circulorespiratory endurance, flexibility, and strength.

On the basis of her findings, she recommended that a test battery, appropriate for both males and females, be used and that coeducational fitness programs be designed in terms of the following nine components:

1. Upper-body strength and endurance
2. Trunk strength and endurance
3. Leg explosive strength, endurance, and speed
4. Arm explosive strength and endurance
5. Balance
6. Upper body flexibility
7. Leg and trunk flexibility
8. Circulorespiratory endurance
9. Body fatness (p. 162)

The Fitness for Life Health-Related Test Battery currently consists of five tests, which parallel the model recommended by Tiburzi with one exception. Balance activities are not yet emphasized in the Fitness for Life program, and no balance test is presently included in the test battery. The tests comprising the battery are the University of Georgia step test, the bent-knee sit-up test, the Baumgartner modified pull-up test, the sit and reach test, and skinfold measurements taken at two sites to determine the percent of body fat.

Personalized Fitness Curriculum

The ultimate goal of school fitness programs is to influence students to develop personal active lifestyles resulting in a continuing high level of fitness and improved quality of life. In seeking increased insight on how the fitness experience can be more meaningful to the individual learner, Norton (1982) investigated the personal reasons of students for participating in fitness activities. She designed the Fitness Activities Purposes Inventory to obtain ratings of 15 purposes for engaging in fitness activities, using a 9-point scale, separating the word pairs *not meaningful—very meaningful*. The Carmack and Martens Commitment to Running Scale (1979) was adapted as a Commitment to Activity Scale by changing the word *running* to *activity*. The Purpose Inventory, the Commitment to Activity Scale, and the five-item Fitness for Life Health-Related Test Battery were administered to 197 Fitness for Life students.

A two-way analysis of variance was used to compare purpose means. Specific differences between any two purposes was established by using the Tukey technique. The most meaningful purposes were identified as: musculoskeletal efficiency, attractiveness, mechanical efficiency, circulorespiratory efficiency, weight control, vitality, and enjoyment. The mean values were not significantly different from each other at the .01 level. The least meaningful purposes for engaging in fitness activities were identified as challenge and self-transcendence.

Chi-square analysis was utilized to determine whether differences existed between groups on ratings of the 15 purpose statements. Independent variables were: sex, activity groups (jogging, running, swimming, and cycling as the major class activity), and high and low levels of fitness and commitment. High and low levels of fitness and commitment to activity were determined by selecting the mean score plus or minus one standard deviation. Correlations were used to determine the degree of relationship between individual purposes and commitment to activity, commitment to activity and fitness level, and individual purposes and fitness level.

Significant differences were found in the way males and females valued competition, movement efficiency, and weight control. Men found competition and movement efficiency more meaningful. Women rated weight control higher. A significant relationship was reported between the activity group and the purpose enjoyment. Most cyclers, runners, and swimmers ranked enjoyment as highly meaningful. Less than half of the joggers ranked enjoyment high.

The level of commitment to activity was a significant variable. Although male and female commitment to activity scores did not differ significantly, highly committed students valued catharsis, movement efficiency, circulorespiratory efficiency, enjoyment, vitality, challenge, self-transcendence, and weight control more highly than did students with a low level of commitment. The only purpose ranked in the high range by over 50% of the students with a low level of commitment was weight control.

The highest correlation coefficient was between enjoyment and commitment to activity. Correlations between commitment to activity and the five fitness scores were significant for males but not for females. Perhaps females can be socially or intellectually committed to fitness activity without actually being fit, whereas male commitment to activity is related to the level of fitness.

Adherence to Personalized Fitness Programs

Gorman's (1983) study was designed to identify and compare the characteristics of Fitness for Life student adherers to a personalized fitness program with nonadherers in order to determine major differences existing between the two groups. A Fitness for Life Student Inventory was administered to students who had completed the UGA Fitness for Life course between 1 and 2 years earlier. Adherers in this study were individuals who participated in regular aerobic fitness or strength/conditioning activities at a minimum frequency of three times per week for a duration of 20 minutes per workout. Descriptive statistics and frequency distributions were used to tabulate and analyze the data provided by 266 respondents and to classify each subject as an adherer or a nonadherer. Chi-square analysis was used to determine whether significant differences existed for the adherence variables: gender, attitude, body weight, perceived stress, moral support, exercise model, and fitness level.

Previous research had indicated that the majority of persons who initiated an organized voluntary adult fitness program discontinued within the first 3 to 6 months. Gorman found a similar drop-out rate for Fitness for Life students. The overall adherence rate for the 266 former student subjects was 47% for aerobic fitness activities and 26% for strength and conditioning activities. However, of the 124 former students classified as regular adherers upon completion of the fitness course, 66% still adhered to an aerobic activity one to two years later; 82% of the 69 students who were classified as regular adherers to a strength and conditioning program upon course completion continued to adhere to regular strength and conditioning activities. It was noted that many nonadherers participated in fitness-related activities, but not regularly enough to meet Gorman's criteria for adherence.

Gorman concluded that the overall adherence rate for students completing the UGA Fitness for Life course could be predicted to be approximately 50%. The fact that adherence to aerobic fitness activities was greater than for strength and conditioning activities is consistent with the program emphasis. Students able to adhere for a minimum time period of 3 to 6 months did tend to become long-term adherers. Eighty-three percent of those former students reported 1 to 2 years later that the course had made a very significant contribution to their personal knowledge and attitudes concerning the importance of regular physical activity as a method of maintaining health. The primary reasons given for individual participation in physical fitness activities were physical fitness and health, weight and figure control, relaxation, enjoyment, and personal commitment. These reasons were consistent with the student purposes for engaging in fitness activities reported by Norton.

Gorman found significant differences between adherers and nonadherers to aerobic fitness activities: "Adherers to aerobic fitness activities were more likely to have been female, possess an attitude of high regard for physical activity, been slightly overweight, and had either a very poor or good to excellent initial fitness level" (p. 86). Significant differences were also found between adherers and nonadherers to strength and conditioning activities. Adherers demonstrated an attitude of high regard for physical activity along with strong beliefs in the moral support of their personal families and friends for their participation. The only variable common to adherers in both aerobic fitness and strength/conditioning activities was that of attitude or personal belief that exercise is important.

Recommendations

It has not yet been demonstrated that typical physical education programs necessarily lead to more active adult lifestyles. The research conducted at the University of Georgia leads to the following recommendations:

1. Required physical education should include at least one major unit directed specifically toward commitment to lifetime fitness in addition to instruction in health-related fitness concepts in all activity courses.
2. Fitness education programs should be designed according to a broader concept of total fitness based on a validated model identifying the major fitness components.
3. A fitness education program should provide for individual fitness assessment utilizing a test battery of reliable measures for each of the specific components.
4. Fitness classes should engage in aerobic exercise at least 3 days per week for a minimum duration of at least 30 minutes. The curriculum should offer as wide a variety of aerobic activity choices as feasible.
5. Individualization of instruction is essential in fitness education; it should encompass the utilization of individual purposes for engaging in fitness

activities as a basis for curriculum development and the planning of instructional strategies.

6. Students and teachers need to be mutually involved in the selection of purposes to be incorporated into the curriculum plan. Purposes in the realm of individual development, both physiological efficiency and psychic equilibrium, should be integrated into the development of a fitness curriculum.

7. The purposes of vitality, weight control, attractiveness, and self-transcendence should be stressed. Norton found these purposes to be the most critical in differentiating between high and low fit individuals. The purpose of weight control should be incorporated in all programs because students value weight control regardless of commitment level.

8. It is well established that enjoyment is critical to the development of commitment to fitness activity. Consequently, methods should be employed to help make fitness experiences as intrinsically meaningful and enjoyable as possible. Exercise should be promoted, not for the purpose of preventing heart disease, but because it is enjoyable, it makes individuals feel good, and it promotes feelings of well-being and self-confidence.

9. Instruction in the personalized fitness curriculum should provide assistance in making the transition from participation in an organized program to regular voluntary participation in a personal lifetime fitness program. Structured program participation or frequent follow-up should be provided for a 6-month period following completion of an organized program.

References

Carmack, M.A., & Martens, R. (1979). Measuring commitment to running: A survey of runners' attitudes and mental states. *Journal of Sport Psychology, 1*, 25-42.

Going, W.R. (1984). *An analysis of the lifetime participation objective of a required basic physical education program.* Unpublished doctoral dissertation, University of Georgia.

Gorman, R.S. (1983). *Fitness program variables associated with adherence to a personalized fitness program.* Unpublished doctoral dissertation, University of Georgia, Athens, GA.

Norton, C.J. (1982). *Student purposes for engaging in fitness activities.* Unpublished doctoral dissertation, University of Georgia.

Tiburzi, A. (1979). *Validation of the construct of physiological fitness.* Unpublished doctoral dissertation, University of Georgia.

25

Analysis of the Research Based on Observation of the Teaching of Physical Education

Maurice Piéron
UNIVERSITÉ DE LIÈGE
LIÈGE, BELGIUM

In the last decade a specific area of research in teaching physical education has developed. It deals with the study and analysis of what happens during the teaching-learning process in the gymnasium or on the sports field. It is based on a systematic observation of teacher behavior, student behavior, teacher-student interaction, and the contextual aspects of teaching. This research effort has provided sport pedagogy with invaluable descriptive data. It has led to a better understanding of the teaching act. It has helped methodologists to move beyond sole reliance on their subjective impressions and to base some of their recommendations on data derived from research rather than on unrealistic or romantic expectations from programs (Siedentop, 1983; Piéron, 1984).

In physical education Anderson (1971) was probably the first to focus our attention on the potential of descriptive-analytic research. Several indicators show how quickly the field has developed:

- An increasing number of doctoral dissertations have been devoted to the topic (to date, more than one hundred).
- An increasing number of papers and publications have been devoted to the topic.

Appreciation is extended to Len Almond, George Graham, and Daryl Siedentop for their comments and editorial assistance with this paper.

• Many national and international seminars and congresses include sport pedagogy in their program.

This progress is reflected also by the broad and deep involvement of several universities in programmatic research on teaching physical education in the United States, in Canada, and in Europe.

In the past 2 years well known authors have underlined the progress that has been made and talked of a "modest celebration" (Siedentop, 1983; Locke, 1983). The purpose of this paper is to move beyond the realm of these subjective impressions of progress and use the research completed as a basis for analyzing this progress.

Delimitation of the Field

Gage (1968) proposed that research on teaching occurs when teacher behaviors serve as independent variables with some measure of pupil learning as the dependent variable. Locke used this proposal to define the field: "Research on teaching physical education includes only studies which employ data gathered through direct or indirect observation of instructional activity" (Locke, 1977).

Among those interested in the study of teaching, few, if any, still consider "eyeballing" as an effective observation technique. Systematic observation now is employed widely. *Eyeballing,* observation based on subjective impression, is no more appropriate for a review of research than it is for a research study. For this reason a multidimensional category system has been developed to classify studies and publications dealing with the analysis of the teaching physical education process. Systematic classification of research completed can be used to analyze more carefully the progress in our field. The category system considers seven dimensions:

1. The main object of the study.
   The first dimension is related to the overall purpose of the study. The categories deal with: teacher behavior, teacher-student interaction, student behavior, process-product studies, coach behavior, and teacher or coach behavior modification.
2. The subject matter taught.
   In a large survey of literature, Piéron (1983) observed that subject matter taught is an influential variable affecting teaching; it is frequently more powerful than context variables such as gender or grade level. Subject matters have been grouped in broad categories of individual sport, dual sports, and team sports. Subcategories enable us to differentiate accurately between sport specialities.
3. The type of documents.
   Documents reviewed have been selected according to strict criteria and ready availability. Three kinds of documents have been reviewed: papers published in journals and/or in congress proceedings, doctoral dissertations available through microfilm and microfiche services, and research reports available from the universities or centers sponsoring the research. Two types of documents were discarded because of their uneven quality and lack of availability: master's theses and unpublished papers delivered at national conventions.

4. The type of study.
   This dimension deals with different approaches: from a mere description of an observation schedule to the complete construction of the instrument (with reliability and validity analysis), and from ethnographic techniques of collecting the information to data gathered through predetermined category systems.
5. The teaching population.
   Categories allow sorting out of studies in which the teaching population is in-service teachers, student-teachers, coaches, and different combinations of these categories.
6. The students and learners.
   Independent of the teaching agency, classes or groups observed varied according to the school grade level (elementary, secondary, university) and the skill level (mainstreamed classes, handicapped, athletes). Different combinations of these groups were accounted for.
7. Context and program.
   The concepts of presage, context, process and product as defined by Dunkin & Biddle (1974) were used in this dimension. Program variables as defined by Tousignant and Brunelle (1982) referred to objectives, class organization, subject matter taught, or teaching methodology.

Results and Discussion

A total of 329 documents were suitable for the analysis according to the delimitation of the field as stated above. Several bibliographies and references in an extended review of literature showed that a large percentage of the documents published before January 1, 1984, have been accounted for.

Approximately one third of these documents do not provide the reader with any kind of data: 9.4% are limited to the description of observation systems, and 22.9% develop only theoretical views on behaviors observed in physical education classes.

The main objective of this study was to analyze research trends; documents expressing only theoretical views or providing no data, such as descriptions of observation schedules, were withdrawn. The 216 documents analyzed in this second step of the study were distributed as follows: teacher-student interaction (30.1%), teacher behavior (28.7%), teacher behavior modification (13.9%), student behavior (11.1%), process-product (6.9%), coach behavior (5.6%), and miscellaneous (3.7%).

Of the documents reviewed, 26.9% were doctoral dissertations (i.e., unpublished documents). Although they are available through several microfilm or microfiche services, they are less accessible than several other types of research documents. Difficulties in locating them and a relatively high cost of obtaining them make it more likely that doctoral dissertations will be reviewed mainly through abstracts published by International Dissertation Abstracts than through review of the original document. Many of these dissertations are probably condemned to accumulate dust on the shelves of university libraries.

Table 1. Distribution of documents according to the type of document

	1	2	3	4	5	6	7	T
A	0	3	0	2	0	2	1	8
B	15	14	0	19	12	0	2	62
C	3	4	2	12	3	0	0	24
D	23	15	0	14	10	0	3	65
E	1	4	0	9	1	0	0	15
F	2	4	1	5	0	0	0	12
G	14	9	0	4	3	0	0	30
T	58	53	3	65	29	2	6	216
%	26.9	24.5	1.4	30.1	13.4	0.9	2.8	

1. Doctoral dissertations
2. Papers published in journals
3. Research reports
4. Papers delivered at convention (Proceedings)
5. Papers directly derived from doctoral dissertations
6. Book
7. Chapter of books or monograph

A. General Studies
B. Teacher Behavior
C. Student Behavior
D. Teacher-Student Interaction
E. Process-Product
F. Coach Behavior
G. Teacher Behavior Modification

Adding the 13.4% of papers published from doctoral studies to the 26.9% of doctoral dissertations means that 40.3% of the research studies in teaching physical education originate from the source that is the final step of graduate preparation programs. These studies do have value and interest. Nevertheless, they are not free from several fundamental problems:

1. They have been done mostly by authors starting their first research work study. It is hard to believe, notwithstanding the invaluable aid of their advisors, that beginners in research have already gained mastery of experimental designs, observational techniques, instruments to be used, and an adequate and extended knowledge of literature enabling them to successfully interpret the data gathered. These researchers are still learners in the delicate field of research in teaching physical education.
2. Doctoral dissertations are undertaken with time and financial constraints that can hinder the quality of the research.
3. Most doctoral dissertations are the result of individual research efforts without the assumed beneficial influence of team research.
4. Conflicting or divergent research interests of the doctoral student and of the long-term research program of the institution can occur. This leads to frequent ''one shot'' studies.

For evidence of these statements one merely needs to look at the many studies dealing with the development of observation systems (including carefully planned assessments of validity and reliability) that never go beyond this first step. A score of observation schedules have been developed but never used to collect descriptive data or to study the influence of program and context variables.

In summary, it appears that only one third of the research work done through the doctorate studies program reaches a larger audience under the form of articles or papers published in journals or in congress proceedings; 24.5% of the research has been published in journals, and 30.1% has been published in congress proceedings. These forms of publication are typically less stringently reviewed and probably less widely distributed than journals.

Teaching Population

About half of the studies (47.7%) focus on observation of in-service teachers, for example, persons already trained. The picture gained through teaching analysis, therefore, seems to validly represent the daily reality of the school compared to information gathered through student teacher observation (24.1%). A student teacher may well change his or her teaching pattern between graduation and field practice.

Results provide three types of highly necessary data, for a sound knowledge of teaching skills, that can be used to improve teacher preparation: knowing where the trainee is coming from (student teacher, 24.1%), where he or she has greater chances of going, (in-service teachers, 41.2%), and where it is worth going—toward a successful and effective teaching career (master teachers, 6.5%).

Coaches' behaviors have been studied in a relatively small number of research documents (6.9%). Moreover, part of this research concerns only case studies of a few outstanding coaches. The percentage clearly shows that the domain has not been extensively analyzed and is not well known yet. The teaching agency is not described with enough accuracy to be accurately identified in 21.7% of the studies.

Students and Learners

A large number of studies (40.3%) do not provide suitable information to identify the students observed. Data are frequently combined in such a way that no differentiation can be made between student levels.

When available, data gathered at the elementary (19.0%) and at the secondary (17.1%) school levels show a well-balanced distribution. Mainstreamed classes and the handicapped accounted for 2.8% of the studies.

This part of the analysis consists of a third phase dealing with data that have been gathered. The same document or publication is not always limited to a single topic or comparison. Comparisons according to grade level, gender, and environmental conditions can be found in the same document. This possibility of involving several topics in the same document has been accounted for in the data processing. A total of 279 research topics have been identified and coded.

One quarter (24.0%) of the research topics dealt with comparative studies of the teaching process according to context variables (grade level, gender,

Table 2. Distribution of documents according to the context and program variables

	1	2	3	4	5	6	7	8	9	10	T
A	5	2	0	0	1	0	0	0	0	5	13
B	29	14	1	0	13	5	0	0	2	28	92
C	15	12	0	2	3	2	0	0	0	7	41
D	18	14	1	2	6	0	0	0	8	27	76
E	0	0	0	0	0	0	15	0	0	0	15
F	0	0	0	0	0	1	0	1	0	8	12
G	0	0	0	0	0	0	0	28	0	2	30
T	67	44	2	4	23	8	15	29	10	77	279
%	24.0	15.8	0.7	1.4	8.2	2.9	5.4	10.4	3.6	27.6	

1. Context
2. Program
3. Teaching vs. Coaching
4. Different types of students (Pygmalion)
5. Presage-Process
6. Process-Process
7. Process-Product
8. Teacher Beavhior Modification
9. Individual Variability
10. Undetermined

A. General Studies
B. Teacher Behavior
C. Student Behavior
D. Teacher-Student Interaction
E. Process-Product
F. Coach Behavior
G. Teacher Behavior Modification

environment, ethnic groups, class size, and equipment). This group of research topics concerns variables on which the teacher has little leverage. Implications of these studies hardly go beyond a simple description. They imply few clear consequences for teacher preparation programs. These studies also rarely evidenced fundamental contextual differences or consistent trends from one study to another. Authors seem to have some predilection for studies such as comparisons between male and female teachers or between elementary and secondary school levels.

Fifteen point eight percent of the topics focused on program variables. This area seems to merit more attention from researchers in teaching physical education. It pertains to a domain in which the teacher selected the activity taught, planned the organization of the class, or chose the methodology with which to implement instruction. Program variables probably have a greater predictive value on the teaching process than context variables do.

Teaching methodology has been more frequently studied than other program variables, but even it is not studied very often. Unfortunately these studies are limited to the unique observation instrument, CAFIAS, and to a single comparison of the teacher making all of the decisions versus the teacher sharing some of the decision making with the students. Teaching styles have been rarely investigated, and usually by inappropriate observation instruments.

Table 3. Distribution of documents according to the subject matter taught

	1	2	3	4	5	T
A	0	0	2	3	8	13
B	4	3	12	37	36	92
C	0	0	0	18	23	41
D	0	1	0	4	71	76
E	11	3	1	0	0	15
F	0	0	6	2	4	12
G	2	0	2	0	26	30
T	17	7	23	64	168	279
%	6.1	2.5	8.2	22.9	60.2	

1. Individual sports
2. Dual sports
3. Team sports
4. Identifiable (several subject matter in the same study)
5. Unidentifiable

A. General Studies
B. Teacher Behavior
C. Student Behavior
D. Teacher-Student Interaction
E. Process-Product
F. Coach Behavior
G. Teacher Behavior Modification

Although the data from classroom research clearly shows that presage variables were of low predictive value on the teaching process, one can find an appreciable amount of studies that focus on the relationship between presage and process variables in physical education teaching (8.2%).

The process-product studies, a promising field of research, amounts to a low 5.4%. However, most of this research has been completed since 1980. To date they are still limited to Experimental Teaching Units or ETU-like studies. It appears that now is the time to start with studies involving full classes.

In classroom teaching research it has been observed that many teaching behaviors that correlated positively with teaching effectiveness (student learning) were subject specific (see Table 3). In physical education it is hard to believe that teaching hula hoop, basketball skills, dance, creative movement, or sports gymnastics routines lends itself to the same kind of interaction or teaching behavior.

It is amazing to observe that 60.2% of the studies do not provide the reader with sufficient information to identify the subject matter taught. This apportionment is particularly high in interaction analysis studies (93.4%). The only area where the subject matter is always clearly described is the process-product studies.

Final Remarks

One could probably proceed as in business and try to achieve a balance between assets and liabilities. However, what is now considered as liabilities could be changed into meaningful outcomes for the body of knowledge of the discipline and for the profession.

1. The final objective of research in teaching physical education is to build one or several theories pertaining to a coherent body of knowledge aimed at improving teaching, and more specifically, teacher preparation. This statement is not particularly original. However, it is important for the following comments. To date it seems that we still are a long way from this coherent body of knowledge when considering the literature in our field. Indicators in support of the above statement include: frequent use of "ornamental" references, reference to unpublished and hardly available documents (they were excluded from our data collection), and "parochial" references. It seems that authors often forget that in every scientific publication a reader or another researcher must be able to go back to the referenced sources and find an accurate description of the observation or experience enabling replication. Abuse of unpublished references constitutes an impediment to serious research and affects the credibility of the author. Furthermore, numerous localization mistakes in references lead us to think that many authors work preferably with documents collected in meetings, congresses, or by exchange rather than in using systematic resources. It is common to find draft or provisional documents still referenced several years after their publication.

2. Establishing a theory of physical education teaching implies hypotheses drawn from the body of knowledge and verified by data gathered through observation and experimentation. Among the documents analyzed in this study (according to the selection criteria), many are not data based. It could be thought that many authors theorize without an adequate research support. The large amount of one shot studies reinforces this comment, too.

3. A lack of rigor, namely in using data from graduate studies like master's theses, and reference to these works as a confirmation of their own data affects the credibility of several authors and, by consequence, the credibility of the whole field as compared to a well-recognized academic field of study. The fact that a large part of the research base (approximately 40%) is from doctoral studies shows that few articulated research groups exist. Although coherent research programs are pursued in more and more departments, they appear to come from outstanding leaders rather than research teams. Nevertheless, such teams exist in a few universities.

4. In many studies, a major problem is that the activities taught (more than 60%) are not identified, which considerably limits the meaning of collected data. Grouping data from different activities could have been tolerated in the early studies when searching for an initial understanding of the teaching process; the practice should not be used now.

5. Authors used the same data (generally from his or her doctoral dissertation) for several presentations of similar papers. Again, questions can be raised about the authors credibility in doing so.

6. Several terminological difficulties must be overcome if researchers want to achieve clearer communication and if integrating and comparing data from different sources is desirable. In research dealing with student

behaviors, so many different labels can be found to account for similar behaviors that they become confusing. Some of those labels are academic learning time, active learning time, skill learning time, time on task, activity time, and motor engagement time.

These comments are mostly critical. However, if they are taken into consideration and the necessary corrections and adjustments are made, the quality of research will probably increase. On the other side, some remarkable results have been achieved so far. Research in teaching physical education has developed reliable and valid observation instruments dealing with general and different specific aspects of the teaching act.

The remarkable Video Data Bank Project of Teachers College, Columbia University (Anderson, 1971) gave birth to many offspring in the USA as well as in other parts of the world, and it provided researchers with data for continuous study. A project to share tapes from these video data collections could be a great achievement as well.

Further improvement of the actual body of knowledge could be made in focusing on program variables rather than on less meaningful context variables. The doors have been opened wide to develop process-product studies and to link quantitative observation with qualitative appraisal.

The descriptive-correlational-experimental loop referred to by Rosenshine and Furst (1973) is far from being completed in the physical education teaching research. Many examples of the first step, the descriptive approach, can be found. But few examples of the second and third steps, correlational and experimental paradigms, in physical education teaching research are yet to be found.

Data-based research in teaching physical education has a sound theoretical background, a clearly defined area of investigation, and many questions to answer. It has valid and reliable instruments and enthusiastic young researchers involved in the process. All of these assets allow us to look to the future of research in sport pedagogy with a reasonable optimism.

References

Anderson, W. (1971). Descriptive-analytic research on teaching. *Quest,* **15**, 1-18.

Dunkin, M., & Biddle B. (1974). *The study of teaching.* New York: Holt, Richard, & Winston.

Gage, N. (1968). *An analytic approach to research on instructional methods.* Phi Delta Kappan, **49**, 601-606.

Locke, L. (1977). *Research on teaching physical education: New hope for a dismal science. Quest,* **28**, 2-16.

Locke, L. (1983). Research on teaching physical activity: a modest celebration. In M. Howell & J. Saunders (Eds.), *Proceedings of the VII Commonwealth and International Conference on Sport, Physical Education and Dance,* **6**, Movement and Sport Education (pp. 189-200).

Piéron, M. (1983). Teacher and pupil behavior and the interaction process in physical education classes. In R. Telama, V. Varstala, J. Tiainen, L. Laakso, & T. Haajanen (Eds.), *Research in school physical education* (pp. 13-30). Jyvaskyla: The Foundation for Promotion of Physical Culture and Health.

Piéron, M. (1984). *Pédagogie des activités physiques et sportivies (méthodologie et didactique).* Université de Liége.

Rosenshine, B., & Furst, N. (1973). The use of direct observation to study teaching. In R. Travers (Ed.), *Second handbook of research on teaching* (pp. 122-183). Chicago: Rand McNally.

Siedentop, D. (1983). *Developing teaching skills in physical education* (2nd ed.). Palo Alto, CA: Mayfield.

Siedentop, D. (1983). Research on teaching in physical education. In T. Templin & J. Olson (Eds.), *Teaching in Physical Education* (pp. 3-15). Champaign, IL: Human Kinetics.

Tousignant, M., & Brunelle, J. (1982). What we have learned from students and how we can use it to improve curriculum and teaching. In M. Piéron & J. Cheffers (Eds.), *Studying the teaching in physical education* (pp. 3-22). Liége: AIESEP.